From Archaeology to Archaeologies:
The 'Other' Past

Edited by

Anna Simandiraki-Grimshaw
Eleni Stefanou

BAR International Series 2409
2012

Published in 2016 by
BAR Publishing, Oxford

BAR International Series 2409

From Archaeology to Archaeologies: The 'Other' Past

ISBN 978 1 4073 1007 7

© The editors and contributors severally and the Publisher 2012

COVER IMAGE *Tera Pruitt (chapter 3, Fig.03)*

BAR Publishing is the trading name of British Archaeological Reports (Oxford) Ltd.
British Archaeological Reports was first incorporated in 1974 to publish the BAR
Series, International and British. In 1992 Hadrian Books Ltd became part of the BAR
group. This volume was originally published by Archaeopress in conjunction with
British Archaeological Reports (Oxford) Ltd / Hadrian Books Ltd, the Series principal
publisher, in 2012. This present volume is published by BAR Publishing, 2016.

Printed in England

BAR
PUBLISHING

BAR titles are available from:

BAR Publishing
122 Banbury Rd, Oxford, OX2 7BP, UK
EMAIL   info@barpublishing.com
PHONE   +44 (0)1865 310431
FAX   +44 (0)1865 316916
www.barpublishing.com

Anna Simandiraki-Grimshaw would like to dedicate this book to past family and friends:
Anna, Menelaos, Stefanos, Menelaos, Eleftheria, Ken, Arthur, Alma and Glenys.
You will always live on.

Eleni Stefanou would like to dedicate this book to her family
who have been so supportive throughout the years.
I am extremely grateful to you.

CONTENTS

AUTHOR BIOGRAPHIES AND DETAILS 6

FROM ARCHAEOLOGY TO ARCHAEOLOGIES: THEMES, CHALLENGES AND BORDERS OF THE 'OTHER' PAST 9
Anna Simandiraki-Grimshaw, Eleni Stefanou

AN INSIDER'S VIEW OF AN ALTERNATIVE ARCHAEOLOGY..14
Michael Cremo

PERFORMANCE, PARTICIPATION AND PYRAMIDS: ADDRESSING MEANING AND METHOD BEHIND ALTERNATIVE ARCHAEOLOGY IN VISOKO, BOSNIA...20
Tera Pruitt

MARGINAL AND MAINSTREAM. RELIGION, POLITICS AND IDENTITY IN THE CONTEMPORARY US, AS SEEN THROUGH THE LENS OF THE KENNEWICK MAN / THE ANCIENT ONE.............................33
Liv Nilsson Stutz

A CLASH OF IDEOLOGIES: ZIMBABWEAN ARCHAEOLOGY AT THE FRINGE....................................45
Paul Hubbard, Robert S. Burrett

ACADEMIC CONSTRUCTS ABOUT THE PAST AND EARLY EDUCATION AS (DIS)ENTANGLED COMPONENTS OF IDENTITY FORMATION PROCESSES...56
Anna Zalewska

ARCHAEOLOGY AS ALLEGORY: THE REPRESENTATIONS OF ARCHAEOLOGY IN CHILDREN'S LITERATURE IN BRAZIL..67
Marcia Bezerra

A LOOK IN THE MIRROR AND THE PERSPECTIVE OF OTHERS ON THE PORTRAYAL OF ARCHAEOLOGY IN THE MASS MEDIA...77
Diane Scherlzler

'LOOTING' UNVEILED, ARCHAEOLOGY REVEALED: CASE STUDIES FROM WESTERN GREECE.........86
Ioanna Antoniadou

VISUAL COLLISION? PREHISTORIC ROCK ART AND GRAFFITI IN AN ARMENIAN LANDSCAPE.........93
Fay Stevens

THE COLOURS OF THE PAST 102
Cornelius Holtorf

Ioanna Antoniadou

Ioanna Antoniadou is a PhD student at the University of Southampton. Her thesis focuses on non-professional physical engagements with the material past amongst local communities in western Greece. Her research interests spring from a fascination with the nature of interaction between people and what we call 'archaeological' objects. Aspects that she aspires to deconstruct include the personal and social factors that trigger this relationship with the past, as well as the social and psychological implications that it leads to.
Correspondence: antoniadou@gmail.com

Marcia Bezerra

Marcia Bezerra has a DSc in Archaeology (USP/2003), is Professor of Archaeology at Universidade Federal do Pará (UFPA) and current Vice-President of the Sociedade de Arqueologia Brasileira. She was Adjunct Faculty Member at Indiana University, Bloomington and General Secretary of Sociedade de Arqueologia Brasileira in 2005-2009. She also currently serves as Junior Southern Representative of World Archaeological Congress (2008/2016), Editorial Member of Latin American Antiquity, Archaeologies and Assistant Editor of Amazônica, Antropology Journal/UFPA. She leads a public archaeology and an ethnographic archaeology project in Marajo Island, Amazon. Her interests include material culture studies, Amazonian archaeology, representations of the past, ethnographic archaeology, community archaeology, teaching of archaeology, archaeological tourism.
Correspondence: Universidade Federal do Pará, PPPGA/IFCH, Rua Augusto Corrêa, nº 1 - Guamá - Belém - Pará - 66.075-900 - Brasil. marciabezerrac14@gmail.com

Robert S. Burrett

Rob Burrett is a trained archaeologist and historian, with particular interests in the pre-colonial and early colonial past of south Central Africa as well as indigenous plants and their social and economic values. He worked for National Museums and Monuments of Zimbabwe and has operated as an independent heritage consultant working in Botswana, Lesotho, Zambia and Zimbabwe. Rob has published widely in a variety of international journals. His recent publications include *Dark Deeds: Some Hunting Memoirs of the Nineteenth Century Czech Traveller Emil Holub* (2005, Gweru: Mambo Press) and *Plumer's Men: the Anglo-South African War in Rhodesia and Bechuanaland* (2008, Durban: Just-in-Time). Currently he works as a cultural and environmental management consultant and is involved in several community-based projects, including the sustainable economic use of rural resources from hardwoods to essential oils.
Correspondence: Bulawayo Zimbabwe, projects@khami.co.zw

Michael A. Cremo

Michael A. Cremo is an independent historian of archaeology. He lives in Los Angeles. His work focuses on introducing into archaelogy concepts of human origins and antiquity with roots in the worldview expressed in the ancient Sanskrit writings of India.
Correspondence: 9701 Venice Blvd Apt 5, Los Angeles, CA 90034, USA, mcremo@cs.com

Cornelius Holtorf

Cornelius Holtorf is Professor of Archaeology at Linnaeus University, Kalmar, Sweden. He directs the degree programme in Heritage Studies. His research interests include contemporary and applied archaeology and he currently works on questions about time travelling, zoos, and nuclear waste. He is an Associate Editor of *Heritage and Society*. Recent publications include *Search the Past – Find the Present* (2012), *Contemporary Archaeologies: Excavating Now* (2nd ed. 2011, co-edited with A. Piccini), and *Archaeology is a Brand!* (2007). The multidisciplinary conference *Places, People, Stories,* which Holtorf co-organised in Kalmar in 2011, has among other formats been documented in a graphic novel.
Correspondence: Archaeology, Linnaeus University, 391 82 Kalmar, Sweden. cornelius.holtorf@lnu.se

Paul Hubbard

Born in Bulawayo, Paul has lived all over Zimbabwe both in town and in the wild - which he much prefers. He holds a couple of degrees in archaeology from the University of Zimbabwe and University College London and worked variously as an archaeologist, university lecturer, editor and researcher. Paul currently works around the country as a professional tour guide specialising in the culture and history of Zimbabwe, but spending most of his time in the Matobo Hills World Heritage Site. He is also the project manager for the Mother Africa Trust, an organisation dedicated to helping the people of Matabeleland live better lives through improved educational and environmental conservation opportunities. On behalf of the Trust, Paul runs several wildlife research projects in both the Matobo and Hwange areas. He continues with his archaeological and historical research in Zimbabwe's past as much as possible and has published several papers, reviews and a few books on these subjects, including his latest book, co-authored with Rob

Burrett, *Madzimbahwe of the Southwest: A guide to Khami, Dhlo Dhlo and Naletale.*

Correspondence: Bulawayo Zimbabwe, hubcapzw@gmail.com

Liv Nilsson Stutz

Liv Nilsson Stutz is a Lecturer at the Department of Anthropology at Emory University. She has a background in archaeology and biological anthropology, and her research interests have focussed on prehistoric burial practices, mortuary rituals and different perspectives on the body in the past. Her published PhD-thesis: *Embodied Rituals and Ritualized Bodies. Tracing ritual practice in Late Mesolithic burials* (Almqvist and Wiksell Intl. 2003) develops these approaches to hunter-gatherer cemeteries in Northern Europe. In recent years she has carried out a research project funded by the Swedish Research Council on the repatriation debate in different academic, historic and political contexts, and role of the archaeologist in contemporary cultural heritage production and use. She has published many papers on different aspects of the archaeology of death, the body in archaeology, ritual theory in archaeology, repatriation and cultural heritage and identity processes. She is an associate editor of the journal *Archaeological Dialogues.*

Correspondence: Department of Anthropology, Emory University, 207 Anthropology Building, 1557 Dickey Dr., Atlanta, GA 30322, lstutz@emory.edu

Tera C. Pruitt

Tera Pruitt is a Teaching Associate and Research Assistant at the University of Cambridge, with special responsibility for the new Archaeology Gallery in the Museum of Archaeology and Anthropology. Her PhD titled "Authority and the Production of Knowledge in Archaeology" addressed the way technologies and methodologies are used in science to construct personal and institutional authority. Her research interests are in the politics of museum display, anthropology of science, post-conflict heritage and public archaeology. She has a range of experience in museums and archaeological fieldwork from Bosnia-Herzegovina, Turkey, Crete, Ireland, the United Kingdom and the United States.

Correspondence: 14423 Kingston Falls Ln, Humble, Texas 77396, United States, tcpruitt@gmail.com

Diane Scherzler

Diane Scherzler works as an editor and journalist for Südwestrundfunk (SWR), a major German Public Broadcaster. As a prehistorian, she regularly covers scientific and archaeological topics. Since 1995 Diane has been concerned with how to communicate archaeology through the media. She is the founder and head of the Euroscience workgroup 'Science Communication' that shares best practices in communicating topics from the 'hard' sciences and humanities with non-experts. She regularly provides media training, advises scientific organizations on their media relations and teaches science communication at the universities of Tübingen and Freiburg. Diane currently serves as vice chairperson of the Deutsche Gesellschaft für Ur- und Frühgeschichte (German Society for Pre- and Protohistory).

Correspondence: Orchideenweg 6 - 72762 Reutlingen – Germany. +49/7121 27 45 41.
www.diane-scherzler.de   mail@diane-scherzler.de

Anna Simandiraki-Grimshaw

Anna Simandiraki-Grimshaw, BA, MA, PhD., is trained in Greek (Prehistoric, Classical and Byzantine) archaeology and specialises in the Aegean Bronze Age, particularly Minoan Crete. Anna has also acquired an interdisciplinary professional background since the completion of her PhD. This has included, among other posts, a Fellowship at the International Baccalaureate for research into international education (based at the University of Bath, UK); and the Margo Tytus Research Fellowship (Department of Classics, University of Cincinnati, USA) for research into Minoan corporeality. She is currently an Associate Lecturer at Classical and Archaeological Studies, the School of European Culture and Languages, University of Kent, UK. She also lectures in archaeology at the Continuing Education Departments of the Universities of Cambridge and Oxford, UK. In addition, she is a Teaching Fellow in Modern Greek at the Foreign Languages Centre, Department of Politics, Languages and International Studies, University of Bath, UK.

As a practising archaeologist and researcher for nearly twenty years, Anna has diverse research interests, on which she has published numerous papers and is preparing three books. Her interests include archaeologies of the body, ceramics, religion, artefact databases and reception studies, the latter with particular reference to identity construction through the use of heritage in education and nationalism.

Correspondence: www.anna-simandiraki.co.uk, collaborations@anna-simandiraki.co.uk

Eleni Stefanou

Eleni Stefanou (BA, MA, PhD) works as an Adjunct Lecturer at the Department of Cultural Heritage Management and New Technologies (University of Western Greece), where she teaches Cultural Heritage Management, and at the Department of Pre-School Education and Educational Design (University of the Aegean), where she teaches Museum Education and Museum Studies.

Her PhD, entitled *Aspects of Identity and Nationhood: Commemorating, Representing, and Replicating the Greek Maritime Past*, was conducted at the Department of Archaeology, University of Southampton, UK, and was funded by the Greek Foundation of State Scholarships (IKY).

Eleni is the 2011 holder of the John Morrison Memorial Fund for Hellenic Maritime Studies, awarded by the British School at Athens.

Her research interests and recent publications revolve around the ideological uses of the past in the present, as these are shaped through museum and heritage representations, memory practices, and education, i.e. the predominant fields that shape the intimate relationship of various social groups with the past.

Correspondence: stefanoueleni@googlemail.com
http://aegean.academia.edu/EleniStefanou

Fay Stevens

Fay Stevens' specialist interests are in British and European later prehistory, phenomenology, photography and archaeology, archaeology and ethics and academic literacies

Her current research focuses on depositional practices in their landscape context and Bronze Age metalwork, with a particular interest in phenomenological research methods, writing in the discipline and the role of material culture in prehistoric societies. Her PhD (submission April 2012) is a contextual and phenomenologically informed analysis of Bronze Age metalwork deposition in south-west Britain. She is also currently collaborating on a project that focuses on the role photography plays in the construction of archaeological knowledge. Tied in with this, is an interest in the interplay between theory and method, landscape archaeology, ethics in the discipline and pedagogy in Higher Education.

Fay has taught archaeology at a number of universities across the UK and recently held a Teaching Fellowship in Academic Literacies at UCL. She has worked on a number of funded projects focusing on the pedagogy of archaeological writing and the construction of identity through academic writing. Fay currently lectures archaeology courses in Higher Education at University of Reading and University of Notre Dame, Department of Anthropology, London and in Continuing Education at University of Oxford. She is a Visiting Lecturer in Academic Literacies at Central School of Speech and Drama, University of London where she runs postgraduate workshops in academic literacies.

Correspondence: UCL, Institute of Archaeology,
fay.stevens@ucl.ac.uk

Anna Zalewska

Anna Zalewska is an archaeologist and historian. She is a senior lecturer (adiunkt) at the Institute of Archaeology at the Maria Curie-Skłodowska University, Lublin, Poland. She is interested in understanding the ways in which attitudes to the material traces from the past and to archaeological knowledge and beliefs function in today's societies. As a practitioner and promoter of the second degree archaeology, she is trying to recognize and interpret the social status of archaeology as a discipline; the consequences of some particular approaches to material traces; the professional and non-professional interactions with some specific carriers of material memory. She strongly believes this can contribute to the appreciation and protection of past remains.

Seeing material traces as durable entities, often burdened by many meanings put on them by the many cultural systems in which they were and are engaged, Anna is trying to recognize: the specificity of dependence between various types of statements and messages comprising elements of archaeological knowledge; the social status of certain material traces of the past; the ways in which the (not necessarily mutable) features of physical data 'can' revise cognitive messages based on it; the impact that specific interpretative change can have on the 'collective imaginations' about the past, the roles played by material traces in awakening and stimulating 'interpretative imperative' among professionals and non-professionals.

Correspondence: Institute of Archaeology, Maria Curie-Skłodowska University, Pl. Marii Curie-Skłodowskiej 5, 20-031 Lublin, PL.

FROM ARCHAEOLOGY TO ARCHAEOLOGIES:
THEMES, CHALLENGES AND BORDERS OF THE 'OTHER' PAST

Anna Simandiraki-Grimshaw, Eleni Stefanou

The field of so-called 'fringe' or 'alternative' archaeology is vast and multifaceted, ranging from pseudoarchaeology, 'bad' archaeology practices, conspiracy theories and claims about lost civilizations to extraterrestrial cultures, (neo)shamanism, religious and/or nationalist demands. All these agendas have in common the fact that, through their differentiated readings and appropriations of the past, they create solidarities amongst their supporters. More importantly, alternative interpretations of the past are usually – though not solely – shaped outside the academic archaeological community. They often reject the discipline's scientific methods of analysis and may view 'mainstream' archaeologists as short-sighted members of a disenfranchising academic or political establishment. On the other hand, the 'mainstream' archaeological community also stereotypes and dismisses what it often perceives as a homogeneous 'alternative' community. In recent years, publications, websites, reports and articles by both academics and non-academics have sought to categorise archaeology either as 'mainstream', 'objective' and 'correct' or as 'alternative', 'distorted' and 'wrong'. Such works tend to attract already dedicated readers, while they repel others who may feel intimidated by one-sided polemic (e.g. see Fagan 2006; Feder 2008).

However, there are also archaeological interpretations which combine the two 'poles', both within and beyond the 'mainstream'. One example is the work of (non archaeologist) Peet (2005), who seeks to question the established narratives about the history of the world, employing science in order to provide answers to famous ancient mysteries. Another example is Cremo's project, which explores the 'hidden story of the human race' and argues that modern humans have lived on earth for several millions of years (e.g. Cremo 1998; 2004; Cremo and Thompson 1993). A blurring of this polarisation is discernible in the work of (anthropologist) Kehoe, who explores pre-Columbian contacts between the Americas and other continents: a taboo topic among American archaeologists. Kehoe uses a scientific approach to challenge the legitimacy of pseudoscientific assertions while simultaneously making reference to controversial issues of American archaeology, such as transatlantic migration and Shamanism (2008). In other words, approaches that are considered 'fringe' can and are developed within, as well as beyond, the 'mainstream' discipline of archaeology; and can originate from 'mainstream' as well as 'fringe' practitioners. But, despite increasing debates about 'mainstream' and 'alternative' archaeologies, there has been little analysis of how positions are assigned or how 'alternative' audiences are created. Discussions rarely go beyond stereotypical explanations, involving popular fantasies,

sensationalism and extremism. Of course, this does not mean that the ideologies involved should not be investigated (e.g. Billig 1995). Such ideologies are endemic, and empowering to many social groups. Notable exceptions, which focus on nationalist, colonialist, imperialist, and postcolonialist paradigms, illustrate how the interplay between local, national and global priorities affects archaeological interpretation through public archaeology, indigenous voices or popular culture. For example, the work of Trigger (1989) discerns between three basic types of archaeology (nationalist, colonialist, imperialist) and discusses their impact on the establishment of perceptions about the past. Silberman (1995) points out the legitimisation of modern political demands through excavated material culture. Hamilakis and Duke (2007) tackle the historical dimension of the discipline of archaeology and suggest a more engaged practice, connected to the communities and the people it represents. Holtorf, a substantial voice in the discourse of archaeological practices (e.g. 2005a, 2005b, 2007a, 2007b), explores archaeology as a discipline, but also as a component of society, as representation, as popular culture, as the interplay between diverse archaeology practitioners and audiences. Habu, *et al.* (2008) overcome the boundaries suggested by Trigger's three archaeological paradigms. They critically challenge the concept of multivocality by empowering the voice of minority groups, while questioning the notion of the concept of multivocality itself (for an overview of which social groups are considered indigenous and a discussion of their involvement with or exclusion from archaeological processes, see Watkins 2005). Nicholas and Hollowell (2008) draw attention to the ethical issues of postcolonial archaeology, as the major stakeholders of archaeological interpretations do not easily accept alternative world views. The work of Wallis (2000) is particularly relevant here. Rather than treating neo-shamanism as a 'fringe' practice, he considers it from the viewpoint of queer theory. For him, it is a self-reflective practice which brings together official and unofficial engagements with the past.

Situated within these discourses, *From Archaeology to Archaeologies – The 'Other' Past* seeks to explore the conflicting relationship between the 'mainstream' and the 'alternative'. The idea for this volume emerged from critical self reflection about our own archaeological practices in a session we co-organised at the 13th European Association of Archaeologists Annual Meeting (2007); and from research that our colleagues have shared with us. We acknowledge that archaeological practice is constituted by complex phenomena which involve not only archaeological narratives but also popular ways of understanding the past. In seeking to unravel these complex phenomena, we are not particularly concerned with the scientific validation or rejection of 'fringe' archaeologies. Nor do we aim to 'set the record straight'. Instead, we are interested in the *reasons* why people diversify and oppose other people's notions about the past. As such, this is a self-reflexive volume which welcomes contributions from diverse perspectives by including various geographical areas; by involving 'alternative' writers and topics; by exploring archaeological epistemologies; by critically investigating different practices; and by appealing to a wider and more heterogeneous readership. The need for an inclusive analysis becomes all the more obvious when one considers the growing worldwide public interest in the consumption of 'mainstream' and 'alternative' archaeological discourses through national politics (cf. e.g. Kohl *et al.* 2007), media, habitual performances, or collective rituals. We also feel that the volume has the potential to add to the current renegotiation of archaeological identities, itself a product of the postmodern renegotiation of the boundaries between communities of practice.

Consequently, the chapters of this volume are deliberately diverse, bringing together a range of perspectives and arguments. The authors, writing as 'insiders' or 'outsiders' of the case studies they present, cover Armenia, Brazil, Bosnia, Germany, Greece, India, Poland, the USA and Zimbabwe. We made a conscious decision to include case studies originating from a variety of geographical locations and exemplifying a variety of debates (e.g. ethics, communication, repatriation, evolution, etc.). We also determined to collaborate with authors who represent different paradigms, viewpoints, archaeological and non archaeological backgrounds, as well as languages. Bearing in mind this diversity, the editing of *Archaeology to Archaeologies* was a challenging but extremely rewarding task, as we engaged in many fruitful discussions and deliberations with the author of each chapter. We do not necessarily share all of the authors' opinions, linguistic particularities or arguments. But ut we feel that the freedom for authors to express themselves and publish about their own cultural and archaeological realities is at the heart of this book.

In this light, *From Archaeology to Archaeologies – The 'Other' Past* poses a series of questions. Several of these are addressed by the contributors, while others provide the stimulus for further exploration. Amongst the key questions are: who determines what is considered 'mainstream' or 'alternative'? and how? Another is: Are non-archaeological reasons also important (e.g. cultural imperialism, rigid academic structures, gender imbalances, race, politics)? Yet another question pertains to the boundaries: How are these set and overcome or blurred? For example, if objectivity is accepted as one such boundary, how is that determined and pursued? And - in a postmodern intellectual milieu - should this notion not be problematised? Another question worthy of exploration concerns the processes, reasons and implications of 'cross-over' practice; e.g. when 'mainstream' archaeology and archaeologists embrace 'alternative' views of the past and vice versa. Furthermore, what needs do 'mainstream' and 'alternative' archaeologies satisfy? Why do people diversify, and how do they identify themselves? Finally, a crucial question concerns the implications for the interpretation of material culture. For example, (how) are we to accommodate multivocality, and when? Does it depend on whose rights may be promoted or violated? For example, extremist, racist, and religious approaches are often condemned, while nationalist approaches are permitted, or even encouraged.

The first four chapters of the book unravel the tensions provoked by archaeological multivocality through the differential, acceptable or unacceptable, (micro)politically motivated readings of the same material culture record.

Cremo begins this thematic section by explaining and problematizing his own voice as 'alternative'. He outlines his epistemic thesis, i.e. his argument for extreme antiquity of the human species, on an Indian religious and philosophical basis. This, he explains, jars with current 'mainstream' interpretations of material culture. However, his thesis is not the main focus of the paper – it rather acts as a case study into how epistemic debates can be contextualized within archaeological, religious and political stratigraphies. Cremo proceeds to explore and self-reflect on his motivations for deviating from the 'mainstream', on his audiences and his methods of communication, as well as on the reaction and criticism that his thesis has encountered. As an 'alternative insider', he argues for a more open dialogue between 'fringe' and 'mainstream' archaeologies, which he feels could be achieved through the empowerment of multivocality in the public domain (e.g. museums, schools etc.).

In the next chapter, *Pruitt* looks at another case of the clash between 'fringe' and 'mainstream' archaeologies: that of the Bosnian pyramids. Pruitt takes as a case study the Bosnian site of Visoko and the practices of the amateur archaeologist Semir Osmanagic. She argues that these exemplify a performative invention of (non)existent material culture. While Pruitt leaves no doubt as to why she considers the Bosnian pyramids project as 'pseudoarchaeology', her concern, we feel, is not necessarily to stop or dismantle this. Instead, her valuable contribution lies in her nuanced and grounded analysis, which demonstrates the ways in which heritage communication can manipulate, engage, challenge, encourage or discourage diverse stakeholders.

Liv Nilsson Stutz follows Pruitt's thread of archaeology and politics with another case study: that of the Kennewick Man. She vividly illustrates how political and ideological issues affect archaeological interpretation. After outlining the multitude of ethical, biological and legal issues with which this case is fraught, Nilsson Stutz eloquently argues for underlying non-archaeological factors which influence the interpretation and treatment of archaeological materials: lineage, property, nationalism, politics, religion and race, among others. In essence, Nilsson Stutz demonstrates how the different stakeholders are constructed and reconstructed, their arguments thus being branded as 'fringe' or 'mainstream'.

Hubbard and **Burrett** conclude this section of diverse archaeological debates and interpretations. They offer a fascinating, stratified overview of a highly controversial issue: the authorship of Great Zimbabwe. Through a chronologically informed account, they trace the non archaeological threads of racial politics in the volatile and shifting southern African milieu of the last century or so. They too argue that the creation of 'fringe' and 'mainstream' theories, identities and proponents in southern African archaeology was greatly dependent on the concurrent acceptance (or not) of theories about black (indigenous) or white (incoming) authorship of sites such as Great Zimbabwe, in turn dependent on black or white political and nationalist discourses.

The next three contributions expand further on two major components of archaeological multivocality, namely that of cultural communication and that of the interplay between specialist and non specialist promoters of archaeological information to diverse publics.

More specifically, **Zalewska** explores, through the case study of the site of Biskupin in Poland, the dissemination of archaeological information via educational materials. This has played varied roles in the construction of national and other identities in Poland. She argues, following a thread previously encountered in Hubbard's and Burrett's southern African debates, that Biskupin's significance has fluctuated over the last century, depending on the strength of debates about indigenous or incoming authorship. Poland's recent political and ideological trajectory, she suggests, should be added into the mix, in order to comprehend how autochthonist or allochthonist arguments have rendered the archaeological site of Biskupin visible or invisible in the official state narrative of Polish school books.

Educational books (curricular and extracurricular) are also the topic of the next chapter, which this time is situated in a Brazilian context. Here, **Bezerra** identifies and analyses persistent archaeological types and stereotypes, with a critical eye towards their origins in colonialism, gender imbalances and the constructs of popular culture. Through her nuanced and insightful investigation, Bezerra demonstrates that the otherwise diverse outlets of archaeological processes in children's literature in Brazil nevertheless create a relatively consistent 'alternative' corpus.

Scherzler takes the issue of archaeological representation in the public domain to the realm of journalism. Using Germany as the backdrop to her case study, she explores why tensions can arise between archaeology and journalism. She takes a closer look at the different methodologies and priorities of the two fields and thus pinpoints the differences of perspective. She argues that some archaeological priorities (e.g. accuracy) can contradict certain journalistic priorities (e.g. immediacy and clarity). Similarly, she makes an important distinction between the archaeologist as journalistic author and the archaeologist as interviewee. She highlights the tensions that exist in the relationship between archaeology and journalism, and therefore the nature of archaeological dissemination through the mass media. These tensions arise not only because of different practices, but also because of the potential gaps between how stakeholders perceive themselves and how they are perceived by others.

In the next two chapters, Antoniadou and Stevens expand on debates of alternative interpretation, stakeholder rights, (micro)politics and identity. The common denominator of these chapters, which forms the core of this last thematic section, is the use of postmodernist methodologies (e.g. archaeological ethnography and graffiti practice respectively) to understand and contextualize past material culture.

Antoniadou, using Greece as the locus of her case study, tackles the issue of archaeological multivocality in terms of the contentious issue of looting. Her ethnographic approach does not necessarily endorse looting but instead problematizes this practice as more complex than a stereotypically clear-cut case of illegal, clandestine practices for financial gain. In her analysis she explores and evaluates the motivations, performances and material culture relationships of two anonymized informants. In the process, Antoniadou illuminates the emotional attachment and negotiation of artefact and informant identities, the complexity of (official and unofficial) archaeological interpretations, as well as the love-hate relationship between official and unofficial heritage stakeholders. Ultimately, she demonstrates how, in these cases, the 'alternative', which pursues a 'mainstream' identity, is denied the latter largely on logistical rather than ideological grounds.

Multivocality is further explored by **Stevens's** postmodern treatment of the rock carvings at the Ukhtasar site in Armenia, drawing links with the ideology, practice and performance of contemporary urban graffiti, e.g. the work of Banksy. More specifically, after situating the material culture of the rock carvings in the Armenian context, Stevens proceeds with the important notion of the coexistence and even interaction between the ancient carvings and the modern ones at Ukhtasar. Based on her analysis of key principles of graffiti (such as positioning, piecing and symbolic exchange), and her application of these to the Ukhtasar specimens, Stevens argues for the value and applicability of 'alternative' or 'unorthodox' readings of material culture. Furthermore, she demonstrates how archaeological debates can label past material culture as either 'mainstream' (e.g. Ukhtasar ancient rock carvings as art) or 'alternative' (e.g. Ukhtasar recent/modern rock carvings as graffiti).

Finally, the epilogue by **Holtorf** completes this volume with a discussion of the threads, challenges and issues argued in the various papers of this volume. It also contextualizes these within the wider debate on archaeological multivocality. Holtorf's *Colours of the Past*, in which he discusses how the past is reconfigurable in the present, thus 'mirrors' our introduction. This contribution is decidedly different but, we feel, complementary to the present section.

The element that all contributions of *From Archaeology to Archaeologies* have in common is that they do not address 'mainstream' and 'alternative' archaeologies as clear-cut cases of 'right-or-wrong', even when they do position themselves regarding 'acceptable' or 'unacceptable' uses of the past. Instead, they critically engage with the tensions inherent in archaeological multivocality. As such, several threads can be followed across chapters, mainly due to the complementary nature of their approaches.

One such thread is *authority and epistemology*. Almost all chapters address these by pinpointing and evaluating the ways in which debates about material culture are branded and performed as 'mainstream' and 'alternative'. For example, Cremo discusses the archaeological and non-archaeological reasons why his thesis is not accepted in Western institutional archaeology. In this case, authority and epistemological credibility are to be found in the institutionalisation of debates and the perceived clash of science and religion. Nilsson Stutz also touches upon these issues when she explores the legal side of the Kennewick repatriation case. This, she feels, is further entangled with legal property rights. In her case study, authority and credibility can be seen to emanate from a legal onto a social plane. Pruitt argues about the construction of authority through the performance of 'mainstream' tropes by the 'alternative' practitioners at Visoko and the successful imposition of such 'tropes' upon the (non)existent material culture. Authority and epistemology also clearly emerge in Hubbard's and Burrett's exploration of the Great Zimbabwe debate. Here it becomes obvious that racial politics decide whose voice is or is not authoritative, and therefore credible.

Another thread concerns *collective identity*. The authors discuss the construction of multiple identities (professional, institutional and national). For example, the use of material culture in the service of national identities comes through very strongly in the analyses of the Armenian rock carvings[1] at Ukhtasar (Stevens), the

Biskupin site (Zalewska), (non)Brazilian archaeology (Bezerra), the Bosnian 'pyramids' at Visoko (Pruitt), the looted finds of Greek Macedonia (Antoniadou) and the site at Great Zimbabwe (Hubbard and Burrett). In all these cases, the importance of the sites/artefacts and their heritage has been differentially interpreted and manipulated in order to benefit localist/nationalist ideologies in war-torn, marginalised or even territorially disputed contexts.

Such explorations are further permeated in some chapters by the consideration of autochthonist or allochthonist, or even (post)colonial, issues. For example, the issue of collective identity acquires another fascinating dimension in the analyses of Zalewska, Bezerra, Pruitt, Nilsson Stutz, Hubbard and Burrett, where 'mainstream' and 'alternative' are not fixed, definable facts, but time-dependent agendas. In other words, the interpretation of whether a site or a collection of finds represent originally indigenous or incoming (i.e. non indigenous) people is dependent upon shifting socio-political circumstances, such as race or perceptions of biological, spiritual, national lineage.

Yet another major thread running through the volume is that of *communication* and its various guises, e.g. journalism (Scherzler), education (Zalewska, Bezerra), outreach (Cremo, Antoniadou, Pruitt) and the dialogue between material cultures (Stevens, Antoniadou). What emerges is that tensions between archaeological voices, as well as between archaeological and non archaeological voices, are primarily created because of the different, often conflicting expectations of heritage stakeholders. In the case of the mass media, the tensions and miscommunication arise from the fact that, while archaeologists are interested in publicizing certain datasets and methods, journalists and the general public are interested in knowing different datasets and expect to be catered for through different levels of detail and discourse. In the case of education and outreach, national, ideological, pedagogical and other filters have distilled the information in ways that archaeologists may or may not have control over. In the case of the dialogue between material cultures, communication is a concern not only between diverse archaeological voices (e.g. 'mainstream' vs 'alternative' practitioners), but also between artefacts themselves ('mainstream'/carvings or finds and 'alternative'/modern graffiti or loot).

All in all, the contributors initiate a dialogue as to why there is archaeological deviation, regardless of whose side may be considered 'mainstream' or 'alternative' at any given point. Readers will, of course, draw their own conclusions. Ultimately, we believe that the reasons for the deviations, interactions and discourses explored here are perhaps the heterogeneous identities and needs (institutional, performative, emotional, spiritual,

---

[1] For a different approach of recent graffiti inscribed on ancient stones, see Hamilakis and Anagnostopoulos (2009), who discuss this issue from the view of historical-archaeological ethnography as an indication of the multi-temporal biography of an archaeological site. Also, see

Hamilakis (2011), who considers recent inscriptions as evocative of the diverse social life of a place.

professional) of heritage stakeholders. And this is what keeps archaeological dialogues alive and challenging.

As a conclusion to our introduction, we would like to thank the people who helped create and publish this volume. First of all, we would like to thank BAR for believing in the value of this project and for encouraging our work. We would also like to thank our contributors for their excellent work, collaboration and patience during this long process. We would especially like to thank Cornelius Holtorf for his friendly support, and for undertaking the task of reading the whole volume in order to offer his insights in the *Epilogue*. In addition, Anna Simandiraki-Grimshaw would like to thank Trevor Grimshaw for useful discussions, suggestions and corrections. Finally, we extend our sincere thanks to the total of seven anonymous reviewers who helped this volume by generously giving some of their valuable time and very constructive comments. We are indebted to you.

Bibliography

Billig, M. 1995. *Banal Nationalism*. London, Sage Publications.

Cremo, M. A. 1998. *Forbidden Archeology's Impact.* Los Angeles, Bhaktivedanta Book Publishing.

Cremo, M. A. 2004. *Human Devolution: A Vedic Alternative to Darwin's Theory.* Los Angeles, Bhaktivedanta Book Publishing.

Cremo, M. A. and Thompson R. L. 1993. *Forbidden Archeology.* Los Angeles, Bhaktivedanta Book Publishing.

Fagan, G. (ed.) 2006. *Archaeological Fantasies: How Pseudoarchaeology Misrepresents the Past and Misleads the Public.* London, Routledge.

Feder, K. L., 2008. *Frauds, Myths, and Mysteries: Science and Pseudoscience in Archaeology.* McGraw-Hill Humanities/Social Sciences/Langua.

Habu, J., Fawcett, C., and Matsunaga, J. M. (eds.) 2008. *Evaluating Multiple Narratives: Beyond Nationalist, Colonialist, Imperialist Archaeologies.* Springer.

Hamilakis, Y., and Anagnostopoulos, A., 2009. What is archaeological ethnography. *Public Archaeology: Archaeological Ethnographies* 8 (2-3), 65–87.

Hamilakis, Y. 2011. Archaeological Ethnographies: A Multitemporal Meeting Ground for Archaeology and Anthropology. *Annual Review of Anthropology* 40, 399–414.

Hamilakis, Y., and Duke, Ph. (eds.) 2007. *Archaeology and capitalism: from ethics to politics.* Walnut Creek, USA, Left Coast Press.

Holtorf, C. 2005. Beyond Crusades: How (Not) to Engage with Alternative Archaeologies. *World Archaeology* 37 (4), 544-551.

Holtorf, C. 2005b. *From Stonehenge to Las Vegas. Archaeology as Popular Culture.* Lanham: Altamira Press.

Holtorf, C. 2007a. *Archaeology is a Brand! The Meaning of Archaeology in Contemporary Popular Culture.* Oxford, BAR Publishing.

Holtorf, C. 2007b. An Archaeological Fashion Show: how archaeologists dress and how they are portrayed in the media, in T. Clack and M. Brittain (eds.), *Archaeology and the Media*, 69-88. Walnut Creek, Left Coast Press.

Kehoe, A. B. 2003. Fringe of American Archaeology: Transoceanic and Transcontinental Contacts in Prehistoric America. *Journal of Scientific Exploration* 17(1), 19-36.

Kehoe, A. B. and Lesser, A. 2008. *Controversies in Archaeology.* Left Coast Press.

Kohl, Ph., Kozelsky, M. and Ben-Yehuda, N. 2007. *Selective Remembrances: Archaeology in the Construction, Commemoration and Consecration of National Pasts.* Chicago, The University of Chicago Press.

Nicholas, G. and Hollowell, J. 2007. Ethical Challenges to a Post-Colonial Archaeology: The Legacy of Scientific Colonialism, in Y. Hamilakis and Ph. Duke (eds.), *Archaeology and capitalism: from ethics to politics*, 59-82. Walnut Creek, USA, Left Coast Press.

Peet, P. (ed.) 2005. *Underground!: The Disinformation Guide to Ancient Civilizations, Astonishing Archaeology and Hidden History* (Disinformation Guides). New York, The Disinformation Company.

Silberman, N. A. 1995. The politics and poetics of archaeological narratives, in P. Kohl and C. Fawcett (eds.), *Nationalism, politics, and the practice of archaeology*, 249-262. Cambridge, Cambridge University Press.

Trigger, B. 1989. *A history of archaeological thought.* Cambridge, Cambridge University Press.

Watkins, J. 2005. Through Wary Eyes: Indigenous Perspectives on Archaeology. *Annual Review of Anthropology* 34, 429-449.

Wallis, J. R. 2000. Queer Shamans: Autoarchaeology and Neo-Shamanism. *World Archaeology* 32(2), 252-262.

AN INSIDER'S VIEW OF AN ALTERNATIVE ARCHAEOLOGY

Michael A. Cremo

Abstract

Since 1984, I have been developing an approach to archaeology with roots in a perspective on human origins and antiquity derived from the *Puranas*, the historical writings of ancient India. The *Puranas* present a picture of extreme human antiquity, incompatible with current mainstream theories. In my project, I have nevertheless made use of conventional archeological evidence. In the paper I will explore how and why I have done that. Ultimately, I seek to introduce into archaeology, and science generally, an alternative perspective on human origins and antiquity with roots in an ontology that includes nonmaterial substance, intelligence and agency. I will offer some suggestions as to how such alternative perspectives should be accommodated within archaeology, and within the world of science generally.

Key words: fringe archaeology, alternative archaeology, evolution, science and religion.

Michael Shanks (1992, 114), a prominent voice in archeological theory, wrote: 'Fringe archaeologies . . . explicitly or implicitly pose the question of the identity of the past, recognizing some element of transcendence, the unsayable, the spiritual. . . . Scientific rationality is conceived as partial at best, harmful or destructive at worst.' As a practitioner and proponent of a fringe, or alternative, archaeology, I find this characterization reasonably accurate.

I advocate an archaeology, or more generally, a science of human origins and antiquity, informed by a complementary relationship between scientific rationality and visions of the past incorporating 'some element of transcendence, the unsayable, the spiritual.' Specifically, I write about archaeology and history of archaeology from a perspective derived from my studies of the Vedic literature, especially the *Puranas*, the ancient historical writings of India.

Nevertheless, I get a hearing within professional circles. I give talks at universities, scientific institutions, and conferences, and I also have had some publications in the professional literature (for example, Cremo 1999; 2002; 2009). All of this makes me an example of a phenomenon noted by Ian Hodder, who said (1997, 699-700): 'The proliferation of special interests on the "fringe" increasingly challenges or spreads to the dominant discourse itself . . . . Within this unstable kaleidoscope, it is no longer so easy to see who is "in" the academy and who is "outside."'

How did my involvement in archaeology from a Puranic perspective come about? In the early 1970s, when I was in my early twenties, I found myself attracted to the yoga and meditation systems of India, and became a student of an Indian guru, A. C. Bhaktivedanta Swami Prabhupada (1896-1977), founder of the International Society for Krishna Consciousness. In the 1980s, I became associated with the Bhaktivedanta Institute, which Bhaktivedanta Swami established in 1974 to explore the relationships between the knowledge of ancient India and the worldview of modern science. In 1984, I began research related to the Puranic accounts of human origins and antiquity. The *Puranas,* like the writings of many traditional cultures (including the Christian Bible), put the origin of humanity at the very beginnings of the history of life on earth. I began looking into the history of archaeology, to see whether or not there was any archeological evidence for such extreme human antiquity, i.e. evidence that anatomically modern humans have been present for far longer periods of time (millions of years) than current theories allow (200,000 years or so). I saw there was such evidence in the primary archeological literature, the reports by original investigators of the past two centuries.

Let me give two examples. My purpose in giving them is not to convince you of the case I am making for extreme human antiquity, but rather just to give you some idea of how I am making use of archeological materiality in my work of establishing an 'other past,' a different collective memory, not just for followers of the Puranas, but for consideration by all thoughtful persons.

In the 1970s, American archeologists were excavating a site called Hueyatlaco, near the town of Puebla in central Mexico. They found many stone tools, including advanced bifaces. The archeologists called a team of geologists to date the site. Geologist Virginia Steen-McIntyre and her colleagues used four methods to establish the age of the artefact-bearing layers: uranium series on associated animal bones, zircon fission track on overlying volcanic ash layers, tephra hydration on volcanic crystals, and standard stratigraphic analysis (Steen-McIntyre *et al.* 1981). From the results of all four methods they employed, the geologists concluded the age of the site must be at least 250,000 years. But the archeologists did not believe the site could be that old. According to their understanding, human beings capable of making the artefacts did not exist 250,000 years ago— they had not evolved yet. Furthermore, according to then current ideas, humans did not enter North America until about 25,000 years ago. So the archeologists refused to accept the age for the site given by their own team of geologists, and instead assigned a far younger age to the site.

Later, Virginia Steen-McIntyre and her colleagues independently published the age they had obtained for the site (Steen-McIntyre *et al.* 1981) in a scientific journal. On March 30, 1981, Steen-McIntyre wrote to Estella Leopold, one of the editors (Cremo and Thompson 1993, 364-365): 'Not being an anthropologist, I didn't realize . . . how deeply woven into our thought the current theory of human evolution has become. Our work at Hueyatlaco has been rejected by most archaeologists because it contradicts that theory, period.' Partly as a result of my publishing the history of the case in *Forbidden Archeology,* new archeological investigations have been carried out at the site, as documented by archeologist Chris Hardaker (2007). Some of the new work contradicts the age estimates given by Steen-McIntyre and her colleagues. For example, geoarchaeologist Michael Waters believes that the Hueyatlaco stone tools were found in a recent channel cut into the older Pleistocene deposits (Hardaker 2007, 231-236). But some of the new work, such as the diatom study by Sam VanLandingham (2006), confirms the original dating by Steen-McIntyre and her colleagues, and explicitly contradicts the inset channel explanation offered by Waters. On balance, I think the original dating by Steen-McIntyre and her colleagues is the correct one, although I am sure some will disagree.

In the mid nineteenth century, gold was discovered in California. To get the gold, miners dug tunnels into the sides of mountains, such as Table Mountain in Tuolumne County, California. Deep inside the tunnels, the miners found human bones and human artefacts. The discoveries were made in auriferous gravels in ancient river channels along with plant and animal fossils characteristic of the early Eocene, which would give them an age of about 50 million years. These ancient Eocene river channels are capped by hundreds of feet of solid volcanic deposits, dated using the potassium-argon method, which gave an age of 20-33 million years. Norris and Webb (1990, 90-93) give a review of the geological history. The discoveries were carefully documented by Dr J. D. Whitney (1880). Whitney said that there was no evidence the artefacts could have come from higher, more recent levels. But we do not hear very much about these discoveries today. Anthropologist William Holmes (1899, 424) said, 'Perhaps if Professor Whitney had fully appreciated the story of human evolution as it is understood today, he would have hesitated to announce the conclusions formulated, notwithstanding the imposing array of testimony with which he was confronted.' This authoritative statement influenced many scientists to ignore or dismiss Whitney's report (see for example Munro 1905, 81-90; Lindgren 1911, 53), and the discoveries were largely forgotten.

Some of the artefacts from the California gold mines are still in the collection of the Phoebe Hearst Museum of Anthropology at the University of California at Berkeley. A few years ago, I was researching a paper about these discoveries. I received permission from the museum directors to study and photograph the artefacts. And by consulting Whitney's old maps and documents, I was able to go out to Table Mountain and relocate some of the old nineteenth century gold mining tunnels where the objects were originally found. I presented the paper at the World Archaeological Congress 5 (Cremo 2003), in Session E-4 (The History of Archeology in the Service of Isms), which I co-chaired. The paper explores the influence of Darwinian evolutionary preconceptions on the interpretation of the discoveries.

The Table Mountain discoveries in Tuolumne Country are sometimes conflated with the discovery of a human skull at Bald Hill in Calaveras County. In the well known case of the Calaveras skull, there were some unsubstantiated contemporary hearsay accounts that the skull was planted in the mineshaft in which it was found (Whitney 1880, 270). Such contemporary accusations were not made in connection with the Table Mountain finds, and many others reported by Whitney. Of course, for those who on theoretical grounds have difficulty accepting a fully human presence in the Tertiary, hoaxing is often assumed as an explanation for all the finds, without direct proof of such hoaxing. But, as in the case of the Hueyatlaco discoveries, I recognize that here also there may be differences of opinion.

I collected hundreds of cases of archeological evidence for extreme human antiquity, like the two mentioned above, in my book *Forbidden Archeology* (Cremo and Thompson 1993). The book was intended for a scientific audience. Its stated purpose was first of all to start a dialog with archeologists about anomalous archaeological evidence for extreme human antiquity, with the further goal of eventually demonstrating that an intellectually defensible case could be made for the picture of human origins and antiquity that emerges from the *Puranas.* One way that I tried to get the dialog going was by submitting the book for review in professional journals, which constitutes a kind of peer review. The effort was successful. *Forbidden Archeology* was reviewed in many of the professional journals of archaeology, anthropology, and history of science, including: *American Journal of Physical Anthropology, Geoarchaeology, Journal of Field Archaeology, Antiquity, Journal of Unconventional History, L'Homme, L'Anthropologie, British Journal for the History of Science, Social Studies of Science,* and *Ethology, Ecology, and Evolution.*

Given the controversial antievolutionary nature of the book, it drew a variety of responses. These responses reflect two basic approaches to alternative or fringe archaeologies, visions of other pasts, in mainstream archaeology: exclusion and inclusion. Some of the reviewers were downright hostile, expressing their unremittingly negative opinions in crude derogatory language. Such reviewers (Marks 1994; Groves 1994) wanted to maintain a strict separation between fringe archaeologies and what they regarded as proper scientific archaeology, or anthropology. But others (Murray 1995; Wodak and Oldroyd 1996) expressed views that allowed for some accommodation of alternative archaeologies like mine within mainstream archaeology.

As an example of the exclusion approach, let us consider the words of Jonathan Marks (1994, 141), who, writing in *American Journal of Physical Anthropology*, called *Forbidden Archeology* 'Hinduoid creationist drivel.' Nevertheless, Marks (1994, 140) grudgingly admitted that 'the rich and varied origins myths of all cultures are alternatives to contemporary evolution.' His use of the present tense ('are alternatives') is a reflection that modern science, in the postcolonial era, feels once more threatened by living alternative cosmologies that not long ago were securely categorized as cognitively dead myths. Also of concern to Marks were subversives in the ranks of the academic community itself. Marks (1994, 141) described sociologist Pierce Flynn, who contributed a favorable foreword to *Forbidden Archeology*, as 'a curious personage.' He went on to castigate Flynn for 'placing this work within postmodern scholarship.'

In short, Marks identified *Forbidden Archeology*, quite correctly in my view, with an array of perceived enemies at the boundaries of his discipline, and within the walls of the disciplinary sanctuary itself. These enemies included fundamentalists, creationists, cultural revivalists, religion-based sciences, populist detractors of science, purveyors of anomalies, and finally, the postmodern academic critics of science.

But other reviewers admitted they found *Forbidden Archeology* of some academic interest and value, and saw some role for the vision of the past it presented. For example, in the *British Journal for the History of Science*, archeologist Tim Murray (1995, 379) noted in his review of *Forbidden Archeology*: 'Certainly it provides the historian of archaeology with a useful compendium of case studies in the history and sociology of scientific knowledge, which can be used to foster debate within archaeology about how to describe the epistemology of one's discipline.' More importantly, Murray acknowledged that the Vedic perspective of *Forbidden Archeology* might have a role to play in the future development of archaeology. He wrote (1995, 379) in his review that archaeology is now in a state of flux, with practitioners debating 'issues which go to the conceptual core of the discipline.' Murray then proposed, 'Whether the *Vedas* have a role to play in this is up to the individual scientists concerned.' That is a position I can respect and support.

Forbidden Archeology attracted not only ordinary book reviews, but also a 20-page review article in *Social Studies of Science* (Wodak and Oldroyd 1996). The authors asked (Wodak and Oldroyd 1996, 207), 'So has *Forbidden Archeology* made any contribution at all to the literature on palaeoanthropology?' They concluded, 'Our answer is a guarded "yes", for two reasons.' First, 'the historical material . . . has not been scrutinized in such detail before,' and, second, the book does 'raise a central problematic regarding the lack of certainty in scientific "truth" claims.' Doubtlessly, some will see the latter statement as undermining the supposed objectivity and truth value of scientific conclusions, and as a

dangerous concession to total relativism, while others will see it as a justifiable epistemological position to take in a multicultural, global academic arena. Today many scientists claim that the evolutionary theory of human origins is absolutely certain in terms of its truth. Wodak and Oldroyd (1996, 207) thought the kind of work we did helped in problematising the claim of absolute certainty.

Altogether, *Forbidden Archeology* was successful in inserting an alternative perspective on human origins and antiquity, with openly acknowledged religious inspiration and content, into professional academic and scientific discourse. Those who wish to assess the reactions to *Forbidden Archeology* in more detail may find useful my book *Forbidden Archeology's Impact* (Cremo 1998), in which I collected the academic reviews and related correspondence. About *Forbidden Archeology's Impact*, Simon Locke (1999) wrote in *Public Understanding of Science*, 'It should . . . make a useful teaching resource as one of the best-documented case studies of "science wars," and raising a wide range of issues covering aspects of 'knowledge transfer' in a manner sure to be provocative in the classroom.'

Of the two different approaches to alternative visions of the past, or fringe archaeologies, represented in the reviews of *Forbidden Archeology,* exclusive and inclusive, I am, of course, more in favor of the inclusive approach, and am happy to see that this inclusive approach is becoming more common and influential among archeologists and other scientists and scholars interested in human origins and antiquity. Indeed, some organizations of archeologists, such as the World Archeological Congress (WAC), seem increasingly willing to seriously discuss practical implementation of this inclusive approach.

For example, archeologist Cornelius Holtorf (2006, 90-91) wrote about WAC, which is already hospitable to non-Western indigenous archaeologies:

> *If non-Western groups are made welcome to represent their accounts of the past or archaeological sites according to their own epistemologies and intellectual traditions, it is difficult to see how the same courtesy could be denied to traditions, both within and outside the Western world, that may be similarly different from what is expected within the academic discipline of archaeology . . . . There cannot be different worlds of Western and non-Western or hegemonic and suppressed archaeologies, and there cannot likewise be different worlds of academic and amateur or orthodox and alternative archaeologies.*

However, even though I myself am an alternative archeologist, my use of archaeological materiality and my understanding of the whole array of alternative archaeologies is not uncritical. I agree with Shanks when he says (1992, 115): '. . . the problem with fringe archaeologies, with their mysterious powers in the past, spacemen and catastrophes, is the overwhelming tendency to mysticism and irrationalism. Intuition, inspiration, extra-sensory perception, initiated wisdoms, mystic energies are fertile ground for nonsense.' But so are blind materialism, presumptuous positivism, and superficial scientism a fertile ground for nonsense of another kind.

So how are we to make decisions about such things? Representatives of alternative archaeologies, with visions of other pasts, desiring to participate in the world of science should be prepared to justify those visions in terms of observation and inferences from observation. For example, although I am guided in my archeological research by my Puranic theoretical perspective, it is not that I uncritically accept every archeological discovery that happens to be consistent with Puranic accounts of extreme human antiquity. My procedure, as an historian of archaeology, is to consult primary published works, commentary in the secondary literature, and to also, whenever possible, visit the sites, examine museum collections of artefacts, and search archives for unpublished correspondence, field notes, and maps. After evaluating all of this, I make my judgment about the case, which may be positive, negative, or undecided.

Some may desire to limit observations and inferences to only those consistent with a particular metaphysical framework. For example, many scientists today favor a metaphysical framework for scientific work that is based on a rather strict materialism coupled with an at least methodological atheism. This is often expressed in a language that proposes a strict separation between science and religion (or the spiritual, or the theological, or the mystical, etc.).

But such strict separation has not always been observed in the history of science, even in the West. In nineteenth century Europe, for example, we find scientists approached the question of the origin of species from many different metaphysical perspectives. Darwin, of course, is well known for championing a materialistic scientific naturalism. But he acknowledged special creation by God as a scientific theory to which he was proposing an alternative. Darwin (1859, 6) wrote in the introduction to the first edition of his *Origin of Species,* 'I can entertain no doubt, after the most deliberate study and dispassionate judgment of which I am capable, that the view which most naturalists entertain, and which I formerly entertained—namely, that each species has been independently created—is erroneous.' The important points here are Darwin's acknowledgement that most scientists of his time accepted special creation as the best explanation for the origin of species and his admission that he himself once accepted this idea. Although Darwin eventually came to reject the independent creation of each species by God, he retained God as a first cause (who set up the laws of nature) in his theory. He (1859, 488) referred to 'the laws impressed on matter by the Creator.' So, in 1859 Darwin pointed out that most scientists of that time had concluded that God had independently created each species, a view with foundations in Judeo-Christian metaphysics and theology. But among Darwin's scientific contemporaries, there were some who were operating according to other metaphysical perspectives. Richard Owen (1849) saw the various animal species as unfolding modifications of an original Platonic vertebrate form. Many European scientific contemporaries of Owen and Darwin also looked at biology through a Platonic lens (e.g. Rupke 2009, 119-134). And it does not end there. Alfred Russel Wallace, cofounder of the theory of evolution by natural selection, saw some room for nonmaterial substances and agency in his picture of the origin of species. Wallace, who did extensive research into what we today call paranormal phenomena, wrote (1870, 359):'A superior intelligence has guided the development of man in a definite direction, and for a special purpose, just as man guides the development of many animal and vegetable forms.' He said (1870, 360) that intelligence may have employed 'means of more subtle agencies than we are acquainted with.' And the variety of metaphysical frameworks in European biological science of the nineteenth century does not end there. So at times, even in the fairly recent history of science in the West, there has been a metaphysical pluralism. And we may be returning to such a situation today. In the postcolonial world, metaphysical pluralism extends beyond the metaphysical diversity in Europe to include a more global metaphysical diversity.

In the late nineteenth century, the negotiation among the competing visions, with their different metaphysical frameworks, led, fairly or unfairly, to a consensus view of scientific reality based on a fairly strict materialism that rules out nonmaterial agency (no special creation by God, for example) and nonmaterial substance (no mind-body dualism, for example). I suggest that this consensus is today being challenged, and that we are entering into a time in which it is once more possible to carry out scientific work within different metaphysical frameworks. It is possible, perhaps even desirable, that a new consensus will emerge from such a pluralistic interaction. In the meantime, we should tolerate metaphysical pluralism and a variety of visions of the past.

If there is to be a new consensus on human origins, what do I think it should be like? Some clues may be found in my book, *Human Devolution: A Vedic Alternative to Darwin's Theory* (Cremo 2004). My book *Forbidden Archeology* simply documents archeological evidence that contradicts modern accounts of human origins and that is consistent with Puranic accounts of extreme human antiquity. *Human Devolution* briefly reviews this evidence and then moves on to offer an alternative account of human origins. Today many researchers believe a human being is simply a combination of the ordinary material elements, but when I look at all the evidence, I find it is more reasonable to say that a human being is a combination not just of matter but also of a subtle (but nonetheless material) mind element and an irreducible element of nonmaterial consciousness. To put things very simply, we do not evolve up from matter but down from pure consciousness. But this process of devolution, whereby pure consciousness becomes covered by mind and matter, can be reversed, through disciplines of contemplative prayer, meditation, and yoga. Indeed, I regard my work as an integral part of my yoga, my meditation, my spiritual discipline. Ultimately, consciousness can be restored to its original pure state, and this restoration is, or should be, the main purpose of human existence. For those interested in how I justify all this in terms of observation and inference, I can only refer you to the book itself.

As was the case with my earlier books, this latest book, *Human Devolution*, has found its way to various audiences, including the academic and scientific audiences. When the book first came out, it came into the hands of an anthropologist at a university in the United States, and by his recommendation I was invited to give a two hour presentation about the book at a conference held by the Society for the Anthropology of Consciousness, a division of the American Anthropological Association.

I regard the whole of what I am doing as a contribution to the program advocated by Paul Feyerabend in his book *Science in A Free Society* (1978, 9-10): 'A free society is a society in which all traditions have equal rights and equal access to the centres of power (this differs from [.. .] equal rights [. . .] to positions defined by a special tradition—the tradition of Western Science and Rationalism).'

But Feyerabend (1978, 83) is careful to point out that what he favors is a political relativism (the idea that all knowledge traditions have equal rights to exist in the institutions of modern society) not a philosophical relativism (the idea that all knowledge traditions are equally true). He just suggests that in a democratic society, the truth value of traditions should be established in fair interactions among the traditions. Today, the conditions for such fair interaction do not always exist, because some scientists and academics see modern rationalistic science carried out within the framework of a materialistic metaphysics as deserving monopoly status. They therefore continue to zealously exclude alternative knowledge traditions from the institutional centers of science. Feyerabend (1978, 103) suggests that these 'traditions can become powerful rivals and can reveal many shortcomings of science if only they were given a fair chance to compete,' adding that 'it is the task of the institutions of a free society to give them such a fair chance.'

What I am proposing is that the scientific institutions of a free society should adopt a policy of accommodating proponents of alternate visions of the past, if they are willing to justify their claims in terms of observation and inference. There should also be an openness to metaphysical pluralism in science, so that the process of justifying claims in terms of observation and inference is not artificially constrained.

Bibliography

Cremo, M. A. 1998. *Forbidden Archeology's Impact.* Los Angeles, Bhaktivedanta Book Publishing.

Cremo, M. A. 1999. Puranic time and the archeological record. In T. Murray (ed.), *Time and Archaeology,* 38-48. London, Routledge.

Cremo, M. A. 2002. The later discoveries of Boucher de Perthes at Moulin Quignon and their impact on the Moulin Quignon jaw controversy. In G. Laurent (ed.), *Proceedings of the XXth International Congress of History of Science (Liege, 20-26 July 1997), Volume X, Earth Sciences, Geography and Cartography,* 39-56. Turnhout, Belgium, Brepols.

Cremo, M. A. 2003. The nineteenth century California gold mine discoveries: archeology, Darwinism, and evidence for extreme human antiquity. Unpublished manuscript.

Cremo, M. A. 2004. *Human Devolution: A Vedic Alternative to Darwin's Theory.* Los Angeles, Bhaktivedanta Book Publishing.

Cremo, M. A. 2009. The discoveries of Carlos Ribeiro: a controversial episode in nineteenth-century European archeology. *Journal of Iberian Archaeology* 12, 69-89.

Cremo, M. A. and Thompson R. L. 1993. *Forbidden Archeology.* Los Angeles, Bhaktivedanta Book Publishing.

Darwin, C. R. 1859. *The Origin of Species.* First edition. London, Murray.

Feyerabend, P. 1978. *Science in A Free Society.* London, Verso Editions.

Groves, C. 1994. Creationism: The Hindu view. A review of *Forbidden Archeology. The Skeptic* (Australia) 14(3), 43-45.

Hardaker, C. 2007. *The First American.* Franklin Lakes, Career Press.

Hodder, I. 1997. Always momentary, fluid, and flexible: Toward a reflexive excavation methodology. *Antiquity,* 71, 691–700.

Holmes, W. H. 1899. Review of the evidence relating to auriferous gravel man in California. *Smithsonian Institution Annual Report 1898–1899,* 419–472.

Holtorf, C. 2006. One World Archaeology today. *Archaeologies: Journal of the World Archaeological Congress* 2(2), 87-93.

Lindgren, W. 1911 The Tertiary Gravels of the Sierra Nevada of California. Washington, United States Geological Survey.

Locke, S. 1999. Review of *Forbidden Archeology's Impact. Public Understanding of Science* 8(1), 68-69.

Marks, J. 1994. Review of *Forbidden Archeology. American Journal of Physical Anthropology* 93(1), 140-141.

Munro, R. 1905. *Archaeology and False Antiquities.* London, Methuen and Company.

Murray, T. 1995. Review of *Forbidden Archeology. British Journal for the History of Science* 28, 377-379.

Norris, R. M. and Webb, R. W. 1990. *Geology of California.* Second edition. New York, John Wiley & Sons.

Owen, R. 1849. *On the Nature of Limbs.* London, J. Van Voorst.

Rupke, N. A. 2009. *Richard Owen: Biology Without Darwin.* Chicago, University of Chicago Press.

Shanks, M. 1992. *Experiencing the Past.* London, Routledge.

Steen-McIntyre, V., Fryxell, R., and Malde, H. E. 1981. Geologic evidence for age of deposits at Hueyatlaco archaeological site, Valsequillo, Mexico. *Quaternary Research* 16, 1–17.

VanLandingham, S. 2006. Diatom evidence for autochthonous artifact deposition in the Valsequillo region, Puebla, Mexico during the Sangamonian (*sensu lato*=80,000 to *ca.* 220,000 yr BP) and Illinoian (220,000 to 430,000 yr BP). *Journal of Paleolimnology* 36, 101-116.

Wallace, A. R. 1870. *Contributions to the Theory of Natural Selection. A Series of Essays.* London, Macmillan.

Whitney, J. D. 1880. The auriferous gravels of the Sierra Nevada of California. *Harvard University, Museum of Comparative Zoology Memoir,* 6(1).

Wodak, J. and Oldroyd, D. 1996. Vedic creationism: a further twist to the evolution debate. *Social Studies of Science* 26, 192-213.

PERFORMANCE, PARTICIPATION AND PYRAMIDS: ADDRESSING MEANING AND METHOD BEHIND ALTERNATIVE ARCHAEOLOGY IN VISOKO, BOSNIA

Tera C. Pruitt

Abstract

Alternative claims to the past, like pseudoarchaeology, are complex social processes which originate from intricate social interactions and contexts. This paper examines the case study of Bosnian Pyramids, exploring how one man's fringe vision of the past has become a preferred account of history for many people in Bosnia. This alternative archaeology serves different symbolic, socio-political, and economic purposes on local and worldwide scales, and it is intimately attached to, and working within, larger conditions of politics and performance.

Keywords

popular archaeology, post-conflict heritage, social studies of pseudoarchaeology

Mainstream archaeologists often define the term pseudoarchaeology as an act of amateur archaeological practice that 'invokes the aura of scholarship without being scholarly in fact and blurs the distinction between real scholarship and "alternative" output' (Jordan 2001, 288–9). Recent literature has gone so far as to develop the notion that there is a classic type of pseudoarchaeology. Academics such as Fagan (2006) and Flemming (2006) have developed something akin to rubrics or diagnoses that map out qualities of pseudoarchaeological enterprises. Such research has carefully listed and defined alternative ideas about the past, has created compelling arguments for why it can disturb genuine science and has even taken a more drastic step by declaring such approaches 'pernicious processes' that should be combated (Renfrew 2006).

Perhaps by recognising a need to address pseudoarchaeology at all, academics are taking a step forward in better understanding how alternative approaches and explanations of past events emerge outside of professional culture. However, simply defining an archaeological act as 'pseudoarchaeology' does not satisfactorily characterise the complexity and breadth of the situation. Cases of pseudoarchaeology are ultimately social processes within larger socio-historical contexts, acting in larger frameworks of participation and performance, and they need to be recognized as such. Wiktor Stoczkowski, from the École des Hautes Études en Sciences Sociales in Paris, writes that:

> What is at stake is rather our capacity to grasp the cultural dimension of pseudoscience. In fact, once we have shown that it is inferior to academic science (which is a truism for most of the scientists and their public), we still have done nothing to understand pseudoscience as a social phenomenon (2007, 1).

This argument - that complex contexts and conditions allow for alternative archaeology to become preferred accounts of history - is key to understanding and addressing pseudoarchaeology.

This paper presents one specific case study of alternative archaeology in order to critically examine and deconstruct how one case of pseudoarchaeology operates, performs and represents itself. This paper examines the *performative* side of alternative archaeology. The case study discussed, commonly referred to as the 'Bosnian Pyramids', is immensely complicated and involves multiple levels of complex socio-political negotiations, representations and social arenas of support or dissent. Since the socio-political and economic issues behind this case study are thoroughly covered elsewhere (Foer 2007; Pruitt 2009; Pruitt 2011; Woodard 2007), this paper primarily addresses the Bosnian Pyramids from a more nuanced, but no less important angle: that of performance, representation and theatrics. The performative side of pseudoarchaeology is one of the most important ways alternative claims about the past are developed and spread. While much has been contributed in recent years to a greater understanding of why these ideas take hold (e.g. for political reasons, for personal gain, to satisfy a community economic need, etc.), less has been written in any detail about how pseudoarchaeology actually operates and performs.

Case Study Background: Pyramids in Bosnia

In 2005, a Bosnian-American businessman and alternative historian named Semir Osmanagić made international news headlines when he announced that he had discovered the largest and oldest man-made pyramids in the world. These ancient pyramids, he claims, are located in the small town of Visoko, Bosnia-Herzegovina, 20 miles northwest of Sarajevo (Figures 3.1, 3.2). Osmanagić is originally from Sarajevo, has a Master's degree in politics and economics, and he has defended a PhD from the University of Sarajevo on unconventional theories about the Maya (Osmanagic 2007d; Osmanagic 2009). He settled in Houston, Texas before the Yugoslav Civil War and owns a successful metal construction business that oversees 100 employees, representing considerable managerial and business skill. Osmanagić claims to have studied pyramids around the world in his free time over the past 15 years and is the author of several works of fringe archaeology (Foer 2007). His book *The World of the Maya*, for instance, suggests that the Maya were descended from aliens from the Pleiades, 'inherited knowledge from their ancestors at Atlantis and Lemuria (Mu)', and that 'pyramids erected on these energy potent locations enabled the Maya to be closer to the heavens and to other levels of consciousness' (Osmanagić 2005, 70). All of Osmanagić's alternative history works espouse the same genre of fringe ideas.

In Visoko, Osmanagić identified five pyramidal-shaped hills in the Visočica river valley which he claims are technological feats of a Palaeolithic Bosnian supercivilisation (BosnianPyramids.org 2006; ICBP 2009). The three largest pyramids purportedly form a perfect triangle, and the four sides of the Pyramid of the Sun align to the four cardinal points of the Earth's compass. According to his hypothesis, these pyramids are connected by an intricate underground tunnel network, whose walls are adorned with the world's earliest writing and letters that resemble ancient Nordic runes. Osmanagić has associated two other sites with

Visoko: a hypothetical rock quarry site in the village of Gornja Vratnica and a river ravine near Zenica filled with ancient 'mysterious stone balls' (Osmanagić 2007a; 2007b).

After the initial press release, these theories quickly gained local and national attention and support, as well as broader support from members of the international alternative history community (Coppens 2006; Foer 2007). However, most professional archaeologists agree that Osmanagić's theories have not been supported by any evidentiary material found at the site, despite Osmanagić's claims to the contrary (Bohannon 2006a; Rose 2006a). In spite of the negative professional academic reaction, Osmanagić's project continues to operate and thrive, with continued support from the Bosnian public, media and government (see Pruitt 2009; Pruitt 2011; Woodard 2007).

Figure 3.1: Visoko is located 20 miles northwest of Sarajevo in Bosnia-Herzegovina. Image rights rest with the author.

Figure 3.2: This is the iconic image of Visoko taken in 1973, offering the best view of Visočica Hill (Pyramid of the Sun) and its striking straight-lined edges. Freely distributed public image (http://en.wikipedia.org/wiki/File:1973_Visoko.jpg), accessed on 29 May 2012.

In 2006, after a successful media campaign raised public awareness, Osmanagić established an officially-registered Archaeological Park, the Bosnian Pyramid of the Sun Foundation (referred to in this paper as simply 'the Foundation'), in order to operate a fully-fledged business and administration centre. His team of 35 to 80 individuals is mostly composed of amateurs with an interest in history, but also includes some PhD holders (ICBP 2009). The Foundation maintains that its ultimate goal is to establish Visoko as a major tourist attraction and get the pyramids listed as a UNESCO world heritage site (Bosnian Pyramid of the Sun Foundation 2009). The team runs fully invasive and extensive excavations in Gornja Vratnica, and at Visočica and Plješevica Hills (renamed by Osmanagić as Pyramid of the Sun and Pyramid of the Moon, respectively). The greatest criticism of Osmanagić and his Foundation by the international professional archaeological community has been directed toward the haphazard and destructive methods used by this amateur team. They have damaged genuine medieval and iron age archaeological remains in Visoko during their search for proof of ancient pyramids (Rose 2006a).

Osmanagić and the Foundation publish voraciously: anything from scientific reports aimed at a general public audience to tourist brochures to boost business in the region. These publications contain everything from excited announcements of new pyramid proofs to bitter insults towards those who criticise them (Bosnian Pyramid of the Sun Foundation 2009; ICBP 2009). Osmanagić has also lectured at Bosnian Embassies throughout the world (Osmanagić 2007b), has hosted his own sizeable international scientific conference (ICBP 2009) and has made frequent appearances in local schools and on television (ABC 2006). The pyramid phenomenon in Bosnia has been an overwhelming success, bringing in important positive economic changes to the post-war town of Visoko (Foer 2007; Woodard 2007). Bosnia experienced a great deal of suffering in the recent war (1991-1995), which divided the country ethnically and politically, leaving its citizens very insecure and its government politically disjointed: 'Fears, hatreds, memories, grief for the dead, nostalgia for the lost native places and homes, shattered dreams, insecurity, disappointment, pessimism are continuing to haunt everybody' (Zhelyazkova 2004, 17). In this context, the pyramid project offers a unifying premise; it provides a positive symbol for post-war Bosnian nationalism, promotes an ideology of all-inclusive peacefulness for all ethno-religious backgrounds, and identifies a time when the extraordinary people in the region once built great things, like the largest pyramids in the entire world, before or since. The story of pyramids in Bosnia incorporates the hope of positive international attention after a devastating civil war, as well as an idealistic narrative of an united prehistoric Bosnian Golden Age.

More practically, much of the enthusiasm behind the Bosnian Pyramid project involves the money it can bring to the region through tourism. Visoko has already changed dramatically from its dilapidated condition. Before pyramids were announced, the town received around 10,000 visitors a year and had high unemployment rates; now authorities report that many visitors in a single day and better employment conditions. Visoko attracted 250,000 tourists to the town in 2006 alone, bringing in a flood of new money to the town and an economic boost (Foer 2007). Many strategising politicians seem to realise that the Foundation's excavations are controversial and potentially damaging to cultural heritage in the region, yet they continue to approve of the project because of its tourism potential. On whether or not the project should be shut down, President Silajdzic infamously said, 'Let them dig and we'll see what they find. Besides, it's good for business' (cited in Harding 2007, 44). A spokesman

for the foreign Federation representative in charge of Bosnian Affairs, Christian Schwarz-Schilling, voiced support for the project, calling it 'the world's first victimless pyramid scheme' (cited in Foer 2007). These ideas have had a profound, if potentially unsustainable impact on the country as a whole (Pruitt 2011, 156-216).

The Role of Media

The media has been the single most important reason that information and support for the pyramid project has spread so rapidly. Print news first released and distributed Semir Osmanagić's positive story, and television and the internet stoked further debate between supporters and opposition. Print media coverage of the pyramid project began in the fall of 2005 when Bosnia's highest-circulation newspaper, *Dnevni Avaz*, ran a story on Osmanagić's theories. International news outlets such as BBC and USA Today followed suit (BBC 2006; Cerkez-Robinson 2005). Most of these initial reports were supportive of the project. Mark Rose of the Archaeological Institute of America commented that 'Every major media outlet that initially covered this story got it wrong…nobody bothered to check the story' (cited in Woodard 2007).

Figure 3.3: Wearing his iconic Indiana Jones style hat and rugged khaki, Semir Osmanagić courts the media at his excavation site at Plješevica Hill, renamed Pyramid of the Moon.
The author is the photographer and owner of the image.

Television media was perhaps the most influential in spreading supportive information to a wide audience (Osmanagić 2007a) [Figure 3.3]. Woodard reports, 'Federation television, the largest Sarajevo-based network, provided extensive coverage, and soon thousands of people were visiting Visoko every day' (2007). Local media stations arranged 'face-off' debates between Osmanagić and mainstream archaeologists and distributed many supportive campaigns for his site. Osmanagić travelled around the world with Bosnian TV to places like Easter Island, Peru, England and Jordan, resulting in a twelve-episode documentary that boosted his site's profile (Osmanagić 2007a). In the meantime, private groups released independent, professional documentaries about the site (Huttinger 2006). With international media attention fuelling the local media, excitement and positive press spread the story like wildfire. Almost overnight, Osmanagić became the poster boy of a national sensation.

Mark Rose wrote that 'Mainstream media has become somewhat more critical of stories emanating from Visoko, but much of the real work in dissecting the claims has appeared on blogs and message boards, such as The Hall of Ma'at' (2006b). It is primarily through the medium of print and television that the project gathered force; and it is mostly through the internet that critical opposition has flourished (e.g. Irna 2009).

Actualities and Virtualities

To further bridge practice and theory in this case, this section deconstructs pseudoarchaeology as performative practice. In her article *Theorizing Heritage* (1995), on the subject of heritage and value, Barbara Kirschenblatt-Gimblett retells a story of a travel writer who visited the historic site of Cluny church in France:

> *Last year 700,000 tourists came to see Cluny and the church that isn't there...A museum dedicated to the church stands a few feet away from the excavation. Inside, I look at an animated, three-dimensional computer re-creation...Back outside, I stare at the void. The computer model is still so fresh in my mind that an image of the enormous edifice seems to appear before me. I'm not alone in this optical illusion: everyone else leaving the museum seems to do the same double take outside. It's as if we're having a mass hallucination of a building that no longer exists* (cited in Kirschenblatt-Gimblett 1995, 376-377).

Kirschenblatt-Gimblett offers this example as 'virtualities in the absence of actualities. It produces hallucinatory effects. On the basis of excavation and historical reconstruction and in collaboration with visitors, the museum openly imagines the site into being—in the very spot where it should be still standing but is no more' (1995, 377). Cluny museum's mediating effect (re)invents a virtual site where 'we travel to actual destinations to experience virtual places' (Kirschenblatt-Gimblett 1995, 377).

This example spotlights a major quality of the pyramid project: the inventing of a site through the blurring of what Kirschenblatt-Gimblett calls 'actualities' and 'virtualities' (1995, 375). In the pyramid case, media communication (using language, images and a combination of performance and participation) acts as a medium in which Semir Osmanagić and others collectively *create* the pyramids. The notion that the 'virtual' is opposed to the 'actual', and the idea that the two can become blurred or that the former can replace the latter, is not new in literature (Hamilakis and Yalouri 1999; Hobsbawm 1983a; Lowenthal 1998). Eric Hobsbawm has argued that there is an underlying and genuine custom in which traditions come to be invented and then exist (1983a). Scottish kilts, for instance, were artificial traditions that later merged with and 'became' Scottish custom (Trevor-Roper 1983), and many nationalistic traditions, such as national holidays and festivals, were mass-invented in state-led generations in Europe between 1870–1914 (Hobsbawm 1983b). These invented traditions, encouraged by contemporary political contexts, were in a sense 'virtualities' that became 'actualities' in pre-existing custom.

Jean Baudrillard goes further with this notion of the 'virtual' as opposed to the 'actual' in his philosophical work *Simulacra and Simulations* (1988). Baudrillard specifically discusses 'simulacrum', a Latin word that essentially means 'to put on an appearance of'. According to Plato and Nietzsche, a simulacrum is an unsatisfactory reproduction of something existing in reality, something like a Roman copy of an original Greek statue (Nietzsche 1990; Plato 2004). However, Baudrillard departs from this, arguing that a simulacrum is not a copy of the real, but rather something virtual that becomes truth or replaces truth in its own right, something that is 'hyperreal' (1988). The 'hyperreal' characterises the inability to distinguish between the 'actual' and the 'virtual'. For example, if media radically shapes and filters an event and a viewer's reality becomes enmeshed in both facts and invented/altered information, then his reality is hyperreal.

This discourse of simulacrum, the actual and the virtual, is useful to view the way pyramids are being constructed at Visoko. The Cluny church 'hallucinations' and Semir Osmanagić's pyramids can be seen as cases of simulacrum, where virtual imaginings are created through a mediating factor (the museum mediates in the case of the Cluny church, and various media sources mediate in the case of the Bosnian pyramids). In the case of Cluny and the Bosnian pyramids, viewers experience the 'hyperreal', where imagined understandings of history merge with an 'actual' site. The Bosnian pyramids do not exist as Semir Osmanagić and his followers say they do. The hills are simple geological formations; no matter how hard Osmanagić may search, he will not produce verifiable evidence of a supercivilisation. One can distinguish the actual from the virtual at Visoko, just like visitors to the reconstructed duplicate Lascaux Caves in France 'could easily be made to understand how they, let alone an art historian, can tell the difference between the real and a fake' (Butler 2002, 114). Osmanagić, however, does claim that pyramids do exist at Visoko, and he has more or less devout followers who support his project and claim to see what he sees.

I argue that this situation is occurring because Osmanagić is successfully creating a simulacrum of the site - a hyperreal history - primarily using mass media outlets as his medium to disseminate his ideas. Osmanagić is presenting a 'virtual' (illogically argued and imagined) story through various communication networks in the same way that the museum at Cluny is mediating a 'virtual' (rationally argued for) image of the inexistent Cluny church. This effect is further magnified by the intense desire by the Bosnian public for something uniquely grounding and truly extraordinary to help the economy of their post-war country. The result is that, to the Bosnian public, the modern physical landscape of mountains and medieval history in Visoko has been transformed into a new reality where Bosnia once led the world in building magnificent pyramids, back when people were supposed to only be making rudimentary stone tools. The socio-political and economic potential of this hyperreality is profound.

Inventing Authority

In 2006, the television network ABC Houston 13 broadcast a special story about Osmanagić and his pyramids. This show exemplifies how Osmanagić and communication networks are creating the idea, or the simulacrum, of pyramids:

[*Image: logo brand of a pyramid with the words: "Houston's Indiana Jones"*]

DESK ANCHOR: Travel to Bosnia to follow this modern day Indiana Jones and his search for Bosnia's great valley of pyramids. [*Footage of Semir Osmanagić walking at the Pyramid of the Sun, wearing a khaki shirt and trousers and an Indiana-Jones style hat*]

OSMANAGIĆ: You are enjoying the most beautiful place on the planet.

ANCHOR: You don't know Semir Osmanagić, but to the people of Bosnia, he is a national hero. [*Cut to a scene with school children clapping for him*]. Congratulated, applauded, and loved wherever he goes. [*Cut to a scene of more children presenting Osmanagić with a pyramid-shaped cake*]. This is a land which has been torn by war and civil conflict, but resurrected in a way by one man [...] Indeed, his story, if true, could change the history of the world.

OSMANAGIĆ: [*Walking at the Pyramid of the Sun*] We are going back thousands of years from the ancient times and the Roman and the Greek.

ANCHOR: As a history buff, a sort of living Indiana Jones, he travels the world, exploring mysteries [...]

OSMANAGIĆ: All you need to do is disregard the trees, the greenery, the soil, and you will see the object, clearly in your mind. [...]

ANCHOR: Semir used satellite, thermal, and topography analysis on tens of thousands of hills in his search for pyramids [...] If a person could look back and just visualize this place as you see it, eight thousand, ten thousand years ago, they would see a massive stone city.

OSMANAGIĆ: What they would see would be the most magnificent city ever built on the face of the planet. (ABC 2006)

This example demonstrates how Osmanagić and his supportive media have performed a virtual pyramid site onto the landscape in Visoko. This evocation of a simulacrum occurs in at least four distinct ways, which are discussed further in the sections below. The first is Osmanagić's specific self-representation, particularly using language and images that provoke associations with pop-cultural icons: the adventurer, the hero, the hard-working academic, the cool socialite, the modest public servant, etc. The second is Osmanagić's deliberate narrative establishment of a villain (mainstream archaeologists) that helps to root the pyramid story as a cause 'for good'. The third is through Osmanagić's penchant for logos and branding, which are rooted in modern pop-culture and stereotypes and actively establish his project. Finally, Osmanagić evokes his site by constructing an *appearance* of methodology and evidence by mimicking genuine scientific documentation and the rhythm of scientific language.

I. Self-Representation: Icons and Personalities

First and foremost, Osmanagić represents himself as a romantic adventurer (see Holtorf 2007, 64-65). He builds on one prevalent icon from media and literature: the khaki-wearing explorer who knows that 'anyone is capable of discovery and the non-professional may participate in the grand adventure' (Ascher 1960, 402). Osmanagić fully endorses this image, always wearing rugged khaki and rarely appearing in public without his wide-brimmed Indiana Jones-style fedora (Figure 3.3). Osmanagić describes his work with adjectives like dangerous, brave, exotic and mysterious. His tone is dramatic, targeting notions like 'secrets', 'mysteries' or 'treasures' of the past. In the ABC Houston transcript above, for example, he is a 'living Indiana Jones, he travels the world, exploring mysteries' (2006).

Osmanagić offsets this adventurous image with two contradictory self-representations: that of the hard-working academic and cool socialite. He asserts that his time is dedicated 'to the intensive research of certain enigmas of the past' involving cultures such as the Maya, Assay and pre-Illyric cultures in Bosnia, and in the past he has 'read 40–50 books a year' (BosnianPyramids.org 2006). Somewhat paradoxically, Osmanagić has also been initiated into the artsy 'just plain cool' side of popular culture: the pyramid excavations have been launched with concerts of popular rock groups and pyramid-themed art installations, and Osmanagić has even appeared in a music video (Hodzic 2007).

Osmanagić also represents himself as a hero-crusader, on a quest for truth, trying to save Bosnia. The ABC show above, for example, explicitly calls him a 'national hero' who will 'resurrect' a war-torn country (2006). The humble public servant image is not far behind (see Hamilakis 1999, 66-68; Holtorf 2007, 91). In one interview, Osmanagić recognises that he is in the spotlight of his project, but says 'affirmation of the project on the world wide scene and of course the contact with the media, are all a part of this process. However I will slowly move away from the center of the attention as more people get involved in various activities' (BosnianPyramids.org 2006). His performance of a modest public servant and determined martyr appear in statements such as: 'I was aware in this initial period there would be critics who will publicly or privately speak out, insult and challenge this vision. That is why I did not want to put anyone else forward, but instead I answered to all provocations with the culture of dialogue and scientific arguments' (BosnianPyramids.org 2006).

With these various and often conflicting personalities, it is perhaps surprising that Osmanagić has achieved such a successful media image. But he has, for two reasons: the first is that these images are stereotypes and they seem to be pulled from a collective understanding of what *is* an archaeologist (from pop-cultural icons like Indiana Jones, to academic notions of public servitude and intensive research). The second reason why these multiple personalities work together to create a whole image for Osmanagić is that he and his team have established one solitary opposite force: the villain. Osmanagić juxtaposes his various self-images against this antagonist, giving his character and project a sense of worth and weight.

II. Narration of Villain

Garret Fagan writes of pseudoarchaeology, 'There is another powerful storytelling feature in this genre, one usually lacking in good archaeological television: a villain. For many pseudoarchaeology shows, the villain is archaeology itself' (Fagan 2003). Vilification 'is a kind of symbol-making that groups engage in under certain conditions in order to…build consensus and morale for certain kinds of social actions' (Klapp 1959, 71). Osmanagić has successfully established mainstream archaeologists as the primary villains against his cause. By setting himself in opposition to his archaeological

antagonists, he has been able to maintain his own narrative.

Like a classic hero, Osmanagić has consistently kept up a performance of good guy versus bad guy with the academic establishment, saying that 'every new idea has oponents [*sic*] in the beginning. The bigger the idea, more aggressive the oponents [*sic*]. But, it does not influence my goals and determination for an inch' (Osmanagić 2007a). Osmanagić and his team began by disparaging professional (Bosnian) archaeology, exploiting the weakness of a system that has unstable or inexistent institutions and funding (Kampschror 2006, 27; Zhelyazkova 2004, 12). Osmanagić has used the fact that the academic establishment is in tatters from the war to his advantage, by saying that professional archaeologists are incompetent and have been lax in doing work. He has accused Bosnian archaeologists of 'long-time carelessness' and has cited foreign scholars as 'clueless about the real situation and state of Bosnian Cultural Heritage' (BosnianPyramids.org 2006).

Osmanagić and the Foundation have represented mainstream academics as insulting, fearful groups who conspire to attack his higher truth. On one website, Osmanagić directly politicizes and polarizes his academic opponents: 'convinced about their conservative views, [they] promptly attacked the hypothesis and tried to debunk its author. Some of them, showed a typical bosnian [*sic*] propensity, by launching labels and insults from behind the scenes' (Osmanagić 2006). He has also used forceful language to demean mainstream scientists as afraid, jealous and small-minded: 'Are they afraid about the material evidence that will make collapse [*sic*] their world views?' (Osmanagić 2006); 'The trades like geology and archaeology will be the last to accept [the pyramids], because it's a revolution' (cited in Foer 2007). Like every good crusader and public servant, Osmanagić refers to his opponents in a tone of humble citizen versus the corrupt establishment, conjuring an image of fighting for truth against all odds.

III. Logos and Branding

Osmanagić and his Foundation also use the authority of logos and branding (cf. Holtorf 2007). They do this in several ways, from the promotion of cultural assumptions about foreign academia, to the use of brand names and signage. They use media, which, by nature, 'enable[s] marketers to project brands into national consciousness' (Muniz and O'Guinn 2001, 413). Osmanagić often mentions that he has been living and working in Houston, Texas. According to some Bosnians, living and working abroad (especially in powerful Western countries) is considered an attractive and authoritative feat in its own right (Hadžabdić 2007). Along with his American label, as mentioned above, Osmanagić builds his self-image on prevalent pop-cultural icons. His 'sort of modern-day Indiana Jones' image is his own personal logo (ABC 2006). Headlines brand him as 'Bosnia's Indiana Jones', 'Houston's

Indiana Jones' or 'Indiana Jones of the Balkans' (ABC 2006; Hawton 2006). This self-branding provides enough drama and assumption to give Osmanagić a look of amateur authority, and he is an easily recognisable celebrity icon in media contexts.

As well as branding himself, Osmanagić also seizes every opportunity to promote other people with official political labels or degrees behind their name. Along with encouraging national political sponsorship (Bohannon 2006a), Osmanagić and his Foundation court professors or students who give an impression of authoritative, scientific presence (Schoch 2007). One example of this fondness for scientific labels manifested during his presentation at the Bosnian Embassy in London in 2007: Osmanagić opened his lecture by saying that his 'excavation team includes an Oxford university archaeologist' (Osmanagić 2007b). Osmanagić showed a brief video clip of a young man at the Pyramid of the Moon stating that he is 'convinced that there's certainly some kind of large-scale man-made structure' (Cartwright 2006). Peter Mitchell, an Oxford archaeologist, told *Science Magazine* that the boy in the

video was only an undergraduate student and 'does not have any expertise and in no way represents the university' (Bohannon 2006b). Nevertheless, Osmanagić continues to promote this video on his website, undoubtedly because of the weight the Oxford name carries.

At the most obvious level, Osmanagić's penchant for logos and brand names appears in the way he trademarks his foundation: a shiny, official-looking logo that directly references the power of government by imitating the Bosnian national flag (see logo on the top centre of the sign in Figure 3.4). He also moved to copyright the names of his pyramids and his Bosnian Pyramid of the Sun Foundation (Bosnian Pyramid of the Sun Foundation 2009). In the town of Visoko, official government signs point toward the pyramids, and an array of formal, authoritative signage mark the site (Figure 3.4). This obsession with logos and branding creates the feeling of establishment and authority, a point that also emerges in the way Osmanagić represents the site as 'scientific'.

Figure 3.4: Authoritative signage at Gornja Vratnica project excavations.
In the foreground, the official Foundation logo is centred on on both the site information sign, as well as on the poster for the 'International Scientific Conference' hosted by the Foundation team.
The author is the photographer and owner of the image.

IV. Scientific Representation

Ironically, Osmanagić moves seamlessly from performing as a modest people's adventurer who despises elite academics to the completely contradictory performance of a visionary amateur scientist who leads a team of elite experts, carrying out intensive and detailed scientific analyses. Historically, Osmanagić and his team have carefully manipulated images and language so that his methods appear scientific, while actually having no basis in real evidence or accepted methodology.

Osmanagić has always argued that he has conducted serious academic work dedicated 'to the intensive research of certain enigmas of the past' involving cultures such as the Maya, the Assay, and the pre-Illyric cultures in Bosnia (BosnianPyramids.org 2006). He continues to stress that his research is a controlled and extensive scientific experiment. In 2007, he released a document called *Scientific Evidence about the Existence of Bosnian Pyramids*, which states:

> *Discovery of Bosnian Pyramids was not simply an ad-hoc affair, but required combination of classic geo-archaeological methods with modern geophysical and remote sensing technologies.*
>
> *The Archaeological Park Foundation believes that only a multi-disciplinary approach, with serious scientific argumentation on internationally recognized level will yield a successful realization of the Bosnian Pyramids project.*
>
> *The team, therefore, includes not only archaeologists, but also geologists (mineralologists/petrologists, hydrologists and sedimentologists), geophysicists, paleontologists, speleologists, anthropologists, mining engineers as well as anthropologists. Each one of these experts brings a new element of problem understanding and integrate their qualifications and expertise into the project with a great enthusiasm and collegiality.* [sic]

(Osmanagić 2007c, 1).

Such language intentionally connects the pyramid project to mainstream scientific work and methodologies. However, rarely are these statements supported with any undisputed evidence, and they never explain why the project has geologists speaking authoritatively about archaeological remains, or why Egyptologists are recruited to speak about the Bosnian Palaeolithic.

Osmanagić's *Scientific Evidence* document contains intricate sections with titles such as 'Apparent thermal inertia measurements' or 'Geodetic topographic contour analyses'. His data, however, are nothing but simple statements which say that 'geospatial anomalies' exist (Osmanagić 2007c, 2) or they only reveal vague generalizations, such as 'the sides of Visocica/Bosnian Pyramid of Sun are exactly aligned with the cardinal sides of the world (north-south, east-west), which is one of the characteristics often noted with the existing pyramids' (Osmanagić 2007c, 3). These data entries each have a corresponding image, which at first glance appears to be technical and evidentiary; however, these generic topographic images and their accompanying legends are meaningless, merely high-definition maps with red lines drawn haphazardly over them.

The *Scientific Evidence* document illustrates that *what* Osmanagić says is less important than *how* he says it. This 'scientific' format heavily relies on the trust and power vested in presentation standards that are backed by institutional authority and scientific tradition, a tactic used as much by professional archaeology and mainstream science as by alternative or fringe groups (Hodder 1989; Pruitt 2011). However, in the case of Semir Osmanagić and his Foundation, their elaborate documents merely mimic language patterns of genuine scientific documents, since their claims are rarely backed by actual evidentiary support or academic argument. Their website and logos are formatted to appear formal, official, yet inviting and inclusive for a wider public. Their documentary tone, coupled with colourful, technical images give their work a feeling of weight and worth, connecting them to established authoritative scientific traditions, establishing authority by performing the imagery of science.

Performative Inventing

Holtorf and Schadla-Hall write, 'it has become a truism that every generation has the past it desires or deserves' (1999, 230). This statement also proves true in a narrower sense with the pyramid case, where a nation is inventing the past it desires and feels it deserves. Through his faux-excavations and scientific-appearing documents, Osmanagić is inventing and constructing the perfect image and physicality of an archaeological park. He and his pyramid team are evoking a simulacrum, a 'virtual' site that is replacing an 'actual' history in the public imagination, through the use of performative language and the crafting of specific narrative images. And through the participation of an eager, avid public on the other end of the media projection, the invented pyramids are actively sustained in a greater public understanding.

Ideologically, the public accepts and actively encourages the notion of pyramids, through their continued vocal support, active public discourse about the site. They continue to endorse the project for complex socio-political reasons, both ideological and economic. Physically, the public encourages the idea of pyramids through their active rituals of visiting, promoting tourism and hype. The public supportively consumes products like souvenirs, news, media and other documents related to the site, and they endorse the project by continuing to volunteer in the Foundation's ongoing excavations (Pruitt 2009). Through their agency and participation, the public is contributing to the construction and continuation of pyramid pseudoarchaeology at Visoko. This is *performative inventing*. It is the process by which Osmanagić and his team are inventing a site by performing the roles of amateur archaeologists, and by which their supportive public keeps the site alive through their continued participation and interaction with the project.

Part of performative inventing involves the way Osmanagić's and his supporters use 'performative language'—the process of saying things that makes things happen—or in the case of the pyramids, making things exist that were nonexistent before. In the book, *How to Do Things With Words* (1962), J.L. Austin distinguishes between 'statements', which are utterances that simply describe something, and 'performative language', which are neither true nor false statements, but rather utterances which perform certain kinds of action. When one utters performative language, and the circumstances are appropriate, the language does not describe something, but rather *does* something (for instance, saying 'I name this ship the *Queen Elizabeth*' in the appropriate circumstances will perform the action as it is said) (1962). Although Austin was certainly discussing more narrow and specific utterances and circumstances, the general idea can be applied to the performances occurring at Visoko. By repeatedly saying that there are pyramids, and describing an inexistent site as existent in what appears to be authoritative circumstances, Osmanagić is *creating* pyramids. By saying on ABC television, for example, that 'If a person could look back and just visualize this place as you see it, eight thousand, ten thousand years ago, they would see a massive stone city' (2006), he is uttering performative language. He is not describing the actual remains of this city, because they do not exist. It is through the narration of this city, and through the appropriate circumstances that give him authority (namely authoritative media), that the city *is being invented*.

This performative behaviour, performative language and mimicry of scientific documents are quite literally inventing a heritage site. This point is perhaps best illustrated by the physical site excavation. When visitors approach the Pyramid of the Moon, they find large-scale excavations of monumental steps leading up the mountain. Visitors like Joshua Foer exclaim, 'Suddenly it dawns on me—and I'm shocked that it has taken me so long to figure this out—that Osmanagić is *carving* pyramids out of these pyramid-shaped hills' (2007, emphasis added). Osmanagić is chipping away at the mountainside until it physically resembles pyramid steps. This behaviour is performative: Osmanagić is playing the part, constructing (quite literally) the right image, and thus inventing heritage.

This project is also sustained through *participatory inventing*. As previous studies have illuminated in much more depth (Pruitt 2009; Pruitt 2011; Rose 2006a; Woodard 2007), the pyramid scheme is deeply ingrained in national and ethnic Bosnian history. A variety of interest groups have attached different values and meanings to the site. Eric Hobsbawm writes:

> *'Invented traditions' have significant social and political functions, and would neither come into existence nor establish themselves if they could not acquire them [...] the most successful examples of manipulation are those which exploit practices which clearly meet a felt -not necessarily a clearly understood - need among particular bodies of people.* (1983b, 307)

Such a *need* for pyramids clearly exhibits itself at Visoko. Osmanagić's pyramid site satisfies specific socio-political needs. It offers a world-class monument that outstands and outsizes every other major national monument in the world, right there in 'little Bosnia', opening up profound economic and ideological opportunities for a post-war country.

Osmanagić is able to invent his heritage only through the continued participation from a supportive audience that allows his ideas to gain momentum and security. Osmanagić presents his simulacrum, his 'virtual' story that overlays the 'actual' truth—but it is only through the full acceptance of and participation in this vision that the site comes to fruition. In the past, the impact of the media on the spread of information and public consumption was thought to occur in a linear progression: message production, transmission and reception, with one entity creating and transmitting a message that another entity passively received. This notion has been challenged in the past decade, and media has been 'examined not so much as definers of "reality," but as dynamic sites of struggle over representation, and complex spaces in which subjectivities are constructed and identities are contested' (Spitulnik 1993, 296).

This sense of dynamic message construction and participation has also arisen in museum literature; for example, in a discussion of museum exhibitions, Baxandall outlines the common paradigm in the museum world where three active agents are involved in exhibitions: the maker of the artefact, the exhibitor and the viewer (1991, 36-37). It is through the dynamic participation of all three levels of involvement that a museum exhibition has meaning. The situation in Visoko can be distilled into more or less similar dynamic and interlinked agents: Osmanagić and his Foundation (the producer/makers), the media (transmitter/exhibitor) and the public (viewers/audience). The participatory role of the media and, especially, the public is what has helped to invent the project and keep it alive. This active, participatory inventing is exemplified in one quote by a local business owner: 'If they don't find the pyramid, we're going to make it during the night. But we're not even thinking about that. There *are* pyramids and there *will be* pyramids' (cited in Foer 2007). This is exactly what the participating public, media and Osmanagić are doing: *constructing* pyramids through their participation.

Conclusion

This study shows a dissonance between the simple mainstream pronouncement 'this is pseudoscience' and the complex story that emerges from a more in-depth examination. Until recently, arguments against pseudoarchaeology in Visoko have been (somewhat condescendingly) directed at educating an ignorant public. However, the public in Bosnia is not exactly ignorant; on the contrary, they want and need pyramids, and they have a stake in keeping the notion alive. These pyramids are created and sustained within an immensely complicated web of performance, theatricality and mimicry, and this interaction is rarely taken into full consideration when professional archaeologists critically engage with these sites. If archaeologists do wish to critically engage with pseudoarchaeology, then they need to be fully aware of what they are addressing. Understanding the social processes which create and sustain pseudoarchaeology is the first step in a productive direction.

Acknowledgements

I offer special thanks to my Bosnian translator and friend, Amna Hadžabdić. I also wish to thank Neil Brodie, Robin Boast, Marie Louise Stig Sørensen, Emily Lanza, Donna Yates and David Price for their advice and comments during my research.

Bibliography

ABC. 2006. Bosnian Pyramid! ABC Houston coverage. *YouTube.com.*
http://www.youtube.com/watch?v=xzDY0EBvCbU
accessed on 29 February 2012.

Ascher, R. 1960. Archaeology and the public image. *American Antiquity* 25, 402-3.

Austin, J. L. 1962. *How to Do Things With Words.* Oxford, Oxford University Press.

Baudrillard, J. 1988. Simulacra and Simulations. In M. Poster (ed.), *Jean Baudrillard, Selected Writings*, 166-184. Stanford, Stanford University Press.

Baxandall, M. 1991. Exhibiting Intention: Some Preconditions of the Visual Display of Culturally Purposeful Objects, in I. Karp and S.D. Lavine (eds), *Exhibiting Cultures: The Poetics and Politics of Museum Display*, 33-41. Washington, Smithsonian Institution.

BBC 2006. Dig for ancient pyramid in Bosnia. *BBC News*, online.
http://news.bbc.co.uk/1/hi/world/europe/4912040.stm
accessed on 29 February 2012.

Bohannon, J. 2006a. Mad About Pyramids. *Science Magazine* 313, 1718-20.

Bohannon, J. 2006b. Researchers Helpless as Bosnian Pyramid Bandwagon Gathers Pace. *Science Magazine* 314, 1862.

Bosnian Pyramid of the Sun Foundation. 2009. *Official website of the Archaeological Park: Bosnian Pyramid of the Sun Foundation.*
http://www.piramidasunca.ba/en/index.php
accessed on 29 February 2012.

BosnianPyramids.org. 2006. Exclusive Interview with Semir Osmanagic. *BosnianPyramids.org.*
http://www.bosnianpyramids.org/index.php?id=6&lang=en , accessed on 29 February 2012.

Butler, C. 2002. *Postmodernism: A Very Short Introduction.* Oxford, Oxford University Press.

Cartwright, A. 2006. Volunteer on site at Visoko. *Video.google.com.*
http://video.google.com/videoplay?docid=27344658165 84485800# , accessed on 29 February 2012.

Cerkez-Robinson, A. 2005. Scientist: Bosnian hill may have pyramid. *USA Today*, online.
http://www.usatoday.com/tech/science/discoveries/2005-12-04-bosnia-pyramid_x.htm , accessed on 29 February 2012.

Coppens, P. 2006. *Europe's pyramid history unveiled*, online article.
http://www.philipcoppens.com/euro_pyrs.html
accessed on 29 February 2012.

Fagan, G. G. 2003. Seductions of Pseudoarchaeology: Far Out Television. *Archaeology Magazine* 56(3), online.
http://www.archaeology.org/0305/abstracts/tv.html
accessed on 29 February 2012.

Fagan, G. G. 2006. Diagnosing Pseudoarchaeology. In G. G. Fagan (ed.), *Archaeological Fantasies: How pseudoarchaeology misrepresents the past and misleads the public*, 23-46. New York, Routledge.

Flemming, N. C. 2006. The attraction of non-rational archaeological hypotheses: the individual and sociological factors. In G. G. Fagan (ed.), *Archaeological Fantasies: How pseudoarchaeology misrepresents the past and misleads the public*, 47-70. New York, Routledge.

Foer, J. 2007. Love Triangles. *Outside Magazine*, online.

http://www.outsideonline.com/adventure-travel/Love-Triangles.html?page=all, accessed on 20 April 2012.

Hadžabdić, A. 2007. Personal communication in Visoko, Bosnia-Herzegovina on 20 March 2007.

Hamilakis, Y. 1999. La trahison des archéologues: archaeological practice as intellectual activity in postmodernism. *Journal of Mediterranean Archaeology* 12(1), 60-79.

Hamilakis, Y. and Yalouri E. 1999. Sacralising the past: the cults of archaeology in modern Greece. *Archaeological Dialogues* 6(2), 115-60.

Harding, A. 2007. The great Bosnian pyramid scheme. *British Archaeology* 92, 40-44.

Hawton, N. 2006. Indiana Jones of the Balkans and the mystery of a hidden pyramid. *TimesOnline.* http://www.timesonline.co.uk/tol/news/world/europe/article705784.ece, accessed on 27 October 2009.

Hobsbawm, E. 1983a. Introduction: Inventing Traditions, in E. Hobsbawm and T. Ranger (eds), *The Invention of Tradition*, 1-14. Cambridge, Cambridge University Press.

Hobsbawm, E. 1983b. Mass-Producing Traditions: Europe, 1870-1914, in E. Hobsbawm and T. Ranger (eds), *The Invention of Tradition*, 263-307. Cambridge, Cambridge University Press.

Hodder, I. 1989. Writing archaeology: site reports in context. *Antiquity* 63, 268-74.

Hodzic, T. (Director). 2007. MUSTE DEDIC – Bosanska piramida [Music Video]. Visoko, Bosnia-Herzegovina. *YouTube.com.* http://www.youtube.com/watch?v=5TaLLJf7vFo accessed on 29 February 2012.

Holtorf, C. 2007. *Archaeology is a Brand! The Meaning of Archaeology in Contemporary Popular Culture.* Oxford, BAR Publishing.

Holtorf, C. and Schadla-Hall, T. 1999. Age as Artefact: on Archaeological Authenticity. *European Journal of Archaeology* 2, 229-47.

Huttinger, R. (Director). 2006. *Pyramids of Bosnia* [Documentary]. Vienna. http://b-br.at/blog/2008/06/04/pyramids-of-bosnia-trailer/, accessed on 20 April 2012.

ICBP 2009. *The First Internationals Scientific Conference about the Bosnian Pyramids.* http://www.icbp.ba/ , accessed on 29 February 2012.

Irna 2009. *Le site d'Irna*, online blog. http://irna.lautre.net/-Bosnian-pyramids-.html, accessed on 20 April 2012.

Jordan, P. 2001. *The Atlantis Syndrome.* Thrupp, Sutton.

Kampschror, B. 2006. Pyramid scheme. *Archaeology Magazine* 59, 22–28.

Kirschenblatt-Gimblett, B. 1995. Theorizing Heritage. *Ethnomusicology* 39, 367-80.

Klapp, O. E. 1959. Notes toward the study of vilification as a social process. The *Pacific Sociological Review* 2, 71-6.

Lowenthal, D. 1998. *The Heritage Crusade and the Spoils of History.* Cambridge, Cambridge University Press.

Muniz, A. M. and O'Guinn, T. C. 2001. Brand Community. *Journal of Consumer Research* 27, 412-428.

Nietzsche, F. 1990. *Twilight of the Idols: Or, How to Philosophise with the Hammer.* London, Penguin Books.

Osmanagić, S. 2005. *The World of the Maya.* New Jersey, Gorgias Press (Euphrates Imprint).

Osmanagić, S. 2006. The Formula to understand The Bosnian Pyramids. *Bosnian Pyramid!?* http://piramidasunca.ba/en/index.php/formula-za-itanje-bosanskih-piramida.html, accessed on 20 April 2012.

Osmanagić, S. 2007a. Personal email communication, 21 March 2007.

Osmanagić, S. 2007b. *Bosnian Pyramids.* Unpublished presentation, recorded, January 2007, Bosnian Embassy, London.

Osmanagić, S. 2007c. *Bosnian Valley of Pyramids: Scientific Evidence About the Existence of Bosnian Pyramids*, digital document. Visoko: The Archaeological Park, Bosnian Pyramid of the Sun Foundation.

Osmanagić, S. 2007d. *Doctoral dissertation on the subject: Non-technological Civilization of MAYAS versus Modern TECHNOLOGICAL CIVILIZATIONS.* http://www.semirosmanagic.com/en/maya.html, accessed on 29 February 2012.

Osmanagić, S. 2009. *ODBRANA DOKTORSKE DISERTACIJE.* http://www.semirosmanagic.com/ba/odbrana.html, accessed on 29 February 2012.

Plato 2004. *Sophist*, translated by B. Jowett, online. http://etext.library.adelaide.edu.au/p/plato/p71so/ accessed on 29 February 2012.

Pruitt, T. C. 2009. Contextualising alternative archaeology: socio-politics and approaches. *Archaeological Review from Cambridge* 24(1), 55-75.

Pruitt, T. C. 2011. *Authority and the Production of Knowledge in Archaeology*. Unpublished Ph.D. thesis, University of Cambridge.

Renfrew, C. 2006. Forward. In G. G. Fagan (ed.), *Archaeological Fantasies: How pseudoarchaeology misrepresents the past and misleads the public*, xii-xix. New York, Routledge.

Rose, M. 2006a. The Bosnia-Atlantis Connection. *Archaeology Magazine*, online. http://www.archaeology.org/online/features/osmanagic/ accessed on 29 February 2012.

Rose, M. 2006b. More on Bosnian 'Pyramids'. *Archaeology Magazine*, online. http://www.archaeology.org/online/features/osmanagic/update.html , accessed on 29 February 2012.

Schoch, R. 2007. *Circular Times*. http://www.robertschoch.net , accessed on 27 October 2009.

Spitulnik, D. 1993. Anthropology and Mass Media. *Annual Review of Anthropology* 22, 213-315.

Stoczkowski, W. 2007. Book Review: Archaeological Fantasies. *Antiquity* 81, 472-473.

Trevor-Roper, H. 1983. The Invention of Tradition: The Highland Tradition of Scotland, in E. Hobsbawm and T. Ranger (eds), *The Invention of Tradition*, 15-41. Cambridge, Cambridge University Press.

Woodard, C. 2007. The Great Pyramids of…Bosnia? *The Chronicle of Higher Education*, online. http://chronicle.com/weekly/v53/i30/30a01201.htm accessed on 29 February 2012.

Zhelyazkova, A. 2004. *Bosnia: Tolerant Hostility*. Bulgaria, International Centre for Minority Studies and Intercultural Relations (IMIR). http://www.imir-bg.org/imir/reports/Bosnia_Tolerant_Hostility.pdf accessed on 29 February 2012.

MARGINAL AND MAINSTREAM. RELIGION, POLITICS AND IDENTITY IN THE CONTEMPORARY US, AS SEEN THROUGH THE LENS OF THE KENNEWICK MAN / THE ANCIENT ONE

Liv Nilsson Stutz

Abstract

The calls to repatriate human remains and cultural items from museums and research collections back to their source communities started out as an activist movement in the 1960s among disenfranchised minorities and indigenous peoples. Today, half a century later repatriation has risen to the surface of the international cultural debate and is embraced by the establishment in many parts of the world. This movement from the marginal to the mainstream has shifted the field of archaeology and museum practices toward engaging with the public and descending communities. But this newly gained influence also invites us to reflect more critically than before over the values and ideas that underlie debates and legislations. Through the example of the *Native American Graves Protection and Repatriation Act*, and with a particular focus on the Kennewick case, this chapter critically examines the underlying values and cultural concerns that frame the repatriation debate in the United States, including a contested relationship between faith and science, the role of race in identity production and the value placed on private ownership. It is argued that these cultural values and beliefs align the repatriation movement with the American mainstream, and while they have been critically examined elsewhere in archaeological and anthropological theory, this critique has taken place predominantly in academic contexts that are completely separate from the repatriation debate.

Keywords

repatriation; identity production; past-present continuity

Introduction

It may seem provocative to discuss repatriation in a volume dedicated to alternative archaeologies. Claims for repatriation often challenge the academic establishment when questioning its role of authority in interpreting and curating the material remains of the past. To challenge this authority is in many ways 'alternative.' Yet, repatriation is viewed differently from other alternative movements within and around archaeology, and it is very rarely discussed with them in the same forum (for an interesting exception, see Zimmerman 2008). There are several reasons for this. First of all, to label something 'alternative archaeology' or 'fringe' can be an effective way of undermining its credibility (a potentially problematic power relationship that is explored by other papers in this volume). In the case of the repatriation debate, this is especially problematic since such labeling can be viewed as a strategy to

effectively undermine the right of oppressed minorities and indigenous peoples to their history. On the other hand, it may be argued, claims for repatriation are not necessarily alternative anymore. While the organized political movement for repatriation started out as an activist movement in the 1960s among disenfranchised minorities and indigenous communities (Bray 2001b; see also Hammil and Cruz 1989; Hill 2001) it has today, half a century later, become a position embraced by the establishment in many parts of the world, having risen to the surface of international cultural debate and become a public concern. This change has taken place in a political, activist arena, circumventing the more academic world of archaeology and the museums. As activist voices have gradually influenced the academic position from the 1980s and onward, the idea of repatriation has gained ground within academic debates, where the aims and relationships involved in repatriation resonate with the post-colonial critique of the disciplines and with the more general *credo* of subjectivity and multivocality within post-processual archaeology. While many activists argue that there is still a long way to go to obtain what in their view would be real justice when it comes to repatriation of cultural heritage and human remains (see for example Riding In *et al.* 2004), I argue that repatriation as a concept has shifted from occupying a marginal position to becoming significantly mainstream among many archaeologists, members of the public and the political establishment. Voices in its support can be heard not only in activist meetings, but also in scientific journals (e.g. *Antiquity*, *American Antiquity*, *Public Archaeology* and *World Archaeology*) academic newsletters (*Anthropology News*) and books (for just a few examples see Bray 2001a; Layton 1989; Fforde *et al.* 2002; Fine Dare 2002; Mihesuah 2000), in academic conferences, in university courses (Killion 2008, 8) and in national and international political discourse.

I realize that these objections to discussing repatriation in the context of alternative archaeology are as divergent as they are important, and this is precisely what I am interested in exploring in this chapter, where I seek to elucidate the dynamics involved in the changing status of claims for repatriation of human remains and cultural items. The purpose is not to discuss whether repatriation is 'right' or 'wrong,' but to investigate the move from the marginal to the mainstream. To engage with the overall theme of this volume, I am interested in looking at both how we can understand the repatriation debate within its cultural and social context, and also what happens when a previously marginal position within the overall archaeological discourse becomes increasingly mainstream. As a movement shifts from the marginal to the mainstream, it gains political momentum, influence and power. Yet, the stakeholders involved in the political process by which a historically oppressed or disenfranchised group has newly gained a position of greater power often do not immediately recognize this power shift in their ongoing practice. This may be the case for activists and representatives of historically marginalized groups, where grasp on power and status may be tenuous and contested, but it may also be the case for stakeholders in the mainstream who define their interests in terms of enfranchising or lifting up the formerly marginalized. What is interesting is how the move from marginal to mainstream occurs in a cultural field where identity may be represented by a history of oppression, even as that identity gains in status, with the group gaining in power and social influence.

Lest I be misunderstood, this chapter is not in any way a reactionary argument against the repatriation movement's shift toward the mainstream. Indeed, elsewhere I have emphasized the importance of rights to history and culture as matters of social justice in a post-colonial world (Nilsson Stutz 2008a; 2008b), and in this chapter, I underscore the constructive change that repatriation legislation in the United States has wrought, establishing a cultural shift toward consultation, collaboration, and negotiation between museums and archaeological researchers, on the one hand, and Native American groups, on the other. More broadly, I offer in this chapter an analysis of the political process, bringing to the fore some largely ignored cultural dimensions of the repatriation movement's success in the United States in the late 20th century, as I seek to contribute to the ongoing academic and public debate over the delicate, contested balance between repatriation and the production of shared cultural heritage in museums and education.

Academic debates do not exist in a vacuum but tend to reflect concerns that can be found throughout their social and cultural context. Thus, this chapter looks specifically at the repatriation debate in the United States and how it reflects mainstream cultural concerns with property, race, ethnic identity, and religion. The much publicized case of the repatriation claims regarding the human remains that washed out of a river bank in Kennewick, Washington, serves to illustrate the place of the repatriation debate within the larger contemporary cultural context. The Kennewick controversy – reviewed in detail in an extensive recent volume (Burke *et al.* 2008) -- provides a concrete example for discussing how the alternative and the mainstream positions in the interpretation and appropriation of the past are relative and fluid in a dynamic, multi-stakeholder process of cultural production.

Repatriation in the United States

Today repatriation is a global phenomenon, but the experience of repatriation varies greatly in different parts of the world (e.g. Fforde *et al.* 2002; Layton 1989). The United States, with its well documented and published

debate on the issue which has been especially intense over the past 30 years - along with its far-reaching legislation - can be seen as one of the forerunners of effective globalization of repatriation. The American movement traces its roots to the spearheading activism among Native Americans in the 1960s. In the 1980s, Native American activists and leaders gained support among the general public, archaeologists, politicians and lawmakers. What started out as a culturally marginal movement has today become a mainstream position, politically as well as academically. It was with the signing into law of the Native American Graves Protection and Repatriation Act (NAGPRA[1]) in 1990 that the pendulum definitively started to swing in favor of repatriation in the United States. The law was the result of negotiations between different stakeholders, including representatives from Native peoples, activists, archaeologists, anthropologists and museum curators. NAGPRA can be seen as a product of negotiation and a political compromise, balancing the interests of the different sides (Kintigh 2008, 200; Lovis *et al.* 2004, 165). As a Federal law, NAGPRA provides a systematic process deciding Native American claims for repatriation of human remains, funerary objects, sacred objects and objects of cultural significance to be repatriated. Under the law claims may be made by Federally recognized tribes, Alaskan village corporations and Native Hawaiian Organizations, and any claim is valid where it is demonstrated that the group can trace lineal descent from the remains or otherwise can demonstrate a cultural affiliation to them. A recent amendment (March 15th 2010, effective May 14th 2010) to the regulations (43 CFR Part 10) also provides for the repatriation of unidentifiable Native American human remains and funerary objects to tribes from whose tribal lands or aboriginal occupancy areas the remains were removed. Under the amendment, transfers can also be carried out to not federally recognized tribes, but only after full consultation with relevant federally recognized tribes. These negotiations involving not federally recognized tribes are not mandatory but at the discretion of the museum or federal agency. NAGPRA applies to all US governmental agencies and institutions that receive federal funding. It transfers the ownership from the museums and research institutions that have been curating these items to the group whose claim is awarded. Most significantly, it 'shifts the historical authority from the sciences of history and prehistory to a dialogue among anthropologists, scholars, native peoples, museums, federal agencies, and the public at large' (McLaughlin 2004, 185). The implementation of NAGPRA put into motion a large scale repatriation of human remains and cultural items.[2]

---

[1] The following references to 25 U.S.C are references to parts of the NAGPRA legal document and this is covered in the legal documents references indicated.

[2] According to the NAGPRA website (www.nps.gov/nagpra, consulted April 20, 2010) the remains of 38,671 individuals, a total of 998,731 associated funerary objects and 144,163 unassociated funerary objects, 4,303 sacred objects, 948 object of cultural patrimony and 822 objects

While it is the part of NAGPRA that regulates the repatriation of items from museums that have gained the most attention outside of the United States, the law also includes provision for both intentional and inadvertent discoveries of Native American cultural items and human remains on federal and tribal lands. NAGPRA gives ownership and control of Native American cultural items that are excavated or discovered on federal or tribal lands to the lineal descendants associated with the items. The legal language is crafted in a way that extends right of ownership to other Native American tribes in case descendents cannot be determined; for example, to the tribe with the closest affiliation, the tribe whose tribal land the items were found on, or the tribe whose recognized aboriginal land the items were found on (25 U.S.C. 3002(a)). Excavation and removal of Native American cultural items from federal and tribal land for purposes of research is only permitted if it is carried out pursuant to a permit, and if such items are excavated and removed after consultation with and consent by the appropriate Indian tribe or Native Hawaiian organization (25 U.S.C. 3002(c)). Needless to say, this shift in ownership and authority, along with the regulated move toward museum- or researcher-Tribal collaboration, has had a fundamental impact on how archaeological field projects are carried out in the United States today especially through the changes in the decision-making structures. Darby Stapp has recently argued that there are mainly three reasons for the impact of NAGPRA on the decision making process. First of all, non-Indians tend to relate to the sensitivity surrounding human remains. Second, non-Indians familiar with the social justice history of Native Americans agree that American Indians 'should have a voice in cultural resource matters', and finally, since NAGPRA imposes a thirty-day work stoppage in the case of inadvertent discoveries, in order to notify appropriate tribes, the economic loss of not taking initial provisions may simply be too great (Stapp 2008a, 220-221). The effects are especially notable in the cultural resource management sector where compliance with the law has become a central concern which has influenced the sector as a whole to move from a focus on scientific research to collaboration, protection and a focus on serving community needs (Stapp 2008a). The consultation process has not only affected the practical routines and methods of archaeology, but also influenced the research questions and definitions, including a change in the definition of cultural resources (Stapp 2008a, 221-224) to new approaches to questions such as traditional history, migration and cultural affiliation (Kintigh 2008, 198-200) Ultimately, NAGPRA works effectively to level the playing field between the different stakeholders. The process, grounded in mutual consultation, has created a platform for collaboration and interaction between representatives of Native American tribes, archaeologists and museum curators (see for example Boyd and Haas 1992; Killion 2001; 2008; Lippert 1997; 2008; Stapp 2008a; and

contributions in Colwell-Chanthaphonh and Ferguson 2008).

NAGPRA is centered on the concept of ownership, but it is important to recognize that while the transactions regulated by NAGPRA ultimately transfer ownership of an item, the transaction encompasses a transfer of the power to control the presentation of cultural heritage and the writing of a group's history. From this perspective, some authors see NAGPRA as a civil rights law that extends the same rights to Native Americans that other groups have long been able to take for granted (Hutt and McKeown 1999).

Today, very few within the academic and museum communities would openly reject repatriation. The resistance that can still be felt in the debate centers on specific issues pertaining to the legislation, such as that of determining cultural affiliation. The issue of affiliation remains, in my opinion, one of the greatest challenges for NAGPRA, whether it is applied in repatriation cases from museums or when regulating the handling of new discoveries.

In NAGPRA cultural affiliation is defined as:

> *[A] relationship of shared group identity which can be reasonably traced historically or prehistorically between the present day Indian tribe or Native Hawaiian organization and an identifiable earlier group.* (25 U.S. C. 3001(2))

Affiliation is established according to the principle of preponderance of evidence, which can be based on geographical, kinship, biological, archaeological, linguistic, folklore, oral tradition, historical evidence, or other information or expert opinion which reasonably leads to such a conclusion [43 CFR 10.2 (e)]. Ousley and colleagues (2005) have outlined in detail the many challenges the establishment of affiliation faces. The procedure requires (1) the existence of an identifiable present-day Indian tribe or Native Hawaiian organization with standing under the act (i.e. that is recognized by the Federal government), (2) evidence of the existence of an earlier group, and finally (3) a link between the present day group and the group in the past. This link becomes especially difficult to establish for items from prehistoric periods. Here, the relationship is often unclear according to the archaeological evidence, and while such ambiguity is appreciated by archaeologists and anthropologists, it is not necessarily viewed as relevant for the tribes who identify with this past and claim to *know* the relationship from tradition. Legally the archaeological evidence does not necessarily carry more significance than any of the other lines of evidence. As we will see below, this fundamental difference in understanding the world, which emerges in sharp focus when we consider the process of establishing affiliation, has given form to the central disagreement in the Kennewick controversies.

NAGPRA, like any other piece of legislation, reflects the values of the society in which it is formulated and

---

that are both sacred and patrimonial had been returned to affiliated communities on September 30th 2009.

implemented. While it is often portrayed as a radical alternative to mainstream hegemonic structures, NAGPRA also simultaneously reflects many mainstream American concerns that cut across the traditional political left-right spectrum. Thus, while NAGPRA embodies a postcolonial critique, as it recognises multiculturalism and supports the democratization of cultural heritage use and knowledge production, it is also based on a deeply rooted respect for ownership (as the principle for control) and a non-negotiable respect for private property (private land and privately funded institutions are exempt from this federal law). This private property exemption constitutes a striking contrast for archaeologists from European countries, where cultural heritage is considered the property of the state or the people and cannot, with some exceptions, have a private individual or corporate owner. The preoccupation with ethnic identity and the desire to (re)appropriate an ethnic past is not simply part of a post-colonial emancipation process; in the Native American context, it may also be a reaction to the positive cultural American value placed on being part of the 'melting-pot' experience. Finally, NAGRPA opens up a legal realm, where the authority of religion and traditional knowledge is protected in the face of scientific perspectives; here, religion and tradition yield an understanding of the world that may often be favored in practice, in the framework of particular repatriation claims, over scientific argument and evidence. Of course, religious values and a religious worldview are not automatically part of a conservative ideology. However, in the contemporary United States there exists a strong link between a conservative political agenda and the emphasis placed on religious values in the public sphere including public school curricula (especially with regards to teaching evolution) and the federal funding of scientific research (for example stem cell research). NAGPRA is thus simultaneously the product of a progressive movement of postcolonial emancipation and an embodiment of American conservative ideals. This has almost certainly contributed to bi-partisan political support for the legislation on a national level, because the legislation resonates with a broader mainstream of values that can be found both to the left and the right of the political spectrum.

Brief background to the Kennewick case

One of the most publicized repatriation cases in the United States is that of 'Kennewick Man,' or 'the Ancient One.' The events that unfolded after the inadvertent discovery of these well preserved human remains—which had washed out of a bank of the Columbia River near Kennewick in Washington state in the summer of 1996—created a perfect storm that not only resulted in a long and highly publicized process of litigation (*Bonnichsen et al. vs United States*), but also dramatically revealed many of the key challenges and contradictions inherent in the NAGPRA repatriation process. At the time of the discovery, NAGPRA had been implemented for little more than half a decade, and a combination of factors including uncertainty over the

protocol (Owsley and Jantz 2001, 570-71) and the fact that the law itself was still considered controversial by many academics contributed to the ensuing controversy. A concrete central contributing factor was the early prehistoric age of the remains, which not only made the affiliation process more complicated, but also elevated the stakes for the scientists who viewed the remains as having significant value for them.

When the bones were first found, they were assumed to be the remains of a murder victim and the discovery was reported to the local police. The local coroner, in turn, contacted William Chatters, an anthropologist who owned a local cultural resource management firm. His preliminary study was inconclusive. On the one hand he argued that the morphology of the skull exhibited 'Caucasoid features' and as lacking 'definitive Native-American characteristics' (Chatters 2004, for a more complete description of the remains see Chatters 2000). This led him to believe that the remains were those of a 19th century European settler. But this interpretation was challenged by the fact that the fragment of a projectile point of a type that is associated with a time period of 8500 B.P. to 4500 B.P. was lodged in the pelvis of the individual, which pointed directly to a prehistoric origin for the remains. To resolve these contradictory indications, radiocarbon dating was carried out, and the result placed the remains at 8410 ± 60 B.P., which corresponds to approximately 9300 calendar years old (Burke *et al.* 2008, 27), which confirmed the prehistoric age indicated by the typology of the projectile point. The result was dramatic, and it would have consequences for several different stakeholders. For the US Army Corps of Engineers who controlled the land on which the remains were found, this meant that they were obliged by NAGPRA to seize the remains from the coroner and anthropologist that were studying them and contact all local Native American Tribes (Umatilla, Yakama, Nez Percé, Wanapum and Colville), in order to inform them about the find and start negotiations for repatriation. The tribes decided to claim the remains collectively under NAGPRA, based on a notion of shared group-identity affiliation. In the process all further scientific study was halted. For the Native American tribes involved, the date confirmed their belief that the individual was a Native American and that they, being the descendants of this ancient man, had the obligation to give him a lasting burial. It was his right, they argued, to be laid to rest in peace (Minthorn 2008). Several scientists, on the other hand, viewed the remains as a remarkable and unique opportunity to study the peopling of the continent, human diversity and the prehistory of North America. To them, the remains were a national treasure with no apparent ties to the contemporary Indian tribes. A collective of scientists (Bonnichsen, Brace, Gill, Haynes, Jantz, Owsley, Stanford and Steele) filed a suit against the Federal government to halt the repatriation process, in order to allow further study. They argued that there was no way of correctly establishing an affiliation without a proper study of the remains. The conflict that arose at this moment went beyond the dispute over the remains themselves and must be understood both as a political conflict and as a difference in worldview which involves fundamentally different understanding of the past, of evolution and religion and of the value of scientific and traditional knowledge, respectively.

Because NAGPRA is centred on the principle of affiliation, the Kennewick case came to rely on the different stakeholders' interpretation of this concept and the interpretation of the evidence provided by the remains. For the biological anthropologists the morphology of the skull was of interest since it provided information that would allow them to better understand the history of the peopling of the North American continent in terms of population biology and history. According to this view, it is understood that while the first humans who migrated to North America initially came from somewhere else, they are still the distant biological ancestors of the populations of contemporary Native Americans. However, it is also recognized that the population history most likely was complex and that these human groups probably migrated long distances throughout history, and while they are the distant biological ancestors to contemporary Native Americans, it is difficult to trace their more precise affiliation with specific contemporary groups or tribes (Owsley and Jantz 2001; 2002). Because of the wording of NAGPRA regarding inadvertent discoveries, the question came to center upon whether or not the remains were those of a Native American, and ultimately how 'Native American' could be defined in this case. The scientists' argument, which directly questioned the possible affiliation of Kennewick (under NAGPRA) to any of the current tribes in the area did not necessarily entail an undermining of the idea of the Native Americans as the indigenous people of North America. What the scientists argued, rather, was that there is no evidence of *cultural* continuity between the prehistoric human remains and a contemporary tribe.

The tribes rejected these arguments. The scientific understanding of the peopling of North America was uninteresting to them, because—based on a worldview grounded in traditional knowledge-they already knew that they had always lived in this region. All prehistoric remains encountered in the area must therefore be those of their ancestors. Their position can be summed up in a quote by Armand Minthorn (of the Umatilla nation): 'From our oral histories, we know that our people have been part of this land since the beginning of time. We do not believe that our people migrated here from another continent, as the scientists do' (quoted in Zimmerman and Clinton 1999, 218). Moreover, and perhaps more importantly, the Native American tribes simply considered it more important to give the Ancient One a lasting burial than to submit the remains to scientific studies, sometimes even destructive ones, that would yield basically uninteresting results based on 'pure speculation' (Sampson 2008, 40; see also Minthorn 2008).

As the legal process continued in the following years, the case became a testing ground for some of the unresolved issues of NAGPRA. It raised questions regarding how to determine affiliation for prehistoric remains, and it also came to focus on who may be considered a stakeholder in the understanding of prehistoric North America. The case has involved so much disagreement and controversy that it has been referred to as the 'worst situation regarding control of the past that has arisen within the repatriation arena' (Watkins 2008, 172), to the point of becoming quite simply a 'negative role model' (Thomas 2008, 74). What makes the Kennewick case so complicated is that different stakeholders in the debate focused on the same key themes such as race, identity and the peopling of America, but they often had very different frames of reference and understanding of the underlying concepts and questions. This resulted in a series of miscommunication and misunderstandings, and with sometimes blatant abuse of the findings to further political agendas.

Discussion of the cultural concerns expressed in the Kennewick debate

When viewed within its social and cultural context, it is clear that the Kennewick litigation and the public debate that surrounded it may be connected to a series of central concerns within mainstream American society. I have chosen to focus on three main themes that I find especially interesting. The first theme is the relationship between science and religion. The second theme that runs through the debate is the concern with cultural identity and how this is conflated with biological identity, relating to the concept of race in the contemporary United States. The final theme concerns the notion of cultural heritage as property. Here, I discuss each of these themes, outline how they have been expressed in the Kennewick debate, how they align with American mainstream values and to what extent they have been critically examined in the repatriation debate.

The following discussion is taking a closer look at the particular case of the Kennewick litigation and the debate that surrounded it. When referring to the group of five Native American tribes (the Confederated Tribes of the Umatilla Indian Reservation including the Confederated Tribes of the Colville Reservation, the Yamaka Nation, the Nez Perce Tribe, and the Wanapum Band) that claimed the remains under NAGPRA, I will use the term 'the group of Native American tribes.' I will also use the more general term 'Native American' when referring to statements made in the repatriation debate in general and with regard to the Kennewick case in particular. I want to clarify that I do not intend to reduce all Native Americans to one homogenous group. Indeed, I have in several publications critiqued the ways in which the repatriation debate reproduces a false dichotomy between indigenous and Western (Nilsson Stutz 2008a; 2008b), but since the purpose of this chapter is to analyse the debate the terminology used in it has been repeated here.

Faith and politics

While many in the debate have argued that it would be reductionist to view the Kennewick case as a conflict between science and religion (Zimmerman and Clinton 1999, 218f; Watkins 2008; Thomas 2008), I argue that this particular relationship remains central to understanding the positions in the conflict and the arguments underlying them. The anthropologists' position, based on evolutionary theory almost immediately clashed with the traditional worldview of the group of Native American tribes who claimed the remains as their ancestor in the legal battle that ensued. To return to the theme of this volume, this may at first glance seem to be a traditional case of an alternative group challenging the scientific establishment, which is supported by mainstream structures of power. Scientists clearly occupy a traditional position of power in their relationship with Native Americans (Watkins 2008, 173; see also Thomas 2008, 73). Not only has Native American traditional knowledge often been ignored by archaeology, but Native Americans have systematically been denied the right to write their own history. Scholars are viewed as 'yet another group of Euro-American colonists, trying to dictate Indian history to Indians and to appropriate another resource for themselves, the very essence of the Indians' understanding of themselves' (Zimmerman and Clinton 1999, 218). In this context the rejection of the scientific perspective becomes a strategy for Native Americans to extract themselves from the majority population and manifest their right to difference (for a discussion, see Nilsson Stutz 2008a). But a closer examination of the case reveals a more complex situation, allowing us to reflect on the intricate balance between the alternative and the mainstream. First of all, it would be wrong to assume that rejection of the theory of evolution and a belief in creationism in any form is a marginal or even alternative position in the contemporary United States. A series of Gallup polls[3] conducted between 1982 and 2010 show that between 40%-47% of Americans believe that God created humans in their present form in the last 10.000 years. During the same time (1982-2010) only between 9% and 16% claimed to believe in the theory of evolution. While we can assume that the majority of those polled were referring to the creation as told in the Bible and not that known through Native American traditions, it still appears that the claims made by the Native Americans in the Kennewick debate resonated with the mainstream

strand of American values and beliefs. In this context it is also possible to see how the scientists could view their position as marginal and even threatened by mainstream society. The skepticism toward the theory of evolution by a majority of the American population is generally viewed as a problem among American academics, who in recent years have responded with extensive public outreach strategies (e.g. Dean 2005). But in repatriation cases, including that of the Kennewick remains, this kind of united response is conspicuously absent. Many academics are quick to point out that there is no parallel to be drawn between a traditional Native American creationism and Christian creationism (Thomas 2008, 73). To make the distinction, most authors stress the political context and point to the power relationship discussed above, or simply view it as a civil right to religious freedom (Hutt and McKeown 1999). The Kennewick case, they argue, cannot be framed according to the same standards used to approach the mainstream skepticism of evolution. While I fully agree that it is important to recognize the historic circumstances and the contemporary political reality, that recognition in itself does not address the problem with creationist views as evidence in a court of law. Moreover, to avoid the religious and spiritual content of the argument and only recognize its political dimension is to implicitly question its authenticity. I suggest that this is surprising coming from those claiming to defend the human and civil rights of Native peoples, but maybe it reflects some degree of discomfort regarding creationism and religion. The strategy of emphasizing the political dimension of the tribes' arguments can also be viewed as a rhetorical strategy. By framing the creationist arguments in the Kennewick case as a purely political matter, the academic defenders of repatriation are able to both distance themselves from the religious dimension of the question, while simultaneously effectively undermining all criticism of the arguments by associating it to a failure to recognize the injustices in the historical and contemporary political power relationships.

The question of race

The Kennewick case also almost instantly focused on the highly contested and inflammatory issue of race. The first study of the remains, which had the primary goal of identifying a supposed crime victim, soon became exploited in several intertwined disputes. At first, the morphology of the skull was used by the scientists as an argument to claim that the Kennewick Man /Ancient One was morphologically different from the contemporary tribes in the area who claimed the remains on the grounds of affiliation. Some voices in this debate, including Chatters' promoted the idea that this morphological difference reflected a racial difference, something which gained great interest in the media coverage (Preston 1997; see also Thomas 2000, xxi). The debate then grew to encompass the wider discussion about the peopling of the Americas (described briefly above). As we shall see below, this issue became conflated with the theme of race.

---

[3] In addition to the results accounted for in the text, it can be noted that during the same period of time (1982-2010) between 35% and 40% claimed to believe that humans had evolved over millions of years, but that God had had some role in this process (theistic evolution). Strict creationism has held a dominating position throughout the time period and among the individuals polled, and is challenged only at the latest poll (in 2010) by the theistic evolution point of view. It can be noted that strict creationism has declined a few percentage points in the last years while the secular evolution position has gained support with a few percentage points. However, despite these trends, the belief in secular evolution with a maximum support at 16% must still be viewed as a minority position. The result of the Gallup poll can be accessed at: http://www.gallup.com/poll/145286/Four-Americans-Believe-Strict-Creationism.aspx

According to the wording of NAGPRA, it is valid to call upon biological evidence, such as skull morphology, when establishing affiliation. This has been done in several cases (Owsley and Jantz 2001, 569), and in recent years there have been efforts to increase this kind of work as a way to allow for more remains to be repatriated (Ousley *et al.* 2005). The idea of using biological criteria in determining affiliation is problematic for many anthropologists and archaeologists, who hesitate to conflate biology and culture. Cultural identity is not reflected in our bones and determined by our biology, but created through social and cultural processes. But contrary to this critique, NAGPRA—by acknowledging biological evidence when establishing affiliation—contributes to reproducing the idea that identity can be derived from morphological traits. NAGPRA as a legal instrument is formulated to provide for a process with clear results that can contribute to effectuating repatriation. It is not a vehicle to problematise and nuance the concepts it employs. We can still ask why the use of such a fundamentally problematic connection was allowed to be included in the legal framework of NAGPRA. While this should be researched in more detail, I suggest tentatively that this may actually be explained by the role of race in contemporary American society. While race as a concept has long been debated, contested and deconstructed in American society and scholarship (see for example Hartigan 2010; Montagu 1975; Mukhopadhyay *et al.* 2007; Stocking 1968), racial labels remain highly relevant in American social life, and many public institutions use racial categories to identify individuals. Racial typologies are constantly reproduced through everyday practices (such as the action of ticking the appropriate box for race and ethnicity when filling in a job application, a questionnaire or a healthcare form). While racial identity and notions of racial equality remain quite politically inflammatory and bitterly contested, race undoubtedly plays a mainstream role in American society. And while the relationship and tension between White and Black racial identities still focally define the cultural phenomenon of race in America—just as the debate over the scientific theory of evolution is still mainly driven by Christian creationism, highlighting the mainstream strain between the secular and the religious in American society—the Kennewick case brought to the surface the underlying mainstream cultural tension and ambiguity over whether racial difference simply reflects social categorization or, pending the next earthshaking scientific discovery, a biological reality.

Indeed, race played a central role in the Kennewick case's gaining widespread media attention, setting it apart from most other similar findings. The old age of the remains was, in and of itself, highly interesting, but it would probably not have sparked the intense media coverage, if it had not been for the supposed racial component of the discovery (Zimmerman and Clinton 1999, 215). As the story was covered and sometimes sensationalized in the media, the initial observations of the remains as 'Caucasoid' were misunderstood and presented as 'Caucasian,' 'white' (Burke *et al.* 2008, 28; see also discussion in Swedlund and Anderson 1999, 571) or even 'European' (Afrasiabi 1997, 805), which in turn led journalists to touch upon the debate concerning the peopling of the Americas with little grasp of the scientific complexity and the political sensitivity of the issue (see for example Egan 1996; Preston 1997). As touched upon above, the scientific consensus today is that anatomically modern humans, who initially evolved in Sub-Saharan Africa, spread out across the globe and eventually populated the American continent. Even if this understanding does not correspond with traditional Native American knowledge, the idea that these people had to have come from somewhere else does not, from a scientific point of view, undermine the aboriginal status of Native Americans. However, due to the interpretations of the shape of the skull in combination with a highly litigious climate and a law that required establishment of affiliation with a now-living group, skeletal biology was conflated with cultural identity. The most radical form of this argument came from the extreme right and white supremacists, who soon became interested in the widely discussed and publicized evidence of a more than 9000 year old 'Caucasoid' skull in North America, which they quickly came to see as potential evidence for the idea that the continent had initially been occupied by 'white' people (see Gardell 2003, 150; Ponte 1999). These original inhabitants, they suggested, had subsequently been wiped out by the Native Americans, ideas we recognize from the colonial and racist 19th century 'Myth of the Moundbuilders' (Trigger 1989, 104-109). In October 1996, as the Kennewick litigation began in the U.S. Magistrate's court, the Asatrú Folk Assembly, a group of asatrúers (representing a self-proclaimed 'ethnic religion native to Northern Europe' [Gardell 2003, 258]) filed a suit (*Asatru Folk Assembly vs United States Corps of Engineers*), claiming that if the remains were Caucasian, *they* may be the rightful descendants. The claim appeared absurd to most, but while it was objectionable and outrageous, it became difficult to reject outright, since the actual arguments used to claim the remains, including the morphology of the skull and arguments of right to culture and cultural continuity, were accepted and used by the other parties of the litigation. While the Asatrú Folk Assembly has no standing under NAGPRA since they are not Native American, they still managed to gain access to the unopened box containing the bones in August 1997 at the Battelle Pacific Northwest Laboratory in Richland where they were deposited at the time, in order to conduct an Asatrú ceremony (Associated Press 1997) under heavy criticism from the Native American spokespersons who rejected the notion that the Asatrúers had any cultural or religious connections to the remains (Lee 1997).

After a series of subsequent studies including additional radiocarbon dating, the Department of Interior announced in January 2000 that Kennewick Man is a Native American. It further clarified that its interpretation of NAGPRA's intent is that anyone who died on this continent more than 500 years ago is Native American (Burke *et al.* 2008, 32). The statement contributed to putting out the immediate fire surrounding the Kennewick case, as the Asatrú Folk Assembly withdrew their claim to the remains. However, the Department of Interior statement must leave many puzzled, including archaeologists interested in the early Viking Age settlements in Newfoundland. This bureaucratic approach served to reproduce NAGPRA's emphasis on accepting as unambiguous certain criteria for establishing plausible or valid claims of repatriation. Where biological similarity may be accepted as legal evidence to support repatriation of more recent—usually historic/contact-period—human remains, prehistoric remains are by definition potentially affiliated, even if the skeletal biology suggests substantial genetic distance between the remains and the living groups. And again, the more critical, but complicating issue of conflating biological similarity with cultural affiliation has little place in the legal process.

Looking back at the Kennewick controversy one could argue that the initial anthropological analysis and the subsequent use of those results in the litigation process gave fodder to the right extremists. But on the other hand, it was not so much the shape of the skull itself as it was the conflation of this shape with culture and identity which caused the many misunderstandings and conflicts. While contemporary anthropological debate has deconstructed the concept of race and criticized the biologisation of cultural identity, these ideas are still present in mainstream society, and in the case of Kennewick they were further reinforced both by the different stakeholders and the media, and ultimately by NAGPRA itself, as it provides a legal process for the reproduction of these ideas.

The past as property

NAGPRA is about claiming the past and claiming cultural items (I have discussed more in depth the central role of these material remains in contemporary identity processes, see Nilsson Stutz 2008a; 2008b). One outcome of this general focus on claiming and controlling the past is that ethnicity, identity and cultural affiliation have become practically instrumental for archaeological work in many parts of the US (see discussion in Adler and Bruning 2008). The cultural affiliation to an item or to human remains constitutes not only a privileged emotional connection but also a basis for actual appropriation, ownership and control. This value on ownership/control motivated surprisingly diverse claimants in the Kennewick case. This leads us to one of the most undertheorised, and therefore perhaps most interesting, dimensions of NAGPRA: its focus on ownership and how that is connected to American mainstream notions of property.

Ownership and property are fundamental concepts for the way in which NAGPRA was formulated. When repatriation is carried out, there is a transfer of ownership, from the museum or Federal agency, to the affiliated tribe. This transaction has no strings attached, reflecting the notion that the tribe is free to do what they decide is best with their property. This is most commonly viewed as a process of regaining the fundamental rights of self definition, as it renders concrete the appropriation of other intangible values such as the right to write one's own history, to define oneself and to have freedom of religion. Hutt and McKeown (1999) even claim that property rights must be viewed as human rights and argue that NAGPRA simply extends the same right to private ownership and community property rights to Native Americans that are already held by more historically mainstream or higher status identity groups. But from an archaeological and anthropological point of view, it also seems important to point out that this focus on property and ownership contributes to a commodification of cultural heritage. Despite the extensive postcolonial critique of museums and museum technologies, it may be argued that museums, with their promise to preserve and display objects for the public, have a role in contemporary society (see contributions in Cuno 2009). And without disregarding their colonial past, or, for that matter, their role in the capitalist present, it may also be argued that the curation of objects in museums actually protects them in the sense that they withdraw them from the market economy of private or exclusive ownership. While NAGPRA to some degree provides for communal ownership by, for example an affiliated group, it still challenges the fundamental idea that cultural heritage belongs to humanity and reproduces the notion that it belongs to the descendants of the people that produced it (see also Brown 2009). Since a transfer under NAGPRA does not impose any demands on those who receive the material – including a responsibility to curate it – it does not constitute protection against commodification. It is important to point out that these transactions rarely result in commodification, since the remains most often are reburied, used in ceremonies or curated in tribal museums or collections. Still, the very idea that cultural heritage can be 'property' is reproduced in the implementation of the law. Here, support for NAGPRA politically relies on the same values as the American mainstream, where private property rights are viewed as fundamental and non-negotiable.

The more damaging effect of this non-negotiable attitude to private property can be seen in the fact that NAGPRA does not concern private collections or remains found on private land (with the exception of tribal lands). The fact is that the United States is virtually alone in the world in giving ownership of archaeological resources to the fee owner of the land (Michel 1997, 131; see also Cameron 1997, 69). The consequences for this exception in NAGPRA are extreme, as thousands of sites fall victim to development and professional looters (Michel 1997, 131). After tragedies such as the infamous sacking of the large Native American burial ground at Slack Farm in Kentucky in 1987 by 10 professional looters, who had simply leased the right to the archaeological remains from the landowner (Fagan 1995, 129-135), there have been moves to increase the legal protection of burial sites, but this has only occurred on a state-by-state basis. Moreover, these efforts have remained insufficient to give full protection to the archaeological heritage, including burials on private land in the United States. The problem with the lack of protective legislation is often discussed with regards to looting, but it has received little attention in the debate on repatriation and NAGPRA. Considering the extreme vulnerability of archaeological sites on private land, this seems surprising. In a recent article that describes fascinating and thoughtful research on the fluid process of affiliation to an archaeological material by different stakeholders at Hummingbird Pueblo in New Mexico, Adler and Bruning (2008) make a point of having chosen for their project a site on private land, since it was 'outside of the purview of NAGPRA' and 'the collaborators did not need to be concerned about the impact of research on the ultimate disposition of the site or its contents' (Adler and Bruning 2008, 41). It is also interesting to note that, while activists have been pushing for clarifications regarding the repatriation and reburial of *unaffiliated* remains (e.g. Riding In *et al.* 2004), there is no similar move to challenge the exception of private collections and private land. The reason for this is probably a sense of political pragmatics. An effort to include private collections and private land in NAGPRA may simply not be realistic, as it probably would never get the required votes to pass in the US Congress, and even if it did, more than two centuries of the development of property law would likely ensure that repatriation of either affiliated or unaffiliated remains located on what is now private property would not stand up to legal scrutiny in the courts. Critique on the implicit reproduction of the strong cultural value on private property is therefore virtually absent. Indeed, I suggest that we need to see NAGPRA in its American cultural context, in a society where private property rights are simply too important to be negotiable. What the private property issue points toward is that the repatriation movement has achieved remarkable success in the US by enmeshing itself quite intimately with vitally mainstream cultural values. As a consequence, the movement also runs the immediate risk of reproducing these values and reinforcing them, not only in people's everyday lives, but also in ongoing debates and negotiations among archaeologists, museum curators, and tribal representatives over the value and management of indigenous cultural resources. NAGPRA exploits the mainstream respect for private property in giving Native American groups the means to achieve civil rights and social justice. Because of the close association between ownership, control and emancipation, it is difficult for archaeologists to critique the concept of commodification of cultural heritage in this particular context. Yet, the idea of private ownership of cultural heritage, and the ways in which it is connected to looting, is seen by most archaeologists today as a primary threat to world heritage, including the cultural heritage of Native peoples in North America. By avoiding any effort to legislate protection for private land and private collections, NAGPRA fails to protect Native American cultural heritage from what is the greatest threat it is facing in contemporary society, that of private land development and professional looting.

Conclusion: between marginal and mainstream

It would take several years of legislative battle over the Kennewick remains until Magistrate Jelderks came down with his final verdict in 2002. He argued that, since it could not be demonstrated that the remains of Kennewick Man / the Ancient One were Native American, the remains were not subject to provision of NAGPRA. Instead, he argued, they should be treated as an archaeological resource and could undergo scientific study. Despite efforts to appeal the decision, the 9th Circuit Court of Appeals upheld the ruling in 2004. The ruling has been analyzed and criticized in detail (Jones and Stapp 2008b). The main critique has been that the decision was directed by science rather than informed by it, as is stated in NAGPRA (Stapp 2008b:63). Opinions still differ on whether Kennewick Man / the Ancient One can be said to be culturally affiliated to a contemporary tribe (compare Stapp 2008b; Zimmerman 2005 and Owsley and Jantz 2002).

The purpose of this article has been to analyze the controversy from a perspective that focuses on the dynamics of what can be considered the marginal and the mainstream in the arguments driving the repatriation movement in the United States. The worldwide repatriation movement is often framed as engaged in a struggle, where marginal or marginalized indigenous communities seek post-colonial emancipation in their right to culture and history from an empowered academic community, supported not only by political structures but also by mainstream attitudes. I have shown here that in the United States, at least, the situation is far more complicated. Since the 1980s, the repatriation movement in the US has become mainstream and is regulated by a strong legal framework (NAGPRA). In this article I have argued that NAGPRA is supported politically in no small part because the legislation resonates with mainstream American values and beliefs spanning the center and right of the political spectrum—values and beliefs about religious faith, ethnic identity and tension over the biological versus social dimensions of race and private property.

In archaeological and anthropological theory all of these cultural values and beliefs, including the role of religion in society; the conflation of race, culture and identity; and the notion of private ownership of cultural heritage have come under critical scrutiny. Yet, the critique has taken place predominantly in academic contexts that are completely separate from the repatriation debate. With repatriation in the US—as marked by the success of NAGPRA-these values and beliefs have become closely associated with the Native American emancipation movement, which makes it difficult to transfer the more general critiques of identity, the past, race, property commodification, and politics. The risk is that by critiquing the repatriation movement by deconstructing the values underlying it, one may be seen as simply reactionary. The judicial outcome of the Kennewick Man/the Ancient One case—falling firmly on the side of scientific investigation—may suggest that, by failing to look critically at the political path toward the mainstream, the repatriation movement and its supporters in academia may fail to establish a more sustainable long-term success in achieving the aims of indigenous rights to culture and to the writing of history.

Acknowledgements

I want to thank to the Swedish Research Foundation for funding my research on the repatriation debate.

Bibliography

Associated Press 1997. Pagan group plans ceremony over Kennewick Man bones, August 20, published on-line: http://www.tri-cityherald.com/1997/08/20/136500/pagan-group-plans-ceremony-over.html , accessed on 29 February 2012.

Adler, M. and Bruning, S. 2008. Navigating the Fluidity of Social Identity. Collaborative Research into Cultural Affiliation in the American Southwest, in C. Colwell Chanthaphonh and T.J. Ferguson (eds) *Collaboration in Archaeological Practice. Engaging Descendant Communities*, 35-54. Lanham, MD, Altamira Press.

Afrasiabi, P. R. 1997. Property Rights in Ancient Human Skeletal Remains. *Southern California Law Review* 70, 805-839.

Boyd, T. H and Haas, J. 1992. The Native American Graves Protection and Repatriation Act: Prospects for New Partnerships Between Museums and Native American Groups. *Arizona State Law Journal* 24, 253-282.

Bray, T. 2001a. (ed) *The Future of the Past. Archaeologists, Native Americans, and Repatriation*. London, Garland.

Bray, T. 2001b. American Archaeologists and Native Americans. A relationship under construction. In T. Bray (ed), *The Future of the Past. Archaeologists, Native Americans, and Repatriation*, 1-8. London, Garland.

Brown, M. 2009. Exhibiting Indigenous Heritage in the Age of Cultural Property. In J. Cuno (ed) *Whose Culture? The Promise of Museums and the Debate over Antiquities*, 145-164. Princeton, Princeton University Press.

Burke, H., Smith, C., Lippert, D., Watkins, J. and Zimmerman, L. (eds) 2008. *Kennewick Man. Perspectives on the Ancient One*. Walnut Creek, Left Coast Press.

Cameron, C. M. 1997. The Loss of Cultural Heritage – An International Perspective. *Nonrenewable Resources* 6 (2), 67-69.

Chatters, J. C. 2000. The Recovery and First Analysis of an Early Holocene Skeleton from Kennewick, Washington. *American Antiquity* 65, 291-316.

Chatters, J. C. 2004. Kennewick Man. In *Northern Clans, Northern Traces: Journeys in the Ancient Circumpolar World*. Smithsonian Institution website, Washington DC. Available on-line at http://www.mnh.si.edu/arctic/html/Kennewick_man.html accessed on 29 February 2012.

Colwell-Chanthaphonh, C. and Ferguson, T. J. (eds) 2008. *Collaboration in Archaeological Practice. Engaging Descendant Communities*. Lanham, MD, Altamira Press.

Cuno, J. 2009. (ed) *Whose Culture? The promise of museums and the debate over antiquities*. Princeton, Princeton University Press.

Dean, C. 2005. Challenged by Creationists Museums Answer Back. *The New York Times*, September 20, F1.

Egan, T. 1996. Tribe Stops Study of Bones that Challenge History. *The New York Times*, September 30, A12.

Fagan, B. 1995. *Snapshots of the Past*. Walnut Creek, Altamira Press.

Fforde, C., Hubert, J. and Tumbull, P. (ed) 2002. *The Dead and Their Possessions. The repatriation in Principle, Policy and Practice*. London, Routledge.

Fine Dare, K. 2002. *Grave Injustice: The American Indian Repatriation Movement and NAGPRA*. Lincoln, University of Nebraska Press.

Gallup n.d. *Evolution, Creationism, Intelligent Design*. http://www.gallup.com/poll/21814/Evolution-Creationism-Intelligent-Design.aspx accessed on 29 February 2012.

Gardell, M. 2003. *Gods of the Blood. The Pagan Revival and White Separatism*. Durham, Duke University Press.

Hammil, J. and Cruz, R. 1989. Statement of American Indians Against Desecration before the World Archaeological Congress. In R. Layton (ed) *Conflict in the Archaeology of Living Traditions*, 195-200. London, Unwin Hyman.

Hartigan, J. 2010. *Race in the 21st Century*. Oxford, Oxford University Press.

Hill, R. W. 2001. Regenerating Identity. Repatriation and the Indian Frame of Mind. In T. Bray (ed), *The Future of the Past. Archaeologists, Native Americans, and Repatriation*, 127-138. London, Garland Burke.

Hutt, S. and McKeown, C. T. 1999. Control of Cultural Property as Human Rights Law. *Arizona State Law Journal* 31, 363-389.

Killion, T. W. 2001. On the Course of Repatriation. Process, Practice and Progress at the National Museum of Natural History. In T. Bray (ed), *The Future of the Past. Archaeologists, Native Americans, and Repatriation*, 149-168. London, Garland Burke.

Killion, T. W. (ed) 2008. *Opening Archaeology. Repatriation's Impact on Contemporary Research and Practice*. Santa Fe, School for Advanced Research Press.

Kintigh, K. 2008. Repatriation as a Force of Change in Southwestern Archaeology. In T.W. Killion (ed), *Opening Archaeology. Repatriation's Impact on Contemporary Research and Practice*, 195-207. Santa Fe, School for Advanced Research Press.

Layton, R. (ed) 1989. *Conflict in the Archaeology of Living Traditions*. London, Unwin Hyman.

Lee, M. 1997. Tribes upset by ritual for Kennewick Man. *TriCity Herald*, August 27.

Lippert, D. 1997. In Front of the Mirror: Native Americans and Academic Archaeology, in N. Swidler, K. E. Dongoske, R. Anyon and A. S. Downer (eds), *Native Americans and Archaeologists. Stepping Stones to Common Ground*, 120-127. Walnut Creek, Altamira Press.

Lippert, D. 2008. The Rise of Indigenous Archaeology. How Repatriation Has Transformed Archaeological Ethics and Practice. In T. W. Killon (ed), *Opening Archaeology. Repatriation's Impact on Contemporary Research and Practice*, 151-160. Santa Fe, School for Advanced Research Press.

Lovis, W. E., Kintigh, K. W., Steponaitis, V. P. and Goldstein, L. 2004. Archaeological Perspectives on the NAGPRA: Underlying Principles, Legislative History, and Current Issues, in J. R. Richman and M. P. Forsyth (ed), *Legal Perspectives on Cultural Resources*, 165-184. Walnut Creek, Altamira Press.

McLaughlin, R. H. 2004. NAGPRA, Dialogue, and the Politics of Historical Authority, in J. R. Richman and M. P. Forsyth (eds), *Legal Perspectives on Cultural Resources*, 185-201. Walnut Creek, Altamira Press.

Michel, M. 1997. Private Property-National Legacy: Protecting Privately Owned Archaeological Sites in the United States. *Nonrenewable Resources 6*, 131-136.

Mihesuah, D. A. (ed) 2000. *Repatriation Reader. Who Owns American Indian Remains?* Lincoln, University of Nebraska Press.

Minthorn, A. 2008. Human Remains Should Be Reburied, in H. Burke, C. Smith, D. Lippert, J. Watkins and Zimmerman, L. (eds), *Kennewick Man. Perspectives on the Ancient One*, 42-43. Walnut Creek, Left Coast Press.

Montagu, A. 1975. *Race and IQ*. Oxford, Oxford University Press.

Mukhopadhyay, C. C., Henze, R. and Moses, Y. 2007. *How Real is Race? A Sourcebook on Race, Culture, and Biology*. Lanham, MD, Rowman and Littlefield Education.

Nilsson Stutz, L. 2008a. Archaeology, Identity and the Right to Culture. Anthropological perspectives on repatriation. *Current Swedish Archaeology* 15-16, 157-172.

Nilsson Stutz, L. 2008b. Caught in the Middle – An Archaeological Perspective on Repatriation and Reburial, in M. Gabriel and J. Dahl (eds), *Utimut. Past Heritage – Future Relationships*. Copenhagen, International Work Group for Indigenous Affairs, Document No 122.

Ousley, S. D, Billeck, W. T. and Hollinger, R. E. 2005. Federal Repatriation Legislation and the Role of Physical Anthropology in Repatriation. *Yearbook of Physical Anthropology* 48, 2-32.

Owsley, D. W. and Jantz, R. L. 2001. Archaeological Politics and Public Interest in Paleoamerican Studies: Lessons from Gordon Creek Woman and Kennewick Man. *American Antiquity* 66, 565-575.

Owsley, D. W. and Jantz, R. L. 2002. Kennewick Man – A Kin? Too Distant, in E. Barkan and R. Busch (eds), *Claiming the Stones, Naming the Bones: Cultural Property and the Negotiation of National and Ethnic Identity*, 141-161. Los Angeles, The Getty Research Institute.

Ponte, L. 1999. Politically Incorrect Genocide, Part Two. *FrontPageMagazine.com*, October 5. Published on-line at http://97.74.65.51/readArticle.aspx?ARTID=22976 , accessed on 10 May 2010.

Preston, D. 1997. The Lost Man. *The New Yorker*, June 16, 70.

Riding In, J., Seciwa, C., Shown Harjo, S. and Echo-Hawk, W. 2004. Protecting Native American Human

Remains, Burial Grounds and Sacred Places. Panel Discussion. *Wicazo Sa Review* 19(2), 169-183.

Sampson, D. 2008. Ancient One / Kennewick Man: (Former) Tribal Chair Questions Scientists' motives and credibility, in H. Burke, C. Smith, D. Lippert, J. Watkins and L. Zimmerman (eds), *Kennewick Man. Perspectives on the Ancient One*, 40-41. Walnut Creek, Left Coast Press.

Stapp, D. 2008a. The Impact of NAGPRA on Anthropology: A View from Cultural Resource Management in the Pacific North West. In: Killion, T. W. (ed.) Opening Archaeology. Repatriation's Impact on Contemporary Research and Practice. Santa Fe: School of Advanced Research Press, 209-226.

Stapp, D. 2008b (with Jones, P. N.). An Anthropological Perspective on Magistrate Jelderk's Kennewick Man Decision, in Burke, H., Smith, C., Lippert, D. Watkins, J. and Zimmerman, L. (eds), *Kennewick Man. Perspectives on the Ancient One*, 45-66. Walnut Creek, Left Coast Press.

Stocking, G. W. 1968. *Race, Culture and Evolution. Essays in the History of Anthropology*. New York, The Free Press.

Swedlund, A. and Anderson, D. 1999. Gordon Creek Woman Meets Kennewick Man: New Interpretations and Protocols Regarding the Peopling of the Americas. *American Antiquity* 64, 569-576.

Watkins, J. 2008. The Repatriation Arena. Control, Conflict, and Compromise. In T. W. Killon (ed), *Opening Archaeology. Repatriation's Impact on Contemporary Research and Practice*, 161-177. Santa Fe, School for Advanced Research Press.

Thomas, D. H. 2000. *Skull Wars: Kennewick Man, Archaeology, and the Battle for Native American Identity*. New York, Basic Books.

Thomas, D. H. 2008. American Archaeology in the Twenty-First Century: Back to the Future? In T. W. Killon (ed), *Opening Archaeology. Repatriation's Impact on Contemporary Research and Practice*, 57-76. Santa Fe, School for Advanced Research Press.

Trigger, B. G. 1989. *A History of Archaeological Thought*. Cambridge, Cambridge University Press.

Zimmerman, L. J. 2005. Public Heritage, a Desire for a "White" History for America, and Some Impacts of the Kennewick Man/Ancient One Decision. *International Journal of Cultural Property* 12, 265–274.

Zimmerman, L. J. 2008. Unusual or "Extreme" Beliefs about the Past, Community Identity, and Dealing with the Fringe, in C. Colwell Chanthaphonh and T.J. Ferguson (eds). *Collaboration in Archaeological Practice. Engaging Descendant Communities*, 55-. Lanham, MD, AltaMira Press.

Zimmerman, L. J. and Clinton, R. N. 1999. Kennewick Man and Native American Graves Protection and Repatriation Act Woes. *International Journal of Cultural Property* 8(1), 212-228.

Legal documents:

Native American Graves Protection and Repatriation Act, 25 U.S.C. 3001 et seq. [Nov. 16, 1990], accessible on-line including subsequent regulations at: http://www.nps.gov/nagpra/MANDATES/INDEX.HTM accessed on 29 February 2012.

A CLASH OF IDEOLOGIES: ZIMBABWEAN ARCHAEOLOGY AT THE FRINGE

Paul Hubbard, Robert S. Burrett

Abstract

The debate regarding the origins and development of the Zimbabwe Culture dramatically shaped archaeological practice in southern Africa. Like many fringe archaeologies, the debates have advocated a state of worldwide archaeological, cultural and governmental conspiracy to keep the 'truth' hidden. The flimsiest of 'evidence' has been invoked to deny the fact that the ruins are the product of an indigenous African society. Few of the authors have been professional archaeologists or historians, but all have challenged professional findings and conclusions. This paper will identify the main actors, their ideas and their intended audience. The proponents identify themselves through established national symbols, drawn from a global context, that mean different things to different people. The agendas behind the representation and edification of some pasts and not others will be explored in a southern African context. Finally the relevance of such a debate to current archaeological practice in Zimbabwe will be evaluated.

Keywords: Great Zimbabwe, Zimbabwe Controversy, race

Finally to those others, too many to enumerate, who helped us in sundry ways, I tender our thanks, not least among them those unknown correspondents of lively imagination, whose letters of advice now lie filed under the heading INSANE

(Caton-Thompson 1931,viii)

This... is typical of the propaganda of this school of thought which, while deficient of real scientific scholarship, calls itself scientific and denounces its opponents as persons without scientific qualifications

(Gayre 1972, 220)

Introduction

Zimbabwe has one of the oldest traditions of archaeological research in sub-Saharan Africa, no doubt spurred on by the presence of hundreds of apparently enigmatic stone-built structures located within its borders. These structures, known locally as *madzimbahwe*, have fired the imagination of generations of visitors and researchers alike, encouraging attempts to discover the origins, development and demise of the culture behind their creation. Unfortunately this debate, at times heated and intense, has become one of the parables of world archaeology about the use and abuse of the past in order to justify certain political, social and ethnic stances. In the modern era, this discussion has become strictly polarised between mainstream archaeologists on the one hand, and on the other a so-called popular 'fringe'. Proponents of either side remain antagonistic and effectively incommunicative.

At the onset it is important to stress that as archaeologists, we are convinced of the autochthonous origin of the Zimbabwe Culture. In this paper, we seek to understand the factors that have conditioned interpretations and fostered the inharmonious relations between academic practitioners and those in the broader public sphere with their own theories. An understanding of this may go some way toward building bridges and formulating a genuine public archaeology, something more than the well-meaning, but in our local case rarely witnessed, practical intersection of heritage management and academic discourse.

How to define fringe? Zimbabwean Perspectives

One could begin, rather facetiously, by stating that technically archaeology is a fringe discipline in Africa, introduced as an integral part of the colonial process (cf. Robertshaw 1990; Shepherd 2002). In Africa, particularly in Zimbabwe, archaeology remains a largely academic subject, sequestered in the secure precincts of universities and museums, but viewed with great suspicion by the general public, for whom it purports to work (Pwiti 1996). We could then argue that to the people of Zimbabwe archaeology is at the 'fringe' of their daily lives, educational experiences and entertainments. Recent developments in the discipline in southern Africa are attempting to transform the subject into a more relevant, engaging and holistic discipline (e.g. Chirikure and Pwiti 2008), although there is still a long way to go; statements of 'public archaeology' are often more rhetoric than real engagement.

Archaeology, defined here as the study of the human past through analysis and interpretation of material culture, is a diverse discipline. This allows a multitude of different viewpoints and specialisations to flourish, although there is usually a commonality of approach grounded in the origins of the discipline (Bahn 1996), as well as in shared theory and practice. We refer to this as 'mainstream' archaeology. Most fringe or alternative archaeologies stress this commonality, placing themselves on, or being pushed to, the boundaries of what is seen as 'acceptable academic practice'. Who defines what is acceptable (or accepted) is another matter. In Zimbabwe, archaeologists have set the rules, placing those not supportive of their ideas, data and theories into the category of the 'other' (e.g. Caton-Thompson 1931; Garlake 1973, 1982a; Randall-MacIver 1906b; Summers 1965).

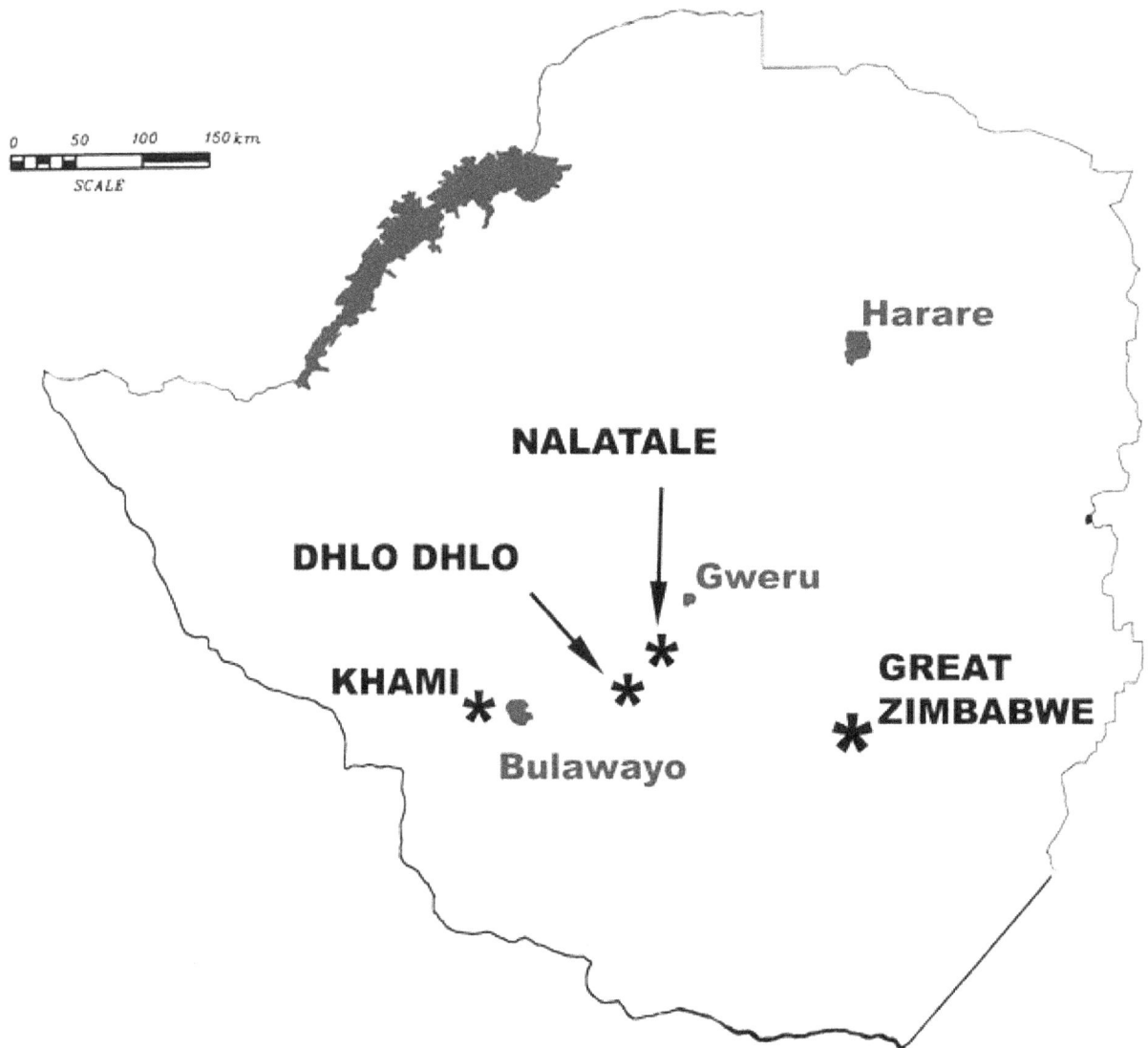

Figure 5.1: Map of Zimbabwe, indicating the location of the site of Great Zimbabwe.
Map by the authors.

We argue that the very concept of the fringe in Zimbabwean archaeology has itself changed considerably over the years, alternating between various camps anchored on their beliefs about the Zimbabwe Culture. This mirrors who controls and is the loudest in the debate, reflecting in turn changing extra-archaeological socio-political dominance. Colonisation, liberation politics, and nationalism have all played a prominent role in the changing entity that is archaeology and its fringe. In more recent times, most archaeologists would argue that the fringe has become easier to define (and thus condemn), given the racial polarisation of the discussion on Great Zimbabwe and its associated sites. We argue that while this may be true, a simple reactionary denunciation of the fringe and a refusal by academics to engage in public debate with alternative views (usually simply ignoring them), has the unwanted consequences of alienating a large portion of our audience (Holtorf 2005) thus exacerbating the gap. This

has, in part, allowed for the continued promulgation and acceptance of inaccurate ideas about the history of Zimbabwe, by successive governments and their supporters. It also misses the opportunity of self-reflection within the discipline. Mere dismissal of 'the other,' the fringe, has had the effect of obscuring and neutralising the nuances of other people's beliefs and our understanding of the construction and practice of archaeology in the country, as well as the dissemination (or lack thereof) of its results.

The Zimbabwe Culture in Zimbabwean Historiography

The Zimbabwe Tradition as a whole falls within the period commonly defined as the Iron Age, an era when the new technologies of semi-permanent residence, agro-pastoralism and metal working became dominant in the subcontinent, starting around 2000 years ago (Huffman

2007). The Zimbabwe Tradition is associated with the development of socio-cultural complexity and state formation in southern Africa. Its more prominent elite sites consist of stone-built enclosures occurring in a variety of sizes and styles, dating from the 12th to the 18th centuries CE. Over 200 such sites are known in southern Africa and of these Great Zimbabwe is the largest and most impressive. Successive studies have shown that the walls were a highly visible symbol of power and prestige for the ruling elite who lived behind them (cf. Huffman 1996; Pikirayi 2001).

Great Zimbabwe has effectively dominated the country's archaeological literature. A recent bibliography of Zimbabwean archaeology (Hubbard 2007b) revealed that of the 1920 publications on the Iron Age of Zimbabwe, 468 were on the site of Great Zimbabwe alone, compared to 272 on all the other ruins combined. The basis for this dominance in the country's historiography revolves entirely around the debate and discussion on the origins, date and function of this single site; a phenomenon often referred to as the Zimbabwe Controversy (Chanaiwa 1973). Succinctly, the debate pits those who perceive great antiquity and exotic origin against those who believe in a local derivation and a comparatively recent date (cf. M. Hall 1984; 1990; Kuklick 1991; Mahachi and Ndoro 1997; Summers 1965). The latter is today defined as mainstream archaeology but this has not always been the case.

Genesis: discovery and myth-making about the Zimbabwe Culture

From their 'discovery' in 1871 by the German explorer Karl Mauch (Burke 1969; the ruins of course were well-known to the local people) the ruins of Great Zimbabwe have captured the imagination of various writers, each espousing their own opinions. Mauch's publications elicited immediate global interest given his claim to have found the palace of the mythical Queen of Sheba, immortalised in the Bible as the consort of King Solomon. He was not the first to make this claim. He was drawing on earlier Arabic and Portuguese legends about the interior and was influenced by several well-read missionaries, primarily Reverend A. Merensky of the Berlin Missionary Society (Burke 1969; Burrett 2008; Huffman 1976). Mauch's ideas were not widely accepted by the academic establishment, yet they gained immediate and widespread popular acceptance due to skilful manipulation of the press by his sponsor, German nationalist Dr A. Petermann (Barnard 1971; Burrett 2008). The varied reactions to Mauch's reports triggered the current divided attitudes and speculative ideas about the site's history.

In 1891 the Middle Eastern antiquarian Theodore Bent arrived at Great Zimbabwe, tasked by British empire-builder Cecil John Rhodes to ascertain the identity of the builders and the age of the structures. Although he began his research with preconceived ideas about a foreign influence, Bent's initial investigations convinced him

that everything was of local origin (Braddock 1999, 39; Garlake 1973, 66). What later changed his mind (and quite possibly the course of Zimbabwean archaeology) was his examination of the soapstone Zimbabwe Birds that, to his mind resembled Phoenician sculptures rather than anything African (Bent 1896, 180-191). The influence of his sponsor can also not be discounted since Rhodes was known to prefer a foreign origin for the ruins (Brown-Lowe 2003). Bent narrowly selected a variety of artefacts and attributes from the site and, through superficial comparison to apparently 'similar' items from the Classical World, concluded that the culture was Egypto-Arabian with a distinct Phoenician influence (Bent 1896).

A significant portion of the white settler community hailed Bent's conclusions. He listened to local knowledge and heeded racially-motivated settler opinion in setting out his final conclusions. This work is still one of the most significant published on Great Zimbabwe, not only for the large amount of primary data it contains, but because it provided the very basis on which almost all of the subsequent fringe writers rest their assumptions (e.g. Brown-Lowe 2003; Bruwer 1965; R. Hall 1905, 1909; Hall and Neal 1904; Willoughby 1893). Although now defined as fringe, in his time Bent's conclusions were mainstream, given the colonial mentality that dominated the discipline and the fact that he was a 'professional'.

The first curator of Great Zimbabwe, journalist Richard N. Hall, undertook the next major excavations. He was employed by Rhodes largely because of his co-authored book on the numerous ruins of the country, a body of data collected by treasure hunters operating under the auspices of the Rhodesia Ancient Ruins Ltd (Hall and Neal 1904). Hall's duty as curator was to ensure the preservation of the buildings but he went further by removing not only vegetation, fallen stones and spoil heaps, but a large proportion of stratified archaeological deposits to the detriment of subsequent archaeological studies (Garlake 1973, 72-73). Although Hall was removed from office in 1904, his later publications played a significant part in promoting and popularising the myth that Great Zimbabwe was the product of a foreign civilisation (Hall 1905; 1909). He was a popular figure who challenged the 'professionals', thus comprehensively defining the divide between fringe and mainstream.

Academics united: the controversy takes shape

It was the heated debate between Richard Hall and a British archaeologist, David Randall-MacIver that initiated the 'Zimbabwe Controversy' (Summers 1971, 230). The British Association for the Advancement of Science and the Rhodes Trust sent Randall-MacIver to Rhodesia to investigate the stone ruins of the country and prepare a report for the 1905 meeting of the Association (Randall-MacIver 1906b). 'As the first trained archaeologist to visit the ruins, Randall-MacIver came to southern Africa prepared to ridicule the amateur methods of his predecessors, and to lament the damage they and others had done in ignorance' (Kuklick 1991, 144). Peter Garlake (1973, 78) claims that it was Randall-MacIver's results that effectively polarised opinion on Great Zimbabwe creating settler disdain for the 'overseas expert'. More than this, we would argue that it was his often high-handed attitude towards the white Settlers, as exemplified in Kuklick's above quote, which hardened public opinion against ideas of a local origin for the culture. As he said in an address to the Geographical Society, 'it is... entirely an archaeological question' (Randall-MacIver 1906a, 325), thereby dismissing out of hand all alternative, speculative ideas without engaging with the pseudo-facts. The 'others', who did not agree with him, were marginalised. It became a clash between personalities and national identities rather than a quest to study this fascinating precolonial civilisation.

Why was it so important to local Rhodesian settler society that a foreign civilisation be responsible for the ruins' origin? It is generally agreed that ideas about European racial superiority and the need to justify the (re)colonisation of the country were important factors (Garlake 1973; 1982a; Mahachi and Ndoro 1997; Shepherd 2002). The Europeans and South Africans (who were to become Rhodesians) had to claim a precedent in the form of some ancestral antiquity for their right to occupy the African territories south of the Zambezi and assigning a foreign authorship for the ruins seemed a perfect solution. Randall-MacIver's conclusions that the ruins were actually the product of the ancestors of the local Shona people directly threatened one of the central tenets of the formative settler psyche that considered that 'their natives' were incapable of such achievements. Thus the fringe was set up against mainstream academia.

Hall's (1909) swan song on the Zimbabwe Culture, *Prehistoric Rhodesia*, is largely a point-by-point rebuttal of Randall-MacIver's (1906b) conclusions. A convoluted and aggressive book, it offered little new archaeological or historical evidence. It has been described as 'a moral tale justifying the establishment of white settler society in southern Africa... a tale consistent with the settler belief that Africans had no clear title to land either by virtue of long occupation or capacity to use natural resources productively' (Kuklick 1991, 146). Hall's work set the tone for all future discussion, or more correctly lack of discussion, between the academic establishment (usually perceived of as under the influence of foreign, liberal tendencies) and the Rhodesian Settlers, who had their own ideas about the site and culture. Hall's combative stance brought a great deal of unnecessary emotion to the argument, dividing the debate into a sharply defined 'them and us' scenario.

Hall's (1909) book was possibly the first, certainly the most well read, publication to explicitly state that black people could not have constructed the buildings due to their alleged racial inferiority (Hall 1909, 10-14). 'Since

Hall's time [racial theories] have continued to be used often to prejudge and negate any contrary archaeological evidence' (Garlake 1973, 79). Race has been the one common factor that unifies a century of what we now call the fringe literature on Great Zimbabwe.

Cries of the right: overt racist ideas and Rhodesian politics

The 'winds of change' that blew across Africa in the 1960s, toppling colonial governments, were strongly resisted in the south of the continent. This was due mainly to the presence of large white Settler populations unwilling to relinquish their political control as well as the lack of any unified opposition (Martin and Johnson 1981). Martin Hall (1990, 65-67) has mapped the change in the Rhodesian State's attitude from promoting a 'partnership' between races and creation of a black middle class to increasing resistance against the growing demands of Black Nationalists (cf. Keatley 1963). The Rhodesian Front, a hard-core white nationalist party, won the limited franchise (white only) elections in 1962, later breaking from Britain in 1965 with the so-called Unilateral Declaration of Independence (UDI). This launched Rhodesia into a 15-year crisis, the latter part characterised by a bitter civil war that ended with independence in 1980.

The publications considered in this section are all overtly political in nature by virtue of their aims and conclusions. Inspired largely as a reaction to the Pan-Africanist independence rhetoric of the time, these Rhodesian, fringe publications sought to actively portray Great Zimbabwe and associated sites as the product of some lost civilisation later destroyed by rampaging African tribes or through the 'weaknesses' brought about by miscegenation. Such books are still being produced (e.g. Brown-Lowe 2003) and they serve more as a moral tale about the 'decline' of white occupation and identity rather than any serious attempt at historical enquiry.

Dedicated to the then-Rhodesian Prime Minister, Ian D. Smith, A.J. Bruwer's (1965) book is a curious mishmash of archaeological fact and fantasy. He drew widely from separate, completely un-associated cultures from across the world, in an attempt to prove that Great Zimbabwe was built by the Phoenicians as part of their struggle with the Greeks over the control of the Mediterranean. Like many fringe writers, Bruwer is dismissive of the aims and methods of academic archaeology: 'I am writing this book not because I am an archaeologist; it is bad enough to be an economist. Anybody, qualified or unqualified, can set up as either the one or the other and nobody seems to be any the wiser for it' (Bruwer 1965, xvii). Bruwer is clearly anti-academia and is explicit in defending his racist departure from orthodoxy. He revels in being on the fringe. This must have been a particularly attractive stance to his readership given that the book appeared in the same year as UDI, a time when white Rhodesians were feeling persecuted and rejected by the outside world due to the imposition of sanctions and loud denunciations of UDI. His whole book is an attack on what he characterises as a largely foreign-based scholarship on the Zimbabwe Culture and reflects the widespread feelings of this time.

Describing a trio of archaeological personalities he met during his researches, Bruwer (1965, xviii) claims the 'politico-archaeologist' is directly responsible for the 'myth' of local origins for the ruins and he sets himself the task of revealing the actual 'truth' about the ancient culture. Like most fringe authors, he dismisses most of the archaeological data as irrelevant to the question of its origins, although unlike other writers he does appear to have read most of the contemporary literature. One reviewer justifiably claimed, 'The author espouses the cause of a Phoenician origin for Zimbabwe and pleads his case with flamboyant allusion, and classic polemic. [The book] is a magnificent parody on archaeological research. The only trouble is that the author takes himself seriously' (Fagan 1970, 321). In common with other writers discussed in this section, Bruwer places himself on the fringe of archaeological consensus in order to score political points with his target audience; in this case, the majority of white Rhodesian society. The fact that scholars did not publicly contest Bruwer's conclusions, instead preferring to limit their discussion to academic arenas, resulted in such fringe claims enjoying wide public support.

By the 1970s, the issue of the authorship of Great Zimbabwe had become increasingly politicised. In part this was due to the intensification of the civil war that led the government to increase its suppression of conflicting points of view in order to maintain its tenuous control over the population (Martin and Johnson 1981; Moorcroft 1980). Archaeology was not immune. 'Scientific and scholarly enquiry were taken hostage as the diffusionist myths and hypotheses were mobilised in the ideological and psychological armoury of white supremacy' (Swanson 2001, 304). Other than the direct censorship of displays and guidebooks (cf. Frederikse 1982, 10-12; Garlake 1982a; but see Cooke 1974 for a denial), this ideology manifested itself most clearly in the form of *The Origin of the Zimbabwean Civilisation* by Lord Robert Gayre of Gayre (1972), a sustained polemic against the idea that local blacks could have been responsible for the Zimbabwe Culture Gayre had seemingly impressive academic credentials having trained as an archaeologist and anthropologist and having acquired professorial status before writing his book. Yet he attacked the most basic tenets of archaeology, more especially radiocarbon dating and interpretation of stratigraphy, dismissing all such evidence. Like Bruwer, Gayre presents most professional archaeologists of his 'Bantu school' as self-important and under-informed; '[o]ne good thing these distortions may have achieved, as the true facts of Zimbabwe come to be recognised, is the dethronement of the pundits who too frequently in our times have arrogantly dominated the scene' (Gayre 1972, 221). Again, the common thread is the need to challenge the supposed arrogance of the academic establishment, as well as to provide historical moral support for current politics.

Due to the intense government interest in the archaeology of the Zimbabwe Culture, local archaeologists began to retreat into the burgeoning scientific esotericism that was to be the hallmark of the 'New Archaeology' (Johnson 1999), compared to the emphasis on culture history that largely characterised studies before the 1950s. As Roger Summers (1965, 37) neatly summarised it, 'the issue is... between antiquarianism, based on the library and the cabinet of curiosities, and scientific archaeology, based on field studies and the laboratory; between the amateur and the professional'. Summers and other local and international authors stressed the primacy of science in most of their publications on Great Zimbabwe, trying and failing to reconcile the opposing camps. Archaeological data was sanitised, in part by the overuse of jargon and sterile nomenclature (e.g. Robinson 1961).

Additionally, many professional archaeologists in Rhodesia often chose to omit or downplay controversial information within publications aimed at the general public, rather than become enmeshed in ugly public debates (e.g. Cooke 1971; Huffman 1976). In Rhodesia and now Zimbabwe and this is a loose characterisation – the mainstream has been propounded and supported by those working for State institutions, namely the National Museums and Monuments of Zimbabwe, and more recently the University of Zimbabwe. It was no easy path for archaeologists working on the Iron Age in the 1970s as the majority of popular white opinion was against them. Most archaeologists active at the time have been taken to task for alienating the general population (ironically both black and white) from contributing their ideas and feelings through presenting archaeology as an unnecessarily complicated and dry discipline (Garlake 1982a). It would have been difficult to buck the trend, as it were, for fear of losing one's job or even worse being deported from the country – as happened to Peter Garlake in the early 1970s.

One of the latest additions to racist fringe literature is by journalist and former Rhodesian radio personality Robin Brown-Lowe (2003). Written during a time of great political and social upheaval in post-independent Zimbabwe, the book is an unwelcome return to the 'antiquarian pastiche' (Wheeler 1973, 7) of the nineteenth century. 'The audience for the book may safely be assumed to be the white Rhodesians scattered about the world as shown by the frequent digressions into more recent Pioneer history and the pandering to extrinsic origins ideas that were a hallmark of the Smith minority government' (Hubbard 2007a). Brown-Lowe (2003, vii-xv) states that he has liberal views about the 'natives' of the country but in the interests of an imagined 'Truth' he cannot believe that the local populations had anything to do with the genesis and development of Great Zimbabwe.

Brown-Lowe is of the opinion that an 'alien influence' is clearly visible in the architecture and building styles at Great Zimbabwe. He argues that certain structures, such as the sinuously curved doorways, were built for aesthetic purposes only; this was supposedly a trait the local Shona were only able to develop with outside influence. He subtly reinforces this idea with reference to the art school of Frank McEwen and the evolution of contemporary Shona sculpture in a manner that completely fails to understand the development of this art form. Brown-Lowe attributes authorship to the Lemba community of southern Africa. This privileged, supposedly alien-influenced artistic class is identified on the basis of their supposedly uncharacteristic dietary preferences and a limited number of cultural traits (Brown-Lowe 2003, 227-246). This conclusion, first proposed by von Sicard (1952), was revived by Mullan (1969), later partially endorsed by Gayre (1972) and advocated today by Tudor Parfitt (2008) and Richard Wade (2009), respectively Professor of Modern Jewish Studies at the University of London's School of Oriental and African Studies (SOAS) and a freelance astronomer of dubious credentials. It seems that if one (of the racist school) has to accept a partial local origin it is always *another* minority group with supposed racial superiority, the result of interbreeding with external parties. In the case of the Lemba this would probably be European, Arab or Asian but certainly they could not be defined as pure African.

Clearly these authors have difficulty in accepting the evidence; both with the African nationalist politicians as well as academics whom they often claim have worked hand in hand with these politicians to hide an alleged exotic truth. For example, Brown-Lowe presents himself as a persecuted seeker of the 'real' story behind the ruins, claiming a conspiracy amongst liberals who do not understand the 'real Africa' and its history. We hope to have shown how such publications mirror political events.

Kooky or crazy? Alternative scenarios in recent times

In addition to the racist perspectives, other fringe groups exist. While some authors have dismissed them as premeditated political attempts to deny or obscure the truth (e.g. Hall and Borland 1982; Phillipson 1986; Pikirayi 2001), we argue there is a little more to it. We need to avoid tarring all fringe works with the same political brush. These authors are not necessarily denying an African origin, but are often seeking to explore alternatives to the official narrative. Sadly they are rarely engaged by academics and their somewhat irregular conjectures have gone unchallenged. Consequently, they often attract popular interest, as people have not been offered an alternative view with the same level of broad appeal, but from a more staid (and thus academic?) angle. Called the 'New Revisionism' (Pikirayi 2001, 23), these fringe publications are often attempts to relate the Zimbabwe Culture to the larger global picture articulating their own personal interests. Facts are distorted not because of explicit racism but in order to fit outlandish associations with issues of language, architecture, religion and trade taken out of context as evidence of long-lost civilisations.

Focusing on supposed linguistic evidence but using a variety of sources in many languages, Cyril Hromnik's (1981) conclusions echo those of the German anthropologist Leo Frobenius (1931). The latter, who worked in Southern Africa in the late 1920s, believed in some mythical community, Erythräa, that was said to be of Asian origin that had effectively colonised southern Africa (Frobenius 1931). The crux of Hromnik's (1981) more recent argument is that metalworking and the building of the impressive stone structures of the Zimbabwe Tradition were not of local origin but were introduced and sustained by specialists who came from Asia long before the arrival of the 'Negroid Bantu'. The 'Negroid Bantu became unintended beneficiaries of the technological progress brought to Africa by Indians. They appear to have been drawn into the Iron Age… because their services were needed for the successful functioning of the metal-based industrial enterprise of the Indians' (Hromnik 1981, 86). Hromnik not only dismisses any chance of African input, but argues for social, moral and economic decline once the creators left or disappeared (Hromnik 1981, 22, 131-5). A large part of his book is devoted to attacking 'Africanist' archaeology, claiming that the mainstream interpretations are shaky, based on misguided associations and error and that what was suggested was inspired by current African nationalist and liberation ideology rather than supposed hard data (Hromnik 1981, 18-19). In his work the African is present, but in the background there is a hidden, foreign force that provided the stimulus. Hromnik's work is 'racism soft,' while the narrative is disjointed and eclectic, while it is written with the flair of an accomplished journalist.

An architect, Wilfrid Mallows (1984), discounted any chance of structuralist and symbolic meaning to the ruins, choosing instead to concentrate on his own idiosyncratic code, behind its design. He concluded that Great Zimbabwe was both a treasure house and an entrepôt prison for the slave trade. Smaller ruins around the country, despite only superficial similarities, had the same function although they were subordinate to Great Zimbabwe. Said to be ruled by Asians, Mallows argues that this foreign culture collapsed when a change in the international trading system brought about a greater inter-Asian focus, as well as a slave revolt and the impact of massive environmental degradation. Not surprisingly, Mallow's concerns mirror the major global political issues of the 1980s. His book is mostly free from overt racial prejudice, although, as Hromnik (1986, 99) put it, his ideas and conclusions are 'buried in a story that is almost ridiculous', drawing unfounded conclusions from a mélange of data.

Two other books deserve mention in this section. The first, arrestingly called *Psychic Episodes of Great*

Zimbabwe (Clarkson-Fletcher 1941), describes a set of séances held in the ruins by the author, during which he claims to have contacted the spirits of the original builders and other descendants. Written with dramatic and romantic flair and 'under the impetus of psychic influence,' (Clarkson-Fletcher 1941, vi), the author relates the rise and decline of the civilisation in much the same vein as Haggard's classic *Elissa and the Doom of Zimbabwe* (1900). Clarkson-Fletcher's tale concludes that the Phoenicians built Great Zimbabwe to control the gold trade. But it was a sad, lonely colonial existence and the Phoenicians committed mass suicide rather than integrate with the local tribes. Not surprisingly, this book has been ignored and has failed to gain mainstream and even fringe attention, although it has been cited by Richard Ganter (2003) as factual proof that the Phoenicians once lived in southern Africa.

Ganter (2003) resurrects the ideas of Richard Swan (1896) and sees the builders of Great Zimbabwe as northerners who worshipped the stars. He firmly identifies these foreigners as the Phoenicians, linking to the Zimbabwe Culture the Biblical stories of a trading journey made by the Phoenicians in alliance with Solomon that came back with several tons of gold and exotic trade goods. Ganter, however, goes a step further and argues for a permanent international trading network established by these intrepid explorers who, while travelling, supposedly created a series of structures to align themselves with their northern homeland. Great Zimbabwe was one of these 'base stations', as were the pyramids at Giza, the statues on Easter Island and the temples at Angkor Wat. Ganter uses a complex web of addition and multiplication of various alleged degrees and measurements of significance to produce his supposed evidence of connections and relationships across the globe. The archaeologically known cultures and societies from these various locations are dismissed as mere accidentals, fairly recent intruders who lived on top of the 'ancient' sites.

Many of these alternative publications have received widespread public attention but were almost universally ridiculed in academic reviews (e.g. Hall and Borland 1982; Ownby 1981; Phillipson 1986). This reflects the ensuing deep divide in southern African public archaeology. There is almost no direct communication between mainstream professional archaeologists and the fringe authors. The public impression is that academics are unsure of themselves and at the same time withholding something. Unfortunately the failure by regional archaeologists to adequately inform the wider public about their research and findings has contributed directly to the continued resurgences of fringe publications on Great Zimbabwe and archaeology in general. The scholarly community has failed to constructively engage with the fringe, so the public grasps at what information it can get, however improbable.

A new ideology: archaeological research in post independence Zimbabwe

With the Independence in 1980, Zimbabweanist academics hoped that a new era had dawned that would provide a relevant and useful history to the people of the new nation (cf. Garlake 1982a; 1982b; Ushewokunze 1982). This was short-lived optimism. Rhodesian-styled fringe literature has continued to capture the attention of many, sometimes across earlier ethnic divides, but more importantly we have witnessed the emergence of a new Pan-Africanist fringe. A pivotal point was the appointment of the first black curator of Great Zimbabwe, Ken Mufuka. At the time of his appointment, he was Associate Professor of African and Western Civilisation at Lander College, South Carolina. Still a controversial figure to some, Mufuka's views have changed with time, but we wish to refer to his 1984 contribution to the literature on Great Zimbabwe and the considerable debate that it generated. As a publication, it has to be examined in the context of the euphoria of independence, as well as in terms of his personal motivations.

Fontein (2006, 125-128) describes the ensuing furore in detail, noting that along with Garlake, Mufuka can be classed as the first of the nationalist and revisionist historians of the post-independence era, albeit at opposite ends of the spectrum. Both of their guidebooks for the site appeared roughly at the same time (Garlake 1982b; Mufuka 1983); yet each employed very different sources and came to different conclusions about the life and times of the inhabitants. Both authors rejected negative colonial stereotypes about the site, stressing its African origins to promote pride in Zimbabwe's past. However, unlike Garlake, Mufuka privileged sketchy oral traditions that he collected from the area, while at the same time embellishing statements that buttressed his romantic and Africanist vision of the past; a veritable paradise lost divorced from all ills that were after all surely only the product of white colonisation! (cf. Beach 1984). The result was a poetic and idealistic story that clearly reflected the socialist mantra espoused by the government of the time.

Unfortunately Mufuka's book, the epitome of post-independence fringe literature, became the 'gospel' at the site (Garlake in Fontein 2006, 127), overshadowing academic works. In a review of the book, Garlake (1984, 123) described it as a great threat to 'scientific' research, an 'atavistic fantasy, grotesque in its exaggerations, [that] entirely replaces reason and logic and if Mufuka has his way, will bring to an end 78 years of scholarly research, albeit always at hazard to other forms of racism'. One should instead consider the context of Mufuka's book. It was an overt African attempt to contest 'the progressive alienation of the general population' (Garlake 1982a, 14) and provided the first home-grown thesis on what had become the country's most enduring symbol of national unity and pride. This is hinted as much in the introduction to Garlake's (1982b) book, in which the then Minister of Home Affairs stated that Zimbabweans need to 'take Great Zimbabwe back from the foreign tourist, settler and expert and restore it to our people - to put them first' (Ushewokunze 1982, 4). This sentiment has become increasingly expressed in Zimbabwe as the new socio-political elite sought to redefine the past to bolster their own place in that past and to legitimise their current activities. It is a phenomenon that Terence Ranger (2004) has described as 'Patriotic History' when referring to the Zimbabwe version of nationalist history.

Aeneas Chigwedere's work has always been controversial and at the edge of conventional historical sensibilities (Roberts 1999). His writings span the whole gamut of Zimbabwe's political changes (Chigwedere 1980; 1982; 1985; 1998; 2001). His earliest works are part of the broader Black Nationalist historiography that aimed at placing the history of black Africa on equal footing with that of the rest of the world (Ranger 2004). Locally trained Zimbabwean archaeologists including Mahachi and Ndoro (1997), Matenga (1998), Ndoro (2001), Pikirayi (2001), Pwiti (1997) and Sinamai (1998) ignored his earlier work in their own publications on the Zimbabwean Culture, perhaps reflecting their disdain for his unsubstantiated conclusions, repackaging of old racial philosophy with a Pan-Africanist prejudice and unusual research methodology (such as appealing to the 'spirits of the ancestors'). Ranger (2004, 224-5), however, has somewhat cynically argued that Chigwedere's influence has undergone a considerable revival in Zimbabwe with his appointment as Minister of Education which lasted until fairly recently. This allowed him to ensure that 'his' version of history became the primary discourse in the nation's schools.

Zanu-PF, one of the liberation parties that successfully fought for independence in Zimbabwe, has ruled the country almost continuously since Independence. Currently part of the schema defined as 'Patriotic History' (Ranger 2004), Chigwedere's later publications (1998; 2001) are an overt attempt to write a history that best reflects the 'aspirations' of the formerly Zanu-PF dominated Zimbabwean government. Patriotic history is a complicated phenomenon, reacting to perceived and often imagined 'threats' against Zimbabwe, or more specifically against Zanu-PF, by the West and former White Rhodesians. The government's aim was, and still is, to present a new monolithic view of history that endorsed and praised the continued rule of a Zanu-PF government at the expense of conventional history (Fontein 2006; Ranger 2004). It is thus ironic that, at the turn of the millennium, Zimbabwean history and archaeology found itself again at the fringe of yet another 'new revisionism' (Pikirayi 2001, 23) created by the State to justify contemporary socio-political prerequisites.

Conclusions

In this paper we have focussed on the so-called Zimbabwe Controversy in an attempt to understand the rationale and changing character of fringe interpretations vis-à-vis mainstream archaeology. How the terms 'mainstream' and 'fringe' are defined is subjective. The exotic origin theories for Great Zimbabwe were 'mainstream' in the nineteenth century. Later these theories were marginalised to the fringe, but they have never disappeared. They remain a substantial part of the public's image of Great Zimbabwe, be it in white racial overtones or black nationalist reactions. We have shown that questions of ethnic identity, nationalism and social competition can all be blamed to a fair degree for the origin and persistence of these fringe interpretations. Also influential has been the role of populist political policy adopted by successive governments from Cecil Rhodes, to successive Rhodesian governments with varying views on racial equality to current post-independence struggles for the hearts and minds of the Zimbabwean public. Academics have failed to become adequately engaged in these debates. Some have sided with the powers that be, but most often they have held back, uncertain of their ability to sway and educate the public and the politicians. Unfortunately several have been overtly confrontational (e.g. Randall-MacIver, Caton-Thompson and Garlake), antagonising and alienating the general public. This has usually generated an anti-academia reaction pushing some into the unquestioning acceptance of fringe interpretations.

But are the public (and politicians) entirely to blame? How much have we as archaeologists sought to popularise our works? Do we in fact publish for anyone other than our in-house peers? Is it comprehensible to the public both in writing style and accessibility? Do we engage the fringe or just ignore them, smirking behind the closed doors of our academic institutions? The old adage of ivory towers unfortunately still dominates southern African archaeology. While there have been many calls for engagement with the public – who often foot the bill for archaeological research through their taxes – these have been largely hollow and unheeded. The oft-cited excuse of being too busy with core research and teaching hides a serious failing in our discipline (cf. Hubbard 2007b).

Zimbabwean archaeology again finds itself at a crossroads. Today fringe theories and unsubstantiated conjecture are again dominating popular imagination. For some it is harking back to old, disproven racial interpretations that cite exotic and most often European origins, for others it is the selective inclusion and exclusion of facts in order to bolster the socio-economic policies of post-independent Zimbabwe. Now, more than ever, the discipline needs to reinvent itself, moving from its current place at the *fringe* of Zimbabwean consciousness to become an active participant in the creation of a history meaningful to the nation. This will only come about if scholars actively engage with fringe authors, but more importantly, with the general public.

Acknowledgements

We would like to gratefully acknowledge the assistance of Anna Mabrey, Rhona Sargeant and James Bower in the production of this article. The editors and three anonymous reviewers helped strengthen this paper in many ways, for which we are grateful. Any errors and all opinions remain our own.

Bibliography

Bahn, P. 1996. *The Cambridge Illustrated History of Archaeology*. Cambridge, Cambridge University Press.

Barnard, F. O. (ed) 1971. *Karl Mauch: African explorer*. Cape Town, C. Struik.

Beach, D. N. 1984. Book Review: K. Mufuka. 1983. Dzimbahwe: life and politics in the golden age 1100-1500AD. Masvingo: Belmont Press. *Prehistory Society of Zimbabwe Newsletter* 57, 4-6.

Bent, J. T. 1896. *The Ruined Cities of Mashonaland: Being a Record of Excavation and Exploration in 1891. (3rd Edition)*. London, Longmans, Green and Co. [Facsimile Reprint 1969, Bulawayo: Books of Rhodesia (Rhodesiana Reprint Library Volume 5)].

Braddock, B. J. 1999. Theodore and Mabel Bent: A Discussion on the work in Great Zimbabwe of this 19th Century Couple. *Zimbabwean Prehistory* 23, 38-44.

Brown-Lowe, R. 2003. *The Lost City of Solomon and Sheba: an African mystery*. Gloucestershire, Sutton Publishing Ltd.

Bruwer, A. J. 1965. *Zimbabwe: Rhodesia's Ancient Greatness*. Johannesburg, Hugh Keartland.

Burke, E. E. (ed) 1969. *The Journals of Carl Mauch: His Travels in the Transvaal and Rhodesia 1869-1872*. Salisbury, National Archives of Rhodesia.

Burrett, R. S. 2008. Karl Gottlieb Mauch (1837-1875). *Heritage of Zimbabwe* 27, 74-88.

Caton-Thompson, G. 1931. *The Zimbabwe Culture: Ruins and Reactions*. Oxford, Clarendon Press.

Chanaiwa, D. 1973. *The Zimbabwe Controversy, A Case of Colonial Historiography*. New York, Syracuse University.

Chigwedere, A. 1980. *From Mutapa to Rhodes*. London, Macmillan.

Chigwedere, A. 1982. *The Birth of Bantu Africa*. Harare, Books of Africa.

Chigwedere, A. 1985. *The Karanga Empire*. Harare, Books of Africa.

Chigwedere, A. 1998. *The Roots of the Bantu*. Marondera, Mutapa Publishing House.

Chigwedere, A. 2001. *British Betrayal of the Africans. Land Cattle and Human Rights. Case for Zimbabwe*. Marondera, Mutapa Publishing House.

Chirikure, S. and Pwiti, G. 2008. Community Involvement in Archaeology and Cultural Heritage Management: An Assessment from Case Studies in Southern Africa and Elsewhere. *Current Anthropology* 49 (3), 467-485.

Clarkson-Fletcher, H. 1941. *Psychic Episodes of Great Zimbabwe: A True Narrative*. Cape Town, Central News Agency South Africa, Limited.

Cooke, C. K. (ed) 1971. *Guide to the Great Zimbabwe Ruins and other antiquities near Fort Victoria*. Salisbury, Commission for the Preservation of Natural and Historical Monuments and Relics.

Cooke, C. K. 1974. Letter to the Editor. *Antiquity* 48 (190), 83.

Fagan, B. M. 1970. Book Review: A. J. Bruwer 1965 Zimbabwe: Rhodesia's Ancient Greatness Johannesburg, Hugh Keartland. *Antiquity* 44 (176), 320-322.

Fontein, J. 2006. *The Silence of Great Zimbabwe: Contested Landscapes and the Power of Heritage*. London, UCL Press.

Frederikse, J. 1982. *None but Ourselves: Masses versus Media in the Making of Zimbabwe*. Harare, Zimbabwe Publishing House.

Frobenius, L. 1931. *Erythräa: Lander und Zeiten des heiligen Königsmordes*. Berlin, Atlantis-Verlag.

Ganter, R. 2003. *Zimbabwe's Heavenly Ruins: A Mystery Explained*. London, Upfront Publishing.

Garlake, P. S. 1973. *Great Zimbabwe*. London, Thames and Hudson.

Garlake, P. S. 1982a. Prehistory and Ideology in Zimbabwe. *Africa* 52 (3), 1-19.

Garlake, P. S. 1982b. *Great Zimbabwe Described and Explained*. Harare, Zimbabwe Publishing House.

Garlake, P. S. 1984. Ken Mufuka and Great Zimbabwe. *Antiquity* 58 (223), 121-123.

Gayre, R. 1972. *The origin of the Zimbabwean Civilisation*. Salisbury, Galaxie Press.

Haggard, H.R. 1900 'Elissa: or, the Doom of Zimbabwe'. In *Black Heart, White Heart and Other Stories*, 69-227. London, Longmans.

Hall, M. 1984. The burden of tribalism: The social context of southern African Iron Age studies. *American Antiquity* 49 (3), 455-467.

Hall, M. 1990. 'Hidden History': Iron Age Archaeology in southern Africa. In P. Robertshaw (ed), *A History of African Archaeology*, 59-77. London, James Currey.

Hall, M. and Borland, C. H. 1982. The Indian connection: an assessment of Hromnik's 'Indo-Africa'. *The South African Archaeological Bulletin* 37 (136), 75-80.

Hall, R. N. 1905. *Great Zimbabwe, Mashonaland, Rhodesia: An Account of Two Years' Examination work in 1902-4 on behalf of the Government of Rhodesia*. London, Methuen.

Hall, R. N. 1909. *Prehistoric Rhodesia*. London, Unwin.

Hall, R. N. and Neal, W. G. 1904. *The Ancient Ruins of Rhodesia (Monomatapae Imperium) (2nd Edition)*. London, Methuen and Co. [Facsimile Reprint 1972, Bulawayo: Books of Rhodesia (Rhodesiana Reprint Library Volume 23)].

Holtorf, C. 2005. Beyond Crusades: How (Not) to Engage with Alternative Archaeologies. *World Archaeology* 37 (4), 544-551.

Hromnik, C. A. 1981. *Indo-Africa: towards a new understanding of the history of sub-Saharan Africa*. Cape Town, Juta.

Hromnik, C. A. 1986. Book Review: W. Mallows 1984. *The Mystery of the Great Zimbabwe: A New Solution*. New York, W.W. Norton and Co. *The South African Archaeological Bulletin* 41 (144), 98-99.

Hubbard, P. 2007a. Review Article: Brown-Lowe, Robin. 2003. *The Lost City of Solomon and Sheba: an African mystery*. Gloucestershire, Sutton Publishing Ltd. http://www.ucl.ac.uk/archaeology/aha/hubbard/PHrevie wbrown-lowe2003.pdf accessed on 29 February 2012.

Hubbard, P. 2007b. *A Bibliography of Zimbabwean Archaeology to 2005*. Available at www.sarada.co.za (under >resources>research) and at African Heritage and Archaeology. www.ucl.ac.uk/archaeology/aha/index.htm accessed on 29 February 2012.

Huffman, T. N. 1976. *A Guide to the Great Zimbabwe Ruins*. Salisbury, National Museums and Monuments of Rhodesia.

Huffman, T. N. 1996. *Snakes and Crocodiles: power and symbolism in ancient Zimbabwe*. Johannesburg, Witwatersrand University Press.

Huffman, T. N. 2007. *Handbook to the Iron Age: the archaeology of pre-colonial farming societies in Southern Africa*. Scottsville, University of KwaZulu-Natal Press.

Johnson, M. 1999. *Archaeological Theory: an introduction*. Oxford, Blackwell.

Keatley, P. 1963. *The Politics of Partnership: The Federation of Rhodesia and Nyasaland*. Harmondsworth, Penguin Books

Kuklick, H. 1991. Contested Monuments: The Politics of Archaeology in Southern Africa. In G. W. Stocking (ed), *Colonial Situations: Essays on the Contextualization of Ethnographic Knowledge*, 135-169. Madison, University of Wisconsin Press.

Mahachi, G. and Ndoro, W. 1997. The socio-political context of southern African Iron Age studies with special reference to Great Zimbabwe. In G. Pwiti (ed), *Caves, Monuments and Texts: Zimbabwean archaeology today*, 69-88. Uppsala, Societas Archaeologica Uppsalensis. (Studies in African Archaeology 14).

Mallows, W. 1984. *The Mystery of the Great Zimbabwe: A New Solution*. New York, W.W. Norton and Co.

Martin, D. and Johnson, P. 1981. *The Struggle for Zimbabwe. The Chimurenga War*. Johannesburg, Ravan Press.

Matenga, E. 1998. *The Soapstone Birds of Great Zimbabwe: Symbols of a Nation*. Harare, African Publishing Group.

Moorcroft, P. L. 1980. *A short thousand years. The end of Rhodesia's rebellion. (Revised Edition)*. Salisbury, Galaxie Press.

Mufuka, K. 1983. *Dzimbahwe: life and politics in the golden age 1100-1500AD. (2nd edition)*. Masvingo, Belmont Press.

Mullan, J. E. 1969. *The Arab Builders of Zimbabwe*. Salisbury, J.E. Mullan.

Ndoro, W. 2001. *Your Monument our Shrine. The Preservation of Great Zimbabwe*. Uppsala, Department of Archaeology and Ancient History, Uppsala University.

Ownby, C.A. 1981. The Indian Rope Trick. *The Journal of African History* 23, 415-416.

Parfitt, T. 2008. *The Lost Ark of the Covenant: The Remarkable Quest for the Legendary Ark*. London, Harper Collins.

Phillipson, D.W. 1986. Book Review: W. Mallows 1985 The mystery of the Great Zimbabwe–the key to a major archaeological enigma London, Robert Hale. *Antiquity* 60 (229), 154-155.

Pikirayi, I. 2001. *The Zimbabwe Culture. Origins and decline of southern Zambezian states*. Walnut Creek, Altamira Press

Pwiti, G. 1996. Let the ancestors rest in peace? New challenges for heritage management in Zimbabwe. *Conservation and Management of Archaeological Sites* 1, 151-160.

Pwiti, G. 1997. The origins and development of stone-building cultures of Zimbabwe. In W. J. Dewey (ed), *Legacies of Stone: past and present*, 77-95. Brussels, Royal Museum for Central Africa.

Randall-MacIver, D. 1906a. The Rhodesian ruins: their probable origin and significance. *The Geographical Journal* 27 (4), 325-336.

Randall-MacIver, D. 1906b. *Medieval Rhodesia*. London, Macmillan.

Ranger, T. O. 2004. Nationalist Historiography, Patriotic History and the History of the Nation: the Struggle over the Past in Zimbabwe. *Journal of Southern African Studies* 30 (2), 215-234.

Roberts, R. S. 1999. Book Review: Chigwedere, A. 1998. *The Roots of the Bantu*. Marondera: Mutapa Publishing House. *Zimbabwe Independent* 15 Jan. 1999.

Robertshaw, P. T. (ed) 1990. *A History of African Archaeology*. London, James Currey.

Robinson, K. R. 1961. Zimbabwe Pottery. *Occasional Papers of the National Museums of Southern Rhodesia* 3 (23A), 193-226.

Shepherd, N. 2002. The Politics of Archaeology in Africa. *Annual Review of Anthropology* 31, 189-209.

Sinamai, A. 1998. Heritage in Politics: Great Zimbabwe in the struggle for self determination, in E.M. Chiwome and Z. Gambahaya (eds), *Culture and Development: Perspectives from the South*, 93-98. Harare, Mond Books.

Summers, R. F. 1965. *Zimbabwe: A Rhodesian Mystery (2nd Edition)*. Johannesburg, Nelson.

Summers, R. F. 1971. *Ancient ruins and vanished civilisations of southern Africa*. Cape Town, Bulpin.

Swan 1896. Chapter V: On the orientation and measurements of Zimbabwe ruins. In J.T. Bent (ed.), *The Ruined Cities of Mashonaland: Being a Record of the Excavation and Exploration in 1891. (3rd edition)*, 141-178. London, Longmans, Green and Co.

Swanson, M. W. 2001. Colonizing the Past: Origin Myths of the Great Zimbabwe Ruins. In E. M. Yamauchi (ed), *Africa and Africans in Antiquity*, 291-320. East Lansing, Michigan State University Press.

Ushewokunze, H. 1982. Introduction. In P. S. Garlake (ed.), *Great Zimbabwe Described and Explained*, 4-5. Harare, Zimbabwe Publishing House.

Von Sicard, H. 1952. *Ngoma lungundu. Eine Afrikanische Bundeslade*. Studia Ethnographica Upsaliensa V. Uppsala, Almquist & Wiksells Boktrycker.

Wade, R. P. 2009. *A Systematics for Interpreting Past Structures With Possible Cosmic References in Southern Africa*. Unpublished Master's Thesis, University of Pretoria.

Wheeler, M. 1973. General Editor's Preface. In P. S. Garlake (ed.), *Great Zimbabwe*, 7-9. London, Thames and Hudson.

Willoughby, J. 1893. *A narrative of further excavations at Zimbabye (Mashonaland)*. London, George Philip and Son.

ACADEMIC CONSTRUCTS ABOUT THE PAST AND EARLY EDUCATION AS (DIS)ENTANGLED COMPONENTS OF IDENTITY FORMATION PROCESSES

Anna Zalewska

Abstract

This article seeks to demonstrate the role of school education in shaping attitudes towards the remote past. Within the broader context of archaeology's potential role in identity formation, the specific question is how and why some of the outcomes of archaeological research actively sustain a sense of belonging and national pride, while others do not. The case study analysed here is the representation of Biskupin in children's textbooks. This 'emblematic' site, which plays a crucial role in many aspects of Polish archaeology, not only offers huge potential for observing the long-term results of exercising 'factual gaps' in archaeological knowledge, but is also presented here as an intriguing issue appealing simultaneously to imagination, emotions, historical consciousness and cultural memory. In the case described here, the 'cultural production' of visions of the past was initially coherent to their creators and recipients. However, the newly emerged academic notions concerning the ethnogenesis of the Slavs, which were to some extent in contradiction with the 'nation building' myths, led to the disintegration of these visions. The phenomenon of multivocality among archaeological stakeholders does not seem unusual. Quite often, simultaneously to epistemological targets and achievements, some other goals, values and meanings can be recognized in the 'archeological realm'. They operate on several, sometimes conflicting, levels of social reality.

Key words: identity, primary school education, second-degree archaeology, social memory

Introduction

This paper is the result of consideration of the ideological uses of archaeology in school settings, and of the roles archaeologists play in validating or refuting some scientific 'legends' and historiographic myths.[1] The extent to which archaeologists can influence visions of the remote past outside academia is considered here at the level of the so-called 'basic' knowledge presented to the youngest pupils. The specific narrow perspective of the mandatory primary school, where the most vivid images of the past are passed down, was chosen because of its strong impact on the opinion of the general public.

As such, education received at this level has a significant influence on the historical/archaeological awareness of the entire society. Additionally, school history education stimulates and is efficiently complemented by parallel and permanent education. Mass media, such as television, radio, documentaries, mass-market publications as well as the more reputable press, incorporate the inclusion of historical material into their long-term plans, which supplements, enriches and broadens people's knowledge. Historically-oriented TV and radio programmes can only become an additional source of knowledge for the youngest, if they are legible by them. In the process of deepening knowledge about the past at the pupils' level, textbooks are essential. Recently, in addition to books, some 'performative communication' (presentations of 'living archaeology', expressions of 'first person history' experiences) has started to play an important role. The influence of factors such as family, mass media, literature, art, church, civil and political organizations, cannot be neglected. However, it is still the school that provides young people with the knowledge and skills 'necessary to properly function in a society and to understand the historical background of the nation and the state'[2] (Składanowski 2004, 7). In theory, engaging with different media in 'teaching' archaeology should confirm the assumption presented by a prominent Polish sociologist that 'the past is the subject of remittance' (Szpociński 2006, 7-63). However, in local practices, the opportunities for presenting archaeological content are not overwhelming.

The case study presented is the representation of Biskupin, an archaeological site in the district of Żnin in the north-east part of the Wielkopolska (Great Poland) Lowland. That site has been elevated to 'the distinctive rank of the symbol' of archaeological inquiries into the most remote past of our land (Dąbrowski 1964, 74). It was chosen as a case study because it has also been given a prominent place in many school textbooks for over 70 years.

Over the decades, Biskupin continued as a symbol and one of the most important references of Slav identity for the Poles, and as such it was extensively presented to the general public (cf abundant bibliography for popularisation, radio broadcasting and fiction in the period 1933-1983 in Piotrowska 2008, 427-428, 381). The unique and complex role of the Biskupin phenomenon in common public awareness seemed to be timeless, despite the fact that for decades Biskupin was

---

[1] A myth, according to its anthropological definition, is seen here as 'immobilized knowledge' and therefore immune to criticism. As in the following case study, such myths can be seen as the sources which reflect the intellectual and social formation not only of the people who constructed them (Kommers 1991, 109) but also of those who maintain their 'mythic' substance. 'Historical myths' are seen here as the 'immanent part' of social life (Maternicki 1990, 66).

[2] All quotes from non English sources are translated by the author. Also, some other sources, further details and examples for the problems examined in that article can be found in Zalewska 2009 (2011), 119-154.

also the 'object of heated discussions and contention, not infrequently, more political than scholarly' (Brzeziński 2008, 11). Terms connected to Biskupin, such as 'proto-Slavonic' and 'proto-Polish', were, from the 1930s to the 1970s, constantly applied by both researchers and teachers. Some archaeologists still feel the 'ethnic burden' of Biskupin is worth being examined. But it cannot be denied that the interpretative situation has changed radically since the 1980s. According to certain researchers, 'the archaeologically evidenced Slavonic culture from the period when it entered history and begun its great expansion to as far as the Elbe and the Balkan Peninsula' should not be associated with periods earlier than the 6th century A.D. (Kaczanowski and Kozłowski 1998, 350). The Biskupin stronghold – dated to the Bronze Age – cannot be seen as Slavonic in the light of the assumptions of allochthonists, correctly naming themselves as a 'majority' among archaeologists. The Polish polemic on the origin of the Slavs continues (Barford 2003; Makiewicz 2005; Tabaczyński 1998, 2005).

The struggle over and the reflection on ethnicity in the Biskupin case can be explained as the element of the social needs driven by 'national interests' and by the requirement for a mythology of common origins (Anderson 1997, 141-143) or as the situational output of the political, e.g. over the lines of national borders (Kobyliński and Rutkowska 2005). Despite the complexity of the interpretative changes over the Biskupin site, one might risk a claim that the foundation of the knowledge about it is still purposefully and consistently formed as a hybrid construct serving the purposes of national 'identity'[3] and, as such, is derived both from popular science publications and the long-lasting processes of education. The intentions of those formulating and advocating the opinion that Biskupin had 'no connection with the Slavs' at the stage of the Lusatian settlement and those who present arguments stressing 'ethnic continuity' since the Neolithic period, or at least since the Bronze Age, in the area around Biskupin may be assumed to be equally sincere. As such, they can be seen as being equivalent from an epistemological perspective. Such questions, however,

raise problems of when and how the contradictory opinions about the representations of the remote past can be presented as a matter of discourse and in a form understandable to the youngest pupils. Should not a calm and measured debate also influence the youngest *via* the differentiated content of the chapters of their textbooks devoted to the remote past? Can the lack of stimulation of critical thinking lead to far-reaching, negative effects in shaping their historical awareness? Can early school education be perceived simultaneously as the cause and as the result of sustaining 'historiographic myths' and, as such, as a sphere of interest of responsible archaeologists? And finally, can such dilemmas be seen by archaeologists as worth thinking about? Is archaeology wide enough to cover not only an academic order within its dominant discourse, but also the complex and often problematic palimpsests of thoughts and opinions build upon it? *Contra spem spero.*

I. School Books – Blame(Less) Remittance

In my opinion, the key to understanding how and why Biskupin is still active in the process of simultaneously building archaeological and historical awareness and establishing strong beliefs in the local origin of the Slavs is to be found in the contents of school textbooks. Of course they must be seen against the background of all existing books, articles and films which contain even a slight mention of the settlement (Piotrowska 2008, 32-33). The somewhat homogenous current representations of Biskupin can be also seen as the long-term result of specific historical circumstances in the 1930s.

The prominence of status benefited in part from certain conditions which enabled knowledge about the site to pass from archaeological obscurity to the general public. For example, shortly before Walenty Szwajcer's discovery of Biskupin (in 1933), the Polish Government (*Sejm*) passed the education act which regulated and unified the schooling system in the country. Primary school was divided into 3 organisational and curricular stages with a 7-year mandatory education period (Składanowski 2004, 15). The reform helped to potentially provide knowledge to everyone. More members of the general public started to read about the 'streets of the sunken settlement' and the 'history of distant millennia' which 'emerges from the peat bog of Lake Biskupin' (Kostrzewski 1934a, 5; Kostrzewski 1934b, 79; Kostrzewski 1934c, 2-3). Images from 'the darkness of the past' fascinated people, since they believed that research in Biskupin 're-creates the everyday life of our ancestors twenty-five centuries ago' (Kostrzewski 1935, 824). The image of 'old Polish culture' became integral, with Biskupin 'a proto-Slavic stronghold' from the Iron Age (700-400BC) (Kostrzewski 1937, 15).

Unfortunately, in 1939 the Polish educational system was liquidated and Polish history was suppressed by the occupants. It was not a Polish school, as Poles had no influence over it whatsoever (Albert, 1989, 318-319).

---

[3] The term 'identity' comes from the Latin root *idem* (the same) and evokes a principle of endurance and continuity, usually in essentialist terms. In archaeological discourse the ways in which 'national identity' was/is conceptualized and studied is analysed with reference to the political implications of nationalism and ethnicity. As in the presented case of the 'fossilised' representation of Biskupin (extensively described as shaped by complex socio-political circumstances, Piotrowska 2004; 2008), it is not surprising that archaeologists have adopted a 'primordialist' perspective rather than its alternative, namely the 'interactionist' perspective (involving a more external, contingent and interactive view of identity) (terms defined after Rowlands 2007, 62-65). However, if one describes the term 'identity' as a process by which the core of each individual is shaped, then difficulties with the 'situating of ego formation in the historical context of particular cultural history elements of inferiority and continuity' (Rowlands 2007, 61) would be crucial, especially for those archaeologists interested in recognizing and understanding elements of the contemporary world of cultural representations (Zalewska 2006; 2009 (2011)).

The German occupiers removed history from the curriculum. Simultaneously, in the regions occupied by the Red Army the Russian policy was introduced. The underground system of schools run by Poles was based on the pre-war curriculum and the preserved textbooks (Składanowski 2004, 15). After the Second World War, the limits of educational reforms were closely connected to the political ones, and a great effort was made to ensure that the messages passed on in schools were coherent with the country's condition at that time.

The demand for something that was 'ours and only ours' was strong not only before, but also after the Second World War. The problems of ethnicity began to be crucial in Poland as much as in other areas where communities were influenced by foreign rule. Interest in the remote past, rather than arising naturally from the traditional and logical connection between power, culture and language (Żelazny 2006, 236), was stimulated by the oppressive circumstances. There is no doubt as to the fact that the sore point, resulting in the more or less spontaneous need to 'defend' or expose ethnic issues, was caused by outside demands of changing the borders and scope of the given ethnos (Urbańczyk 2000; Leube 2004). This was the case when, in the 1930s-40s, both Poland and Germany attempted to again challenge the problem of inseparability between the Germanic and Slavonic *ethne* and the lands in question (Strzelczyk 2003, 19-24). One could risk a conclusion that the conflict resulting from a discussion of Biskupin's ethnic identity – intentionally entangled with the national identity - appeared to be a perfect catalyst for Poles' 'ethnic assumptions' created on a base of 'facts' visible and understandable for researchers during years of excavations (among others, Piotrowska 2004, 102-135). The 'second circuit' of information, such as the continuity of the Slavic ethnos within contemporary Polish borders since the Neolithic period, created conditions for an 'ethnic myth', fortified in order to strengthen national awareness and identity.

In 1946, *Tales from the history of our country for the 4th and 5th forms of primary school* referred to Biskupin as an ancient Slavic settlement and presented finds and reconstructed houses from the site (Hoszowska *et al.* 1946). Also in the book *How people lived ages ago,* the chapter entitled 'In the fortified village beside the lake' presented a tale about Lusatian Biskupin (Przeworska 1946, 105-108). Worth stressing is the active participation of archaeologists held in highest esteem in the shaping of the picture of the remote past passed to the youngest. For example school book *Tales from the history...* was reviewed immediately in 1946 by Józef Kostrzewski (1946) and by Witold Hensel (1946), who wrote some critical remarks concerning the description of the settlement in that book which was reprinted many times. Interestingly enough, *The earth tells a story. A textbook for teaching prehistory for class 3 of primary school* (Sarnowska *et al.* 1948, 73-78, 122) was also commented upon by the prominent archaeologist Roman Jakimowicz, in his polemic *Prehistory at school. On the*

margin of the textbook...' (1947, 127-136). This significant engagement of archaeologists in primary education – worthy of imitation yet invisible – can be seen as expressing the fact that 'archaeology has given us, Poles, the certainty that our land has belonged to us for thousands of years' (Jasienica 1952, 355). Not surprisingly, expression of such certainty was also present in the following period. This was reflected in increasingly popular references to the 'proto-Slavonic settlement from 2500 years ago' and the introduction of the 'Biskupin episode' into virtually every text book published before 1999 (*Program* 1990, 5-6). The scientific and vernacular appeal of primeval cultural phenomena for national awareness, social identity, the categories of stereotypes, perceptions of 'otherness' and other social myths is due to their multifaceted character. Therefore, the discussion surrounding a 'symbolic *universum* of Polishness' continues among researchers from various fields of the humanities (historians, sociologists, psychologists, linguists, literature researchers, etc.), but it engages archaeologists in a very narrow sense. This passivity does not help to establish a dialogue with the pedagogical sphere responsible for preparing educational reforms and correcting textbooks.

As a result, even a selective analysis of textbooks accompanied by pedagogical 'instrumentalisation' illustrates that the state of knowledge connected with Biskupin underwent far-reaching fossilisation until the end of the 1990s. When examined through the prism of school textbooks and popular books, archaeology in Poland can be considered as traditionally engaged in identity-shaping processes (Tabaczyński 2004; Gediga 2004; Piotrowska 2004). As such, archaeological knowledge can be perceived as influenced by patriotic attitudes (understood here as 'the strongly emotional sense of connection with one's own ethnic or national group', after Kłoskowska 2005, 16). In the eyes of the Polish people, archaeology was strongly associated with patriotism (Milisauskas 1997-8, 225). This could be one of the reasons why during the postwar period the two overlapping issues of Slavic ethnogenesis and the origins of the Polish state were so crucial (Bursche and Taylor 1991, 585; Marciniak and Rączkowski 1991; Urbańczyk 2000). Until the mid-1960s, the link between archaeology and state objectives had been very strong (Kobyliński and Rutkowska 2005). The attempts to demonstrate past Slavic occupations in the territories acquired from Germany also strengthened the position of Biskupin (Godłowski 2000). However, the site's emblematic character should also be seen as the indirect long-term effect of national(istic) 'intellectual policy', which had continued in Great Poland since the end of the18[th] century (Kaczmarek 2004).

The 'production' of interpretations of past material culture (among others, 'Lusatian Culture') can be viewed as having 'the spontaneity of a kind of unconscious speech, a taken-for-granted, commonsense existence' that simply demonstrates that the ancestors of current people have always existed in that place (Anderson

1997; Rowlands 2007, 65). Archaeologists have contributed to the primordialist view of identity, even at the time (by the 1970s) when the Polish government no longer relied on archaeologists to justify western borders (Milisauskas 1997-1998, 226; Rączkowski 1996, 212-213).

During the communist period, new objectives for social sciences were presented. It was considered that the teaching of history 'should serve as a preparation of students to actively and intentionally participate in the political, social, economic and cultural life of the country and to creatively contribute to the welfare of socialist Poland' (*Program* 1990, 3). Archaeological knowledge also had a chance to facilitate the building of a 'new order' in Poland, one that would encourage a creative outlook and a sense of responsibility. However, it is pointed out that among archaeologists ideological pressure was negligible in comparison with that in other social sciences (Schild 1993).[4] The accomplishment of Polish archaeology ranked very highly within the former Soviet Bloc and 'the Marxist period benefited scholarship in new excavations and new interpretations (Milisauskas 1997-1998, 233).

There is also a lot of evidence suggesting that archaeological knowledge about Biskupin could have been updated regularly by history teachers during history courses. The didactic superstructure built around history books, popular science literature, tourist information materials and research papers on Biskupin available at the Pedagogic Resource, had a potential chance to enrich knowledge obtained but rarely updated on introductory courses on protohistory during the first year undergraduate course for Historians. For example, as early as the 1980s, it was stated in a text book for history students (future teachers) that 'using the archaeological-settlement method, Józef Kostrzewski, a distinguished representative of the autochthonic school, attempted to verify the existence of cultural continuity between the Lusatian culture and the early Medieval history of the Polish lands. Referring to written sources and linguistic evidence, he identified the Przeworsk and Oksywie cultures with the Slavs' (Chomentowska 1980, 153). However, 'researchers challenging this opinion point to the cultural discontinuity in the 3rd and 2nd centuries B.C., as well as in 4th and 5th centuries A.D.' (Chomentowska 1980, 153).

For at least the last 20 years, future teachers at some Polish universities have been confronted with the notion that 'the views advocated by Józef Kostrzewski are

oversimplified'. According to certain researchers, 'the archaeologically evidenced Slavonic culture from the period when it entered history and begun its great expansion to as far as the Elbe and the Balkan Peninsula should not be associated with periods earlier than the 6th century AD' (Kaczanowski and Kozłowski 1998, 350). An accessible review of the current discussion (with an allochthonistic standpoint explicitly stated by the authors) was included in Volume 1 of *Great History of Poland* (Kaczanowski and Kozłowski 1998, 343-352), which is commonly accepted as a standard university textbook for history students. By this recommendation, I do not advocate that we support the acceptance and spread of the allochthonist version of the 'Biskupin Legend' only, since I do not believe in the chance of spontaneously shifting from biased to neutral, from subjective to objective. Decampment from positioning shaped by the context to the non-contextual is delusion (Szachaj 2004, 183-4). Such delusion would involve nothing more than clearing the space after one (ethnic) myth for another, that of infallibility. I just encourage emphasizing the need to raise awareness that archaeologists are also agents created by current cultural convictions (cognitive and axiological), shaped right from the beginning *via* primary education. Despite being potentially active creators of the representations of the past, we (current archaeologists in Poland) are primarily products of an existing historic process of socialization and education which differs from the one experienced today by Polish children.

Following a number of reforms, the goals of education for the new millennium are now defined as follows: 'to learn about the world, to observe, understand and interpret the process taking place in it, to stimulate and strengthen the sense of cultural, historical, national and ethnic identity, as well as to shape conscious patriotic and civil attitudes, to stimulate the desire to responsibly participate in the social and public life of the country' (Marciniak *et al.* 1999, 125). In practice, the participants of educational processes in the 1990s, who were expected to make creative efforts and find individual meanings in equivocal culture, even had several textbooks from which to choose. Also, radical educational reforms and the free trade in publications produced an impressive selection of simultaneously printed yet differing textbooks. School teachers were left with only personal intuition in selecting the way in which Biskupin would be presented to pupils (as one episode among other more decisive elements of the book).

Interestingly, some of the educational material present in the 1990s was still helpful in constructing a multitude of myths: 'the settlement continuity' strengthens the Slavonic *cliché* attributed to the Lusatian people; 'egalitarianism' builds upon social equality in the Biskupin stronghold. Since that period, the omission of some arguments from the constantly actualized knowledge about Biskupin should be seen exclusively as an 'historiographic myth' created by autochthonists and

---

[4] The Communist Party card 'was helpful, but never essential in the career, at least to the level of professorship' (Schild 1993, 146). However, describing the extent to which archaeologists were (not) under significant pressure to conform to Marxist ideological pressure (or/and under the influence of Marxist materialism) is problematic. The whole period of archaeological thought 'between captivity and freedom', within the borders of our country, is estimated in many - often contradictory - ways and requires further reflection. For detailed information cf. Barford 2002; Lech 1997-1998.

left for public consideration rather than as indispensable and understandable in the context of current social and political conditions. In the late 1990s children could read: 'the settlement in Biskupin was erected around 2600 years ago, its inhabitants most certainly spoke a language different from ours. The population was approximately one thousand people. They cultivated land, reared animals, knew how to process bronze' (Małkowski 1998, 24-25). This message differs significantly from that still found circulating in school history courses, which states that '2500 years ago, ancestors of the Slavs arrived at the lake, whose descendants were later to become Poles. The peninsula was an island in those days…' (Centkowski and Syty 1991, 14). Such 'multivocality' (even if generously termed) is additionally problematic because of factual differences presented in textbooks. One can read: 'Archaeological research has provided us with a lot of information about the life of people in the territory of modern Poland nearly 3000 thousand years ago' (Julkowska *et al*. 1999, 80-81). The updated information (calibrated dating) is also used in *History and Social Sciences Coursebook for Grade 4. Family, Poland and Europe*. There, next to a photograph of a reconstructed palisade gate, we read: 'Around 2600 years ago, visitors entered Biskupin through this gate'; and next to a picture of houses and streets: 'The stronghold of Biskupin had 102 wooden houses located in several rows along streets…' (Baran and Bobiński 1999, 81-82). Interestingly, the text itself lacks any reference to Biskupin.

In the late 1990s, the inseparable pairing of Biskupin with the Slavs had not only been weakened, but we can even observe emerging breaks in the close association of Biskupin with archaeology, which had been unimaginable earlier. The eradication of the Biskupin ambiguity was taken one step further by the author of *History – grade 4. Let me tell you a story*, who neglected Biskupin altogether. The lack of reference to Biskupin, despite using a relatively large amount of archaeological content (Wołosik 1999, 61, 65-67), is as surprising as it is depressing, when one considers the multicultural and extraordinarily well-preserved specificity of that emblematic site. Can the absence of Biskupin in textbooks used today by some pupils be considered as the result of poorly examined factual gaps by professionals? Is this 'accident' the reason for posing the question concerning the role of an archaeology deprived of its identity-building features?

Society started to face the outcome of the interpretative change at the ground level. This observation leads to another, that the sense of common identity which began with reconstructing the 'factual' or even 'mythical' past of Biskupin after 60 years of circulation in the public sphere began to vary even at its base. The canon of 'advocated' values through which a nation sees its own past, present and future (often referred to as 'historical awareness'), which has until now been an indispensable element of the sense of common identity, is now

wavering or being differentiated. This was not observed as long as narratives of the remote past were enriched with a national ideology which underlined the need to protect independence in all its aspects and to care for the ethnicity of the regained territories. It can be claimed that the 'national awareness' created in those days at primary schools was treated with the highest form of 'ethnic awareness'. Nowadays, the trend has changed. When faced with often contradictory messages about Biskupin, children – soon to become teenagers and adults – will have no difficulty in realising the complexity of the problem of the poly-representations of the past.

Summing up, in the light of the latest publications on the ethnogenesis of the Slavs, all of the conclusions reached in the exhaustive research process appear to be a subjective category, whose objectivity is no longer guaranteed by the state or by the hierarchy of academia. Archaeology, like history, 'abandoned its claim to bearing coherent meaning and consequently lost its pedagogical authority to transmit values. The definition of the nation was no longer the issue, and peace, prosperity, and the reduction of its power have since accomplished the rest' (Nora 1989, 11). Archaeologists are situated now in a social 'jungle', with recipients not always focused on what we are communicating with our polysemous achievements. Is this inseparability frightening enough to mobilize a greater research effort, allowing us to better understand the dependence between the centre (strictly archaeological activities) and the outer rim (the functioning of the outputs of the former in society)? Let us hope.

II. Archaeologists: Identity (Co)Creators Or Self-Focused Creators?

The fact that archaeologists investigate the remote past under the pressure of social (and individual) interests, of intellectual trends and of current political and market circumstances is quite obvious. But the extent to which they are susceptible to each factor and the roles which the separate factors play in activating the outputs of archaeological activities are not clear. Also challenging are the roles of material vestiges from the past and casual force of materiality in conditioning our present. Yet, archaeology does have at its disposal certain means (tools, methods, interpretative strategies) allowing it to penetrate the specificity of materiality (including *memory of materiality*) and the vicissitudes and the status of said material remains in the social *imaginarium*. The idea of applying archaeology to the instances of secondary exploitation of material traces of the past, and to archaeological knowledge as such follows the concept of *second degree history* proposed by Pierre Nora (2002). Therefore, the terminological isolation of *second degree archaeology* from *second degree history* does not stipulate that archaeology is disconnected from the framework of human memory. On the contrary, it is inherently dependent on the latter, as a discipline shaped within the confines of specific social contexts, and as a result of actions by individuals subject to acculturation processes driven by the development paths of the societies in which they function. However, archaeology can possibly also (re)present something that should not or could not be normally noticed. The unique durability and agency of material traces of the past (and/or stimulated by the past) provoke interest in emphasising *how* material remains mean and what thoughts they stimulate(d). All such dilemmas and practices may provoke and support investigation within *second degree archaeology*. They can, among others, affirm the plurality of meanings obtained by remains being re-read, translated and negotiated by new people in new contexts. What can be conceived as the crucial role of archaeology is an understanding, with its own grammar, of the trajectory of the past into the present and that would be placed as (alluring as much as challenging) an agenda for further study in *second degree archaeology* (for further information about the theoretical aspects of the proposed archaeology of second degree cf. Zalewska 2009 (2011), 119-122). Such a perspective follows some of the rules and prompts of '*histoire au second degré*' (proposed by Nora 2002). It also denotes a departure from the static positivistic attitude to the past towards the active and symbolic past, serving to boost various fragments of collective imagination (Kończal 2009, 211).

Biskupin, seen from the perspective of second degree archaeology, does not need to struggle with 'unexplained mysteries' and 'unverified hypotheses' to maintain its powerful status within contemporary society. The question is whether conscientious archaeologists can trust the second degree archaeologists' suggestion? The answer depends on the priorities chosen by the archaeologists whose opinions (in that case) are decisive (!) but only to some extent. That is why, despite the fact that since the 1930s 'the research carried out at Biskupin opened a whole new chapter in Polish archaeology', its status is ambiguous. When 'the 'Biskupin fever' had subsided and Biskupin was no longer a barometer of sorts to measure the national state of mind' (Brzeziński 2008, 12), it started to be an indicator of a different type. As such, Biskupin can be seen not only as the 'totemic pride' of Polish archaeology (Kurnatowska and Kurnatowski 2005, 13-27) but also as its 'shameful defeat'. While the first is obvious, in order to clarify the latter, the following parameters need to be taken into consideration:

> 1) unquestionably the most important site in the history of Polish archaeology has not been given yet a comprehensive analysis based on materials recovered during the long excavations (Balcer 2005, 103-104; Brzeziński 2008, 12);
> 2) Biskupin is seen by a critical group of archaeologists (mainly allochthonists) as a 'symbol' of 'anachronism' which 'lacks critical source-based thinking' (Parczewski 2000, 10);
> 3) Biskupin allows an indirect insight into the complex problem of 'consuming' the past. Some, especially elder, archaeologists see the involvement of the Archaeological Museum's employees, i.e. the people directly responsible

for protecting the site in various educational-cum-entertainment-cum-economic activities, as an attempt to evade the more serious tasks of interpretation.

As such, Biskupin is a clear-cut case of conflicting interests between what was found, what was stipulated and what is expected. It is hard to resist the impression that the situation at that archaeological site is no longer dominantly fuelled by an intellectual game of interpretations, but rather by a free market struggle to maintain the unique status that the site once enjoyed. Although this issue is not really an element for consideration here, it is certainly interesting to observe that scientific constructs concerning this particular defensive settlement may in fact be treated as an emanation of the purposefulness and intentionality of contemporary needs and opportunities. This observation allows one to suggest that the picture of Biskupin functioning as the 'Slavonic cradle' is shaped out of the archaeologists' indecisiveness on how the site is going to sustain a sense of belonging in the future. The question 'if' it is going to sustain such a sense seems here inadequate, since that place can (and, in my personal opinion, should) be treated as a 'site of remembrance'. For the purposes of disambiguation, it should immediately be clarified that this is in no way synonymous with any element of the so called 'forefathers' legacy adhering to it. Neither does it imply any sense of biological or ethnic connection. 'Remembrance' may simply refer to the presence of this legacy as one of the elements co-constituting the context which underlies the meaning of various products, occurrences, educational messages and forms of entertainment associated with the site in contemporary culture. It is assumed that the constituting basis for the establishment of a site of remembrance is provided by a certain sense of 'intergenerational connection' (Szpociński 2008, 15-16).

Summing up, the practice of neglecting the interpretative controversies (not only in school textbooks, as I tried to describe above, but also on the official website of the Biskupin Museum and in many scientific and popular publications) may additionally be interpreted as a specific remedy to the excessive 'noise' surrounding the emotional and long-lasting (Wiwjorra 2008, 85-89) discussions over ethnogenesis and 'autochthonists and allochthonists' relations (Godłowski 2000), as well as a result of apprehensive, pragmatic calculation. Thus, the standstill in academic archaeology has made its way into the general archaeological awareness of the nation. At the same time, there seems to be some convincing rationale behind the commonsense supposition that this failure to update the representations of Biskupin is due to the institutional or personal communicational deficiency observed between universities and the bodies responsible, among others, for writing actual textbooks (as I pointed out earlier). Symptomatic of the same is the change observed in the subject matter of texts commenting on the relationship between archaeology and teaching.

Consequently, observing the 'Biskupin Legend' through the medium of schoolbooks directs the attention to the transformation from the 'strict codification of concepts' relating to the site, towards a situation where the only remaining codified interpretative principle is the classification of the site as a 'trace of the past' (term after Szpociński 2008, 12-14). This allows us to perceive not only Biskupin but also other archaeological sites presented in schoolbooks (Simandiraki 2004) as the 'contested domains' within which different 'fields of cultural politics' are strongly entangled with archaeological discourses. 'Pedagogy', understood here after Y. Hamilakis (2004) as a public sphere where knowledge, views and perceptions on the past and the present are debated, valorized, reproduced and legitimized, is situated as one such 'field'.

III. Anxiety, Complexity And 'Edutainment' – The Allies Of The 'Biskupin Legend'

By exploring the circumstances and ways in which some elements of Biskupin's (hi)story became the 'fuel' for historiographic myths, it is easier to understand its very different contemporary representations which are transferred to the general public *via* primary education. The 'ethnic activation' around the issue of Slavdom, and therefore also the 'proto-Polish' origin of Biskupin, has gone through a number of phases. It began with anti-German sentiment (Wiwjorra 2008, 85-89) and progressed through ethnicity and continuity, also underscored by archaeological discoveries, to a sense of self-creation which is now being gradually suppressed as national identity and slowly replaced by a European identity. This, in turn, stimulated a reactivation of sentiments towards what was 'ours and belonging to us only', what is individual and uncontaminated by modernity (Frasunkiwicz 2006, 253-264).

It may be suggested that the initial increase and more recent decrease of interest in prescribing 'ethnogenetic values' to Biskupin were characterized for the political elite, the archaeologists and the public mainly by anxiety. The initial fear about the stability of Poland's borders (after the First and before and after the Second World War) was replaced by the threat of melting into the 'global village' of the EU. Within both the upper level of school books and the personal observation of local educational practices, continuous verification of scholarly views of the past (especially those connected with the ethnic issues) emerges as dangerous. The latter assumption can explain the continuing application of concepts dating back to the 1970s in contemporary schooling. The case of Biskupin shows that some ethnic aspects of the historical curriculum were for a long time emphasised as an 'integral part of the patriotic education of young people' and 'the stimulation and development of patriotic attitudes and feelings' (Historia 1975, 31). In the case of the problem analysed here, cultural

phenomena, such as social stratification, religion or race (typical 'ethnic activations' in many other countries cf. Żelazny 2006, 238), were not widespread.

If we assume that a myth is 'any tale, representation or idea with its accompanying images, widely popularised, passed down from generation to generation, which provides a given (social) group with both cultural unanimity and moral coherence', as defined by Charles O. Carbonell (after Grabski 1996, 32) – then dozens of textbooks, studies, tourist guides, novels etc. can be also seen as a specific collection of beliefs stimulated, among others, by archaeologists. Here also the issue of a nostalgic attitude towards the space 'directly connected' with ancestors which is worth paying to be experienced can be pointed out. Openness for the unique *simulacrum* (here applied to the remote past) from the global perspective can be explained as the element of the 'industrial production of differences', understood here after Baudrillard (2006, 104-114; Zalewska 2006, 207-208) as the process which, on the one hand allows the consumer to feel integrated within society, while on the other, helps him/her to establish the functional difference between 'consumption' of 'national' and 'global' products.

This leads to the conclusion that limiting interpretations of Biskupin to just the problem of ethnic issues would be the worst we can do to that unique site. Its richness and uniqueness can flourish now. With the exception of a few individuals, archaeologists now commonly agree that, since (as in the case of other archaeological cultures) the ethnicity of the 'Lusatian culture' cannot be conclusively established, more attention should be directed to presenting the general public with a new vision of Biskupin. So far, the general public is relatively unaware of even the radical changes in the way in which the site has begun to be interpreted within academia (Tabaczyński 2004). The information the public receive is still strengthened by books written in the past, some of which are now still being reprinted and is the result of the passivity of archaeologists who are, in general, not spontaneously interested in correcting at least some of the school textbooks. The phenomenon facilitated by the extraordinary social and political circumstances of the 1930s, in which the excavation was initiated (Kurnatowska and Kurnatowski 2005), can easily be understood and justified. The perception of the interrelated network of cognitive and didactic phenomena encourages a more in depth and systemic analysis of the factors which were responsible for the generations' long cognitive inertia around the interpretation of the ethnic issue in Biskupin (cf. Urbańczyk 2006, 151-153; Barford 2003), and the lack of updated information in early schooling.

Luckily, nowadays some interesting and constructive activities can be observed around Lake Biskupin. One of the many initiatives is the undertaking of challenging topics for discussions during scientific conferences, publishing proceedings and, last but not least, organizing what might be called 'transcultural' archaeological festivals and experimental archaeology workshops. Archaeologists connected to the Biskupin Museum present a wide-ranging and vivid picture of the remote past of the area - from the era of hunters, gatherers and fishermen to the medieval period. Recently a group of professionals and volunteers successfully led by the extremely engaged Biskupin museum's headmaster Wiesław Zajączkowski and supported by Warsaw University, have acted as agent provocateurs in reenergizing that extraordinary space around Lake Biskupin. One of the greatest archaeological, popular-scientific festivals in Europe takes place in Biskupin annually in early September (see http://biskupin.pl). Because of these events Biskupin is still the best and most popular Open Air Museum in Poland. The current proposal of 'edutainment' has a chance to influence and enrich the representation of the past among visitors, also to constructively stimulate among non-professionals the 'interpretative imperative' (more about it Zalewska 2011, 130-132) and, finally, to strengthen the relationship between modern man/woman and material traces of the past.

The archaeological site of Biskupin is therefore seen (in the eyes of today's children) as more attention-worthy than the nearby Jurassic Park. As a result, it is increasingly becoming considered by today's children more as an interesting destination for a weekend trip rather than a Polish Zion or the *Urheimet of the Poles*. This shows that in today's Poland too, the free market policy has pivotal meaning as the 'provider of identity'. People today, justifying this as determined by their roots, regard a feeling of connectedness with national traditions as central to their identity (Mathews 2005, 25-26): 'In the supermarket of culture we may select the traditions within which our ancestors lived, but from the point of view of our experiences, they will not be the actual roots but a selection' (Mathews 2005, 152).

Treating Biskupin as a complex, unique social construction shaped by contemporary reality provides an opportunity for departing from the radically idiographic, analytic and erudite description of archaeological knowledge and moving towards the observation of what and why has been selected from that knowledge to be 'incorporated' into the world of cultural representations.

Such perspective is not preoccupied with placing artefacts in the development of archaeological explanation, and thus would not contribute to the cognitive status of archaeology directly. In general terms, it rather helps to recognise the social status of archaeology as a discipline, the pressures and consequences of the particular approach of practicing it (theoretical aspects of proposed second degree archaeology, see Zalewska 2009 (2011), 121-122). What is most important is that such reflection has a chance to contribute to the appreciation and protection of material traces from the past.

Conclusions

It seems that the attachment of the Poles to 'fossilised' ideas (myths) may be seen as influenced by the education received in their early schooling, which is deprived of critical thinking about representations. The Biskupin case was presented here as a point for developing in children's minds the sense of belonging (or more conventionally of 'identity'/ 'nationality'). Not only the manner but also the constant care for preserving debatable 'fragments of our prehistory' confirmed the radical opinion that 'there has never been a historical study completely free of myths; the only variable is the extent of their presence, their prevalence and the place they occupy in the structure of historical knowledge' (Grabski 1996, 29). It is very clear at the level of history textbooks that the constantly changing information pool about the past has a very slight influence on the 'archaeological awareness' of the general public. Fortunately, the framework for the present condition of Biskupin and its reception among recipients is shaped by those who underscore, so far mainly *in situ*, the uniqueness of that archaeological site without recalling the post-war demand for an ethnic myth required for the process of reviving the (too) often wounded Polish national identity.

Biskupin shows that the initially uniform vision of the past (preferred by those who created it and by its recipients), was finally dissolved not only by newly-emerging scientific notions concerning 'ethnic issues' (the ethnogenesis of the Slavs), but also by the drastic changes in the ways in which archaeology was examined and practiced by different stakeholders.

It is fascinating to observe the ways by which the results of archaeological investigations circulate within societies. By exploring the circumstances in which some elements of Biskupin's (hi)story gave rise to Poles' 'ethnic myth' while others were used to stimulate creative thinking ('interactionist' rather than 'primordialist' view of identity), curiosity and fun ('edutainment') – it is possible to better understand the contemporary changes in archaeological representations. Even if largely underappreciated from inside academia, that system of 'circulation' can be seen as being pivotal in positioning outcomes of archaeological studies. That is because, in many cases, it was those who performed secondary interpretations, who moderated the so-called archaeological awareness that decided what has a 'better' chance of becoming an indispensable element of the historical awareness of individuals.

Acknowledgements

I am grateful to the editors for their patience and constructive suggestions, to Geoff Carver, for linguistic help, to Dorota Cyngot for her advice (smartness) and time (good-heartedness) and to the anonymous reviewers for their constructive comments and advice on an earlier version of this paper.

Bibliography

Albert, A. 1989. *Najnowsza historia Polski, 1918*-1980. London, Polonia Book Found.

Anderson, B. 1997, *Wspólnoty wyobrażone: Rozważania o źródłach i rozprzestrzenianiu się nacjonalizmu* (*Imagined Communities. Reflections on the Origin and Spread of Nationalism*). Kraków, Znak.

Balcer, B. 2005. Badacze Biskupina po II wojnie światowej – do lat 60, in A. Grossman and W. Piotrowski (eds), *Badacze Biskupina*, 101-124. Biskupin, Wyd. ZET.

Baran, B. and Bobiński, W. 1999. *W rodzinie w Polsce w Europie. Podręcznik do historii i społeczeństwa dla klasy IV*. Warszawa, PWN.

Barford, P. 2002. Reflections on Lech's vision of the history of 'Polish' archaeology. *Archaeologia Polona* 40, 171-184.

Barford, P. 2003. Crisis in the Shadows: Recent Polish Polemic on the Origin of the Slavs. *Slavia Antiqua* XLIV, 121-155.

Baudrillard, J. 2006. *Społeczeństwo konsumpcyjne. Jego mity i struktury*. Warszawa, Sic!

Biskupin
http://biskupin.pl, accessed on 29 February 2012.

Brzeziński, W. 2008. Biskupin - a Living Legend. In D. Piotrowska, *Prolegomena do archeologii Biskupina, tom I: Bibliografia archeologiczna Biskupina 1933-1983*, 9-12. Warszawa, PMA.

Bursche, A. and Taylor T. 1991. A panorama of Polish archaeology. *Antiquity* 65, 583-592.

Centkowski, J. and Syty, A. 1991. *Historia-klasa czwarta szkoły podstawowej. 'Z naszych dziejów'*. Warszawa, Wydawnictwo Szkolne i Pedagogiczne.

Chomentowska, B. 1980. *Najdawniejsza historia ziem polskich*. Warszawa, Wydawnictwo Uniwersytetu Warszawskiego.

Dąbrowski, K. 1964. *Przymierze z archeologią*. Warszawa, Ludowa Spółdzielnia Wydawnicza.

Frasunkiwicz, D. 2006. Sentimental Identity, in M. Bieńkowska-Ptasznik, K. Krzysztofek and A. Sadowski (eds), *Obywatelstwo i tożsamość w społeczeństwach zróżnicowanych kulturowo i na pograniczach*, 253-264. Białystok, Wydawnictwo Uniwersytetu w Białymstoku.

Gediga, B. 2004. Poznanie naukowe a społeczne oczekiwania, in B. Gediga and W. Piotrowski (eds),

Archaeologia. Kultura. Ideologie, 213-221. Biskupin - Wrocław, Elma.

Godłowski, K. (1972) 2000. W sprawie 'nihilizmu etnicznego' w archeologii. In M. Parczewski (ed), *Pierwotne siedziby Słowian. Wybór pism*, 50-57. Kraków, Wydawnictwo Instytut Archeologii Uniwersytetu Jagiellońskiego.

Grabski, A.F. 1996. Historiografia - mitotwórstwo – mitoburstwo. In A. Barszczewska-Krupa (ed), *Historia, mity, interpretacje*, 29-62. Łódź, Wydawnictwo Uniwersytetu Łódzkiego.

Hamilakis Y. 2004. Archaeology and the politics of pedagogy. *World Archaeology* 36(2), 287- 309.

Hensel, W. 1946. Recenzja. *Przegląd Wielkopolski* 2(6), 186-187.

Historia. Wstępna wersja programu 10 letniej szkoły średniej 1975. Warszawa, WSiP.

Hoszowska, W., Szczechura, T., and Tropaczyńska-Ogarkowa W. 1946. *Było to dawno... Opowiadania z dziejów ojczystych dla kl. IV i V szkoły podstawowej*. Warszawa, Instytut Wydawniczy 'Nasza Księgarnia'.

Jakimowicz, R. 1947. Prehistoria w szkole. Na marginesie podręcznika 'Ziemia opowiada'. *Z otchłani wieków* 16, 127-136.

Jasienica, P. 1952. *Świt Słowiańskiego jutra*. Poznań, Państwowy Instytut Wydawniczy.

Julkowska, V., Konieczka – Śliwińska, D., and Skórzyńska I. 1999. *Historia i społeczeństwo. Podręcznik dla klasy IV szkoły podstawowej adaptacja dydaktyczna*. Poznań, Graf Punkt.

Kaczanowski, P. and Kozłowski, J.K. 1998. *Najdawniejsze dzieje Ziem Polskich (do VII w). Wielka Historia Polski. Vol I*. Warszawa, Fogra.

Kaczmarek, J. 2004. Archaeology in the dispute over the national character of Great Poland (Wielkopolska) region in the 19th and 20th century. *Archaeologia Polona* 42, 129-154.

Kłoskowska A., 2005. *Kultury narodowe u korzeni*, Warszawa, PWN.

Kobyliński, Z. and Rutkowska, G. 2005. Propagandist use of history and archaeology in justification of Polish rights to the 'Recovered Territories' after World War II. *Archaeologia Polona* 43, 51-124.

Kommers, J. 1991. Between Structure and Context: Sources, Source Criticism, and Alterity Studies, in R. Corbey and J. Leerssen (eds), *Alterity, Idenity, Image.*

Selves and Others in Society and Scholarschip, 105-121. Amsterdam, Atlanta.

Kończal, K. 2009. Bliskie spotkania z historią drugiego stopnia. In A. Szpociński (ed), *Pamięć zbiorowa jako czynnik integracji i źródło konfliktów*, 207-226. Warszawa, Scholar.

Kostrzewski, J. 1934a. Na ulicach zatopionego osiedla Ostatnie wiadomości z ekspedycji wykopaliskowej na półwyspie jeziora Biskupińskiego pod Gąsawą. *Ilustracja Polska* 7(32) (12.VIII), 5-6.

Kostrzewski, J. 1934b. Zatopiona wieś przedhistoryczna Biskupinie. *Z otchłani wieków* 9(6), 79-90.

Kostrzewski, J. 1934c. Patrzymy w przeszłość Wielkopolski. Z torfowisk jeziora Biskupińskiego pod Gąsawą wyłaniają się dzieje zamierzchłych tysiącleci-Uniwersytet Poznański bada osadę nadwodną z przed 2500 lat. *Ilustracja Polska* 7 (27) (8.VII), 2-3.

Kostrzewski, J. 1935. Obraz w mrokach przeszłości. Nowe badania w Biskupinie odtwarzają życie codzienne naszych przodków sprzed 25 wieków. *Ilustarcja Polska* 8(35) (1.IX), 824-825.

Kostrzewski, J. 1937. Kultura staropolska w świetle nowych odkryć. *Kurier Poznański* 32(404) (5.IX), 15.

Kostrzewski, J. 1946. Recenzja książki 'Życie ludzi w dawnych wiekach...'. *Przegląd Archeologiczny* 7, 117-120.

Kurnatowska, Z. and Kurnatowski, S. 2005. Archeologia polska w dobie podejmowania badań Biskupinie. Polish Archaeology in the period of Biskupin excavations before World War II, in A. Grossman and W. Piotrowski (eds), *Badacze Biskupina*, 13-27. Biskupin, Wydawnictwo ZET.

Lech J. 1997-1998. Between captivity and freedom: Polish archaeology in the 20th century. *Archaeologia Polona* 35-36, 25-222.

Leube, A. 2004. Zur Germanen- Ideologie in der NS-Zeit, in B. Gediga and W. Piotrowski (eds), *Archeologia. Kultura. Ideologie*, 83-90. Biskupin – Wrocław, Elma.

Makiewicz, T. 2005. W sprawie aktualnego stanu badań nad problemem kontynuacji kulturowej pomiędzy starożytnością a wczesnym średniowieczem w Polsce. Punkt widzenia autochtonisty. *Slavia Antiqua* XLVI, 9-31.

Małkowski, T. 1998. *Historia dla klasy IV Szkoły podstawowej. Dzieje Cywilizacji*. Gdańsk, Gdańskie Wydawnictwo Oświatowe.

Marciniak, A. and Rączkowski W. 1991. The Development of Archaeological Theory in Poland under Conditions of Isolation. *World Archaeological Bulletin* 5, 57-65.

Marciniak, E., Hensler, M., and Syty, A. 1999. *Historia i społeczeństwo dla klasy 4*. Warszawa, WSiP.

Maternicki, J. 1990. Mity historyczne, ich geneza, struktura i funkcje społeczne. In M. Maternicki (ed), Metodologiczne problemy badań nad dziejami myśli historyczne, 66-80.Warszawa, Wydawnictwo UW.

Mathews, G. 2005. *Supermarket kultury. Kultura globalna a tożsamość jednostki*. Warszawa, PIW.

Milisauskas, S. 1997-98. Observations on Polish archaeology 1945-1995. *Archaeologia Polona* 35-36, 223-236.

Nora P. 1989. Between Memory and History: Les Lieux de Mémoire. *Representations* 26. Special Issue: Memory and Counter-Memory (Spring), 7-24.

Nora P. 2002. Pour une histoire au second degré. *Le débat* 122. Mémoires du XXe siècle, 24-31.

Parczewski, M. 2000. Kazimierz Godłowski jako badacz początków Słowiańszczyzny (uwagi redaktora tomu). In K. Godłowski (ed.), *Pierwotne siedziby Słowian. Wybór pism*, 7-14. Kraków, Wydawnictwo Instytut Archeologii Uniwersytetu Jagiellońskiego.

Piotrowska, D. 2004. Biskupin-ideologie-kultura, in B. Gediga and W. Piotrowski (eds), *Archeologia. Kultura. Ideologie*, 91-155. Biskupin – Wrocław, Elma.

Piotrowska, D. 2008. *Prolegomena do archeologii Biskupina, tom I: Bibliografia archeologiczna Biskupina 1933-1983*. Warszawa, PMA.

Program *szkoły podstawowej. Historia. Klasy IV- VIII.* 1990. Warszawa, Wydawnictwo MEN.

Przeworska, J. 1946. *Życie ludzi w dawnych wiekach. Z 68 rysunkami Janiny Rosen*. Warszawa, Państwowy Zakład Wydawnictw Szkolnych.

Rączkowski, W. 1996. 'Drang nach Westen'?: Polish Archaeology and National Identity, in M. Diaz-Andreu and T. Champion (eds), *Nationalism and Archaeology in Europe*, 189-217. London, UCL Press.

Rowlands, M. 2007. Configuring identities in archaeology. In T. Insoll (ed), *The Archaeology of Identities: A Reader*, 1-18. New York, Routledge.

Sarnowska, W., Tropaczyńska-Ogarkowa, W., and Podolak, W. 1948. *Ziemia opowiada. Podręcznik do nauki prehistorii dla klasy III szkoły podstawowej*. Wydanie Drugie, Warszawa, Nasza Księgarnia.

Schild, R. 1993. Polish archaeology in transition. *Antiquity* 67, 146-150.

Simandiraki A. 2004, Minopaidies: the Minoan Civilisation in Greek Primary Education. *World Archaeology* 36(2), 177-88.

Składanowski, H. 2004. *Stosunki polsko - sowieckie w programach nauczania i podręcznikach historii w szkole powszechnej (podstawowej) w Polsce w latach 1932-1956.* Toruń, Wydawnictwo Adam Marszałek.

Strzelczyk, J. 2003. Początki Polski i Niemiec, in A. Lawaty and H. Orłowski (eds), *Polacy i Niemcy. Historia- kultura-polityka*, 13-24. Poznań, Wydawnictwo Poznańskie.

Szachaj, A. 2004. *Zniewalająca moc kultury. Artykuły i szkice z filozofii kultury, poznania i polityki.* Toruń, Wydawnictwo Uniwersytetu im. M. Kopernika w Toruniu.

Szpociński, A. 2006. Formy przeszłości a komunikacja społeczna, in A. Szpociński and P. Kwiatkowski (eds), *Przeszłość jako przedmiot przekazu*, 7- 65. Warszawa, Scholar.

Szpociński, A. 2008. Miejsca pamięci (lieux de mémoire). *Teksty drugie. Miejsca realne i wyobrażone* 4 (112), 11-20.

Tabaczyński, S. 1998. Procesy etnogenetyczne: doświadczenia badawcze, archeologia i przyszłość. In M. Miśkiewicz (ed). *Słowianie w Europie wcześniejszego średniowiecza. Katalog wystawy*, 79-99. Warszawa. PMA.

Tabaczyński, S. 2004. Archaeology: dealing with the Past in the Present, in B. Gediga and W. Piotrowski (eds), *Archaeologia. Kultura. Ideologie*, 9-31. Biskupin – Wrocław. Elma.

Tabaczyński, S. 2005. Procesy Etnogenetyczne jako problem badawczy archeologii, in P. Kaczanowski and M. Parczewski (eds), *Archeologia o początkach Słowian*, 37-50. Kraków, Księgarnia Akademicka.

Urbańczyk, P. 2000. Political Circumstances Reflected in Post War Polish Archaeology. *Public Archaeology* 1 (1), 49-56.

Urbańczyk, P. 2006. Polski węzeł słowiański. In P. Urbańczyk (ed). *Nie-Słowianie o początkach* Słowian, 133-153. Poznań-Warszawa, Mała Biblioteka PTPN.

Wiwjorra, I. 2008. 'Germanen' Und 'Slaven' Ostmitteleuropas als Autochthone oder Allochthone. Historiographische Konflikte als Vorlage für politische Konzpetionen, in H. Kircher, J. Suchoples, and H. H. Henning (eds), *Miejsca pamięci. Mity i stereotypy w Europie*, 85-101. Wrocław, ATUT.

Wołosik, A. 1999. *Historia. Szkoła podstawowa klasa 4. Opowiem Ci ciekawa historię.* Warszawa, Wydawnictwo Edukacyjne Zofii Dobkowskiej.

Zalewska, A. 2006. Knowledge as a socially active substance. Our interpretations versus Others' 'self-interpretations'. *Archaeologia Polona* 44, 203- 211.

Zalewska, A. 2009 (2011). Archaeology (of Second Degree) as the Element of the World of Cultural Representations. *Analecta Archaeologica Ressoviensia* 4, 119-154.

Zalewska, A. 2011. Archeologiczny palimpsest jako specyficzna forma interakcji teraźniejszości z... (Archaeological palimpsest as a specific form of the present interacting with...), in A. Marciniak, D. Minta-Tworzowska, and M. Pawleta (eds), *Współczesne Oblicza Przeszłości*, 115-132. Poznań, Wydawnictwo Poznańskie.

Żelazny, W. 2006. *Etniczność. Ład – Konflikt – Sprawiedliwość.* Poznań, Wydawnictwo Poznańskie.

ARCHAEOLOGY AS ALLEGORY:
THE REPRESENTATIONS OF ARCHAEOLOGY
IN CHILDREN'S LITERATURE IN BRAZIL

Marcia Bezerra

Abstract

In this chapter I examine the iconic repertoire of Archaeology in children's literature. I focus especially on the illustrations found in twenty-two books published in Brazil by Brazilian and non-Brazilian authors. The reflections presented here constitute a first step towards understanding children's perceptions of archaeologists, archaeology, populations and landscapes of the past. The first results indicate: 1) a resonance between those 'visual artefacts' and the images produced by children in various projects around the country; 2) the appropriation of iconic discourses of Archaeology as a means to maintain, reproduce and legitimize dominant ideologies.

Keywords: archaeology – representations – children's literature – images – Brazil

Introduction

The field of representations in archaeology has attracted an increasing number of researchers (Molyneaux 1997; Russel 2006). Some scholars, such as Moser (2001), Holtorf (2007a; 2007b) and Russel (1997) have devoted special attention to the modes of visual representation of the discipline and their contents in popular culture (Gero and Root 1996). Others discuss the Poetics of Archaeology, according to which it is necessary to investigate the forms and styles for representing knowledge produced by the discipline in constructing the past (Hodder 2001). However, there is a consensus as to the fact that the images generated by non-archaeologists to communicate the past have been neglected in these studies (Holtorf 2006; 2007a; 2007b; Molyneaux 1997; Moser 2001; Moser and Gamble 1997). Among them, it is possible to highlight the pictorial element present in media directed towards children, who have rarely been the focus of such analysis.

The distortions caused by fiction have damaging effects on the preservation of archaeological heritage, given that they promote a stereotyped vision of archaeology constituted by adventurous characters, mysterious places and fantastic treasures. To those images one may add simplified, outdated and/or incorrect information contained in the texts - and in other media such as films, cartoons and games. This set of images and information has a great impact on the relationship between the public – in this case children – and archaeology and is also essential for the comprehension of their attitude towards material heritage.

Eco (2009) in dealing with narrative texts argues that readers are led to choose paths in the 'forest of fiction' based on their own experiences, on their 'private memory', transforming that forest into a 'private garden', where fantasy allows free creation. For Benjamin (2002, 66), children 'inhabit the images' and 'learn in colors' (Eco 2009, 62).

In this light, I believe that examining children's literature is crucial for visiting the 'colored' 'forest of fiction' of archaeology as presented in twenty-two children's literature books published in Brazil (Disney 1996; Fairbairn 2000; Funari 2001; Girardet and Salas 2000; Gusmão 2006; Hoffman and Lebrun 1999; Larry 2008; Leite 2006; Loibl 1994; Loibl 2002; Loibl 2006; Loibl 2008; Masson 2007; Olivieri 2000; Olivieri 2008; Pavanello 2009; Pirozzi 2007; Prominska 2004; Rius and Vergés 1997; Rodrigues 2003; Sousa 2003; Stine 2007).

Children's Literature

Children's literature, in general, constitutes a literary genre that has been given little attention by scholars. Nevertheless, it is a valuable research subject that allows reflections about children's worldviews. This literature developed together with schools, and has become an instrument in the service of education. It is through it that, since the 18th century in Europe, children have been indoctrinated regarding values and principles of life in society (Zilberman 2003).

Within the last few centuries, there has been a decrease of this canonical role, but the strong pedagogical focus has been maintained and in part still exerts today its pragmatic and formative power (Souza 2006). Thus, children's literature has not been able to easily become a literary genre, and has always remained within the domain of pedagogy, within and outside of the school. According to Zilberman, children's literature up to the present 'remains as a colony of pedagogy', whose didactic nature makes it a means of control (Zilberman 2003, 16).

The history of children's literature in Brazil is more recent and dates back to the end of the 19th century and the beginning of the 20th. According to Souza (2006), there are three distinct phases of children's literature in Brazil: a) initial – importation and translation of texts (19th and 20th centuries); b) transition – elaboration of Brazilian texts (20th century – 1960s); c) expansion – consolidation of the literary process (1970s). In the beginning of the 20th century, the texts directed to children's audiences were deeply concerned with cultural roots and folklore. One of the leading exponents from this period, Monteiro Lobato, revolutionized children's literature with his nationalistic, amusing and aesthetic concerns (Souza 2006; Zilberman 2003). The 1970s were marked by a growing interest in invigorating national memory and identity in children's books, as well as by intense efforts in preparing illustrations, which were created by specialists of that art. The period was further characterized by a concern with pedagogical matters. This phase was partly substituted by a literary approach in the 1990s (Souza 2006; Zilberman 2003).

In 2006 3,031 titles were published and 12,808,625 copies were produced in the children's genre in Brazil (FIPE 2007), the small quantity of which is less than 10% of all national production. However, there is a continuous increase in supply and demand for children's literature, which has been adopted in many schools – especially private ones - as complementary educational materials.

Children's literature stories are an opportunity for children to organize their experiences (Zilberman 2003, 45). Images have an important role in this process because they: a) constitute a unique communication system; b) enhance a degree of cognitive autonomy and c) provoke confrontation with children's individual experiences. Their pre-established representations of the world are reaffirmed or challenged by this repertoire of images.

Illustrations in children's literature may thus be considered as 'visual artifacts' (Hernandéz 2000, 54) that act as mediators between present and past. Unfortunately, concepts of those 'artifacts' or the visions of the world represented in them do not always take children's perceptions into consideration. James (1997, 24), pointing out the problems caused by a lack of such partnership, underlines the importance of interaction between the archaeologists/authors and the illustrators. In the sample examined here, rarely may one infer any dialogue among those professionals. The result in many cases is a stereotyped vision of the past and of archaeology, probably anchored in the representations of the illustrators and/or writers themselves.

Fantasy plays a central role in those representations. It is a crucial element for amusement and a path towards stimulating curiosity, which allows children to construct '(...) their own world of things, a small world inserted in a larger one' (Benjamin 2002, 58, my translation). One of the 'artifacts' utilized in this cognitive process is certainly the image. Despite that, in '(...) sliding freely from reality to the wonderful world' (Zilberman 2003, 47, my translation), one runs the risk of making the vision of the past excessively fantastic, which is somewhat harmful for an adequate understanding of archaeology and the apprehension of scientific knowledge.

The Representation of Archaeology in Children's Literature in Brazil

The twenty-two books examined here were selected during a survey carried out in Brazilian bookstores, especially two large chains – Livraria Cultura and Livraria Saraiva - that have branches in various regions of the country and also have online stores[1] (Disney 1996; Fairbairn 2000; Funari 2001; Girardet and Salas 2000; Gusmão 2006; Hoffman and Lebrun 1999; Larry 2008; Leite 2006; Loibl 1994; Loibl 2002; Loibl 2006; Loibl 2008; Masson 2007; Olivieri 2000; Olivieri 2008; Pavanello 2009; Pirozzi 2007; Prominska 2004; Rius and Vergés 1997; Rodrigues 2003; Sousa 2003; Stine 2007). The child group that has access to those titles is found in the so-called economic classes A and B. The children from less privileged classes – who usually study in public schools - do not have frequent contact with children's literature. The standards of public school libraries in Brazil are not good. This means that students may not have easy access to this kind of literature at school. Prices range from USD 9.97 to USD 16.63 – a variation of between 4.3% and 7.2% of the total income of families with salaries of up to USD 302.76 per month[2]. This keeps such materials, including their repertoire of narratives and collection of images from the past, outside the domains of such children.

Here I consider the illustrations that help understand the representations of: 1) archaeologists; 2) archaeology; 3) populations of the past and 4) landscapes of the past in books that were written by two Brazilian authors and eight non-Brazilians. Moreover, I analyze two comic books published in Brazil – one Brazilian (Sousa 2003) and the other non-Brazilian (Disney 1996) - which, in one of its volumes (Disney 1996), deals with the theme of archaeology. According to their professional experience, the authors are divided into professional, writers, a journalist, a doctor, a schoolteacher, a biologist, an engineer and only one archaeologist. All authors who are neither professional writers nor archaeologists seem to have justified their authorship of the books by their 'passion' for archaeology. Most of them declare their fascination for archaeology, which can be observed on their romantic views of the discipline into the stories.

The Archaeologists

'The Archaeologists' is the title of volume 155 of the comic book published by Disney (1996) and on whose cover one may see the media icons of archaeology: a mummy, a sarcophagus, a magnifying glass, explorer's clothes and a dinosaur. The association between archaeology and dinosaurs is recurring and constructs of that image are strongly influenced by the mass media. In earlier research with ten-year-old students in a private

---

[1] Livraria Cultura (www.livrariacultura.com.br) and Livraria Saraiva (www.livrariasaraiva.com.br).
[2] Available at: http://www.mte.gov.br/.

school in Rio de Janeiro, I verified that the children who watched the film Jurassic Park[3], for example, considered the dinosaurs to be the objects of the study of archaeology, even though their non-contemporaneous relationship with prehistoric populations is vigorously discussed in the early scenes of the film (Bezerra 2003; 2005).

During that same research, I examined the image of the archaeologist who, for many students, corresponds to the 'archaeologist in Jurassic Park' (not to mention the Indiana Jones series[4]). The researchers in the film are paleontologists – a couple – but the children only referred to the man. The idea that archaeologists are men, that they use a certain type of hat, excavate in the desert and wear khaki-colored clothes made the children not even hesitate to consider 'Dr Alan Grant' as an archaeologist, since his character encompasses all of the elements cited. However, 'Dr Ellie Sattler' was not classified as an archaeologist because the gender representation determined the choice (Bezerra 2003).

Representations of archaeologists in the media follow certain canons. The attributes of that 'character-type' are: men, white, Westerners, with a beard, goatee or moustache, wearing khaki shirts with pockets, hats (usually 'pith helmet' style), boots and using magnifying glasses. It is curious to note that this is a popular image noted by other authors in different contexts (Bird and Von Trapp 1999; Cury 2006; De Boer 1999; Thomaz 2001) (see Figure 7.1).

One perceives that there is always an incorporated allegory, be it in the body, or in the clothing make one character distinct from the others. This takes us back to a discussion by Holtorf (2007b) about our image in the media when considering the messages transmitted by our way of dressing. Holtorf states that: 'By choosing what to wear, archaeologists have always been making fashion statements about who they are as archaeologists' (Holtorf 2007b, 86). We frequently end up reinforcing the idea that archaeology is not a profession, but a lifestyle that presupposes the use of 'costumes', be it at work, be it at a private domain (Holtorf 2007b). Holtorf (2007b) observes that many archaeologists today let themselves be photographed using hardhats, instead of the fedoras or ball cap, and health-and-safety wear used by engineers and builders, in order to support an image connected to professionalism and safety, among other things.

In research with children in a Rio de Janeiro school, Ricon (2005) confirms that for child audiences scientists are men, white, bald, with full moustaches and pens in pockets, wearing lab coats in laboratories, eyeglasses and surrounded by test tubes. It is interesting to observe that this image at the same time approaches and distances itself from the image of the archaeologist in the children's literature and the drawings produced by children in some public archaeology projects in Brazil (Bezerra 2003; Thomaz 2001) (Figure 7.1). That is because there are points of convergence, such as gender, but in terms of clothing and personal appearance the characteristics seem to move in opposite directions. With the exception of the researchers represented in Masson (2007), who wear lab coats, ties and eyeglasses and have full moustaches, all the others appear in the traditional khaki uniform and are bearded, which leads us to reflect on the vision of Archaeology as a technique and not as a science.

As for gender, the women, who are underrepresented in this sample, appear in four books: two that portray Brazilian archaeological sites that have been researched by two female archaeologists and two in which there are two archaeologist couples, one of which is relative to Brazil and also the only one visually represented. Both have long hair, tied in a ponytail, wear eyeglasses, are dressed in a manner similar to the men – boots, hats – but with some distinctions: one has a bandanna tied around her neck and the other wears a lab coat. In general, women scientists are stereotyped by the media. In children's cartoons, they are represented with short and relatively well-cared for hair, white lab coats and eyeglasses. They are distracted and eccentric (Ramos and Olschowsky 2009).

The insignificant role of women as archaeologists/scientists in the media, including children's audiences in Brazil (Bezerra 2003; Thomaz 2001), does not correspond to the registered archaeologists with the Sociedade de Arqueologia Brasileira – the Brazilian Archaeology Society -, which indicate a balance between women and men working in the discipline in the country (Schaan 2009, 98). This is not a Brazilian prerogative: in a survey conducted with 40 children in six British schools, Emmot (1994, 25) concludes that students could hardly name women who have contributed significantly to the world's history. In this sense, the media depiction, including the examined sample, points to a stereotype concerning a historically established gender division of labour (for a discussion about this issue in the North American archaeological community see Zeder 1997).

There is a singular kinship relation between archaeologist characters and the children who are protagonists in the books. Most of them are in the categories of parents, uncles or cousin. The parents are represented in two publications, while the uncles appear in eight stories and the cousin in only one. In the other books, the character is substituted by an archaeology professor – a paternal figure - or is not identified.

---

[3] *Jurassic Park* (Spielberg 1993).
[4] Indiana Jones as a fictional character was created by Steven Spielberg and George Lucas and performed by actor Harrison Ford in four movies: *Raiders of the Lost Ark* (Spielberg 1981), *Indiana Jones and the Temple of Doom* (Spielberg 1984), *Indiana Jones and The Last Crusade* (Spielberg 1989) and *Indiana Jones and the Kingdom of the Crystal Skull* (Spielberg 2008).

Figure 7.1: Archaeology Drawings. Anonymous. 2001.

Adults are a fundamental element in those and in many other children's stories. It is they who guide the children through the narrative, leading them to learn about distant and exotic places and saving them from perils. Nonetheless, there is a distinction: in the stories where the parent-archaeologists are represented, there is no emphasis on the dangerous aspect of the adventure, but instead on its educational side; on the other hand, the uncles and the cousin are the transgressor characters, without a fixed residence, untidy, and providing the children with a universe interdicted by their parents.

In dealing with the image of scientists in children's media, Ramos and Olschowsky (2009) affirm that, besides being stereotypical, the representation of the latter is excluding, since it 'does not include ´normal´ (sic) persons in this profession' (from Ramos and Olschowsky 2009, 10, my translation). Another aspect highlighted by Ramos and Olschowsky (2009) is the lack of allusion to any aspect of the social and family life and the residence of those professionals. This reinforces the association of science, and by extension archaeology, with loneliness and unconditional dedication to work.

Nonetheless, in one of the stories the archaeologist assumes a maternal role in gently helping a girl who in a dream becomes lost in a cave (Pirozzi 2007) - a metaphor for the maternal womb and/or to the Bachelard´s oneiric house as 'our [safe, comfortable, warm] place in the world' (from Bachelard 2008, 32, my translation). As for the archaeology professor, he generally personifies a zealous paternal figure. In one case, however, the author introduces a guide who presents the image of the fearless hero (Gusmão 2006), whose outfit includes all of the archaeologist's icons; in another, the professor at the end of the story is unmasked as a relic thief (Pavanello 2009).

This means that the parents, despite being archaeologists, are presented as dedicated adults, as opposed to the uncles and cousin. As these characters are not assigned to a nuclear family, they are free and somewhat daring and dangerous like in the case of the thief. This in part is compensated for by their extreme ability of extricating themselves from threatening situations by means of instruments such as knives and sticks. These turn them into heroes.

The representations of archaeologists for children (Bezerra 2003, 2005; Thomaz 2001) coincide with the attributes that constitute children's literary characters, but their personalities are amalgamated with other representations related to science, gender and family relations.

Archaeology

With regard to the profession of archaeologist, the publications evaluated differ little among them. The images corroborate the statements by Holtorf (2007a; 2007b), as they depict 'doing archaeology' more than the result of archaeological research, even if the stories refer to archaeological sites that have already been studied. The scenes suggest that archaeology's main objective is that of seeking a treasure and unraveling immemorial secrets.

The results of the study by Moraes, Vianna, Freitas, Pinto and Braga (1990) about the representations of science to a group of children in five schools in Rio de Janeiro pointed to the fact that children understand science as something that exists *a priori*. According to their perceptions, the researcher has the task of exposing and not constructing science. I believe that it is pertinent to make an analogy with the image of archaeology in children's literature, and in other media, in which archaeological knowledge is conceived as a sudden and magical knowledge of the past.

This revealing nature of archaeology propagated by the media reinforces the image of the discipline as a treasure hunt and disregards the importance of interpreting those same objects as a construct of the present and the nature of archaeology as a process. What is implied in those scenes is that the past exists as an intrinsic reality to be discovered, a premise vigorously opposed by contemporary archaeology (Tilley 1998).

Archaeological investigation as presented in those books has maps, picks, shovels, magnifying glasses, tents and sleeping bags as its major components. The images seem to depict the beginnings of archaeology, and include none of the various pieces of equipment utilized by researchers in fieldwork today. This indicates that representations of the archaeologists' practice consider neither innovations nor technological advances, such as some of the geophysical methods, nor the professional nature of the discipline.

That confers a precarious, rustic and questionable aspect to archaeological research that is represented as an activity that is not a career but instead a bucolic adventure, an accessory to daily life. The archaeology of those books not only studies the past, but lives in the past.

The Populations of the Past

In most of the books examined, the past is conceived through stereotypical elements. The men are represented in greater number than the women, who appear in seven books; the children appear in six and the elderly in four. Women's invisibility has been highly debated in archaeology, but such discussions have no impact for the authors and/or illustrators of the books. Contrary to the changes identified by Moser and Gamble (1997, 210) in representations of archaeology in popular culture, the female figure in the books researched is still depicted in typically 19th century European romanticism images and in activities such as cooking, caring for children and sewing. The illustrations show a scenario in which the woman has a smaller role in social organization and where the division of labour, clearly represented, always places her in a secondary role, both in the activity carried out and in the perspective adopted by the illustrator. The man, always in the foreground, has reserved for himself the scenes connected to activities that refer to the defense of the family and its subsistence. The art appearing in the majority of the books examined is made up of men, at times accompanied by children, usually boys, who are presented in apprenticeship positions.

It is curious to observe that the books directed towards child audiences mostly do not include children, who always appear in situations of passive learning. Only one of the books (Masson 2007) shows a group of children learning how to chip rocks and having fun with the bruises resulting from that activity. The elderly, for their part, are little represented, but their images suggest a pattern: they are depicted as wise elders in majestic poses, with a wooden scepter in their hands, guiding or teaching skills to the children.

One study with students in a school in São Paulo suggests that the objectification of the concept of old for the children is done through white hair, beard and eyebrows, through wrinkled skin and through support objects such as canes, wheelchairs etc. (Lopes and Park 2007). In this sense, the presence of a wooden artefact such as a scepter, in illustrations depicting the elderly, may be connected to these symbolic reasons. Only men are portrayed as old. The women are always depicted as young. This reinforces their reproductive capacity and essentialises their role as mothers. The sexist approach strengthens masculinity and reaffirms feminine frailty.

Men are mostly shown wearing only animal skins tied to their bodies. In two cases, the clothes that are made from animal skin had their style updated to modern times (Hoffman and Lebrun 1999; Masson 2007). Men wear trousers, long-sleeved shirts with pockets and women wear skirts, blouses or dresses. All wear fur-lined skin boots and hoods for protection from the cold. Long hair and beards seem to be essential elements in these drawings, in which most men are depicted with sparse body hair. A grotesque appearance is identified in two books (Olivieri 2008; Rodrigues 2003), but in general the populations are portrayed with features from modern Anglo-Saxon populations, even though we are dealing with Brazilian prehistory.

In three books concerning Brazilian prehistory, the stereotype of the Brazilian Indigenous societies was used to represent the past. In the national literature, especially school textbooks, they are portrayed as unchanged cultures, the living fossils – as in the 19th century - and with no regard to their ethnic diversity (Grupioni 1996, 427). Grupioni affirms that, in these educational books, the Indigenous populations are always mentioned in a '(...) secondary manner; in relation to the colonizer' and characterized as lazy, passive, free, which implies the need for indoctrinating and civilizing them (Grupioni 1996).

One of the Brazilian books includes a representation of a modern Indian (Gusmão 2006). The scene takes place in a small city, where a group of students led by a professor of archaeology rests before a trip to the archaeological sites. The image depicts the Indian selling handicrafts and dresses with elements that more closely resemble clothing of North American Indians. The asymmetrical relation between the Indian and the group may be observed in the perspective adopted by the illustrator: the Indian is sitting and the group is standing, which may suggest the inferior place of the indigenous collectives in Brazil. But it is not only the Indian who appears in an unfavorable position: further along, in the same city, a woman wearing simple clothes also appears to be selling objects in a small stall. She is also sitting, her arms held close to her curved body, indicating a subservient attitude in relation to the students/tourists/consumers.

Market scenes appear in another book set in Egypt (Loibl 2006), where a group of children accompanied by an uncle are on an archaeological expedition. The Egyptian population is depicted as poor, corrupt (there is the suggestion that archaeological material is being sold in the market), undeveloped and threatening. This image was created by the West to justify politics of dominance over the East, (Bhabha 2007; Gosden 2004; Said 2001; Shobat and Stam 2006) and is perpetuated in those books. It is worth mentioning that the image of archaeology is strongly linked to Egypt and to all that refers to it, namely pyramids, mummies, hieroglyphs, scarabs, etc. A study performed by Raquel Funari (2006) with 347 students at six schools in the southern and southeastern regions of Brazil revealed that the image the students have of Egypt is inexorably associated with those icons explored in children's literature, especially the idea of mystery and exoticism, which matches the reflections of Orientalism as developed by Said (2001). The contrasting images/discourses of the West and the Orient legitimize imperialism and imply the western political, cultural and economic dominance over third world nations.

To a certain degree, we may say that the illustrations found in such books recreate the colonialist imaginary by 'civilizing' prehistoric populations with clothes and domestic artefacts in typical middle-class scenes. It seems that the burden imposed by colonization has also affected children's books.

The Landscapes of the past

The locales chosen for the stories may be divided into caves and shelters, forests, islands and the hinterland. All represent hard to get to and isolated places, which are thus propitious for safeguarding the 'treasures of the past'. The idea is that archaeological discoveries occur in distant places, untouched by time, which would be sanctuaries of the past waiting for the archaeologist-hero to unveil them to the civilized world.

The landscapes that serve as the background for the various stories are always hostile: deserts, glaciers, dense forests, caverns, which recall the assertion by Moser and Gamble (1997, 190) that there is a limited set of scenarios that '(...) conceived [men] in terms of their ecological settings (...)'. It is thought-provoking to observe that caves - the preferred loci for the stories presented in those books - regardless of their association with archaeology, are permeated by elements that qualify them as 'landscapes of fear' (Tuan 1980).

According to research carried out in Brazil (Figueiredo, Travassos and Silva 2009), the representation of the cave in films is associated with situations of conflict, confrontation, difficulties, limits, and also with struggle, power and domination, refuge, ambushes, hostility, danger and so on. Such portrayal evokes the 'Allegory of the Cave' in Plato, which depicts the trajectory of humans when leaving the darkness of ignorance for the light of true knowledge. The image is repeated in several books (Girardet and Salas 2000; Olivieri 2008; Rodrigues 2003) that depict caves as dark and deep places where humans seek refuge from the external and dangerous world and where shadows created by internal fireplaces are projected onto cave walls.

In fact, the scenarios of the struggle for survival are recurrent. In them, humans appear as victims or as aggressors. The scenes reinforce the idea of the ceaseless struggle for survival, which is marked by images of drowning and attacks of ferocious animals, where human groups passively observe the death of one of their members. In those images, the illustrator, in bestializing the features of men and animals, suggests a minimal evolutionary gradient between the two. For Ingold (1994, 14), there is a Western tendency to associate 'animality' to the dark side of human nature and '(...) the threat that it apparently poses to cherished values of reason and civilization' (Ingold 1994, p.14).

The complexity of management strategies adopted by groups of hunter-gatherer and farmer societies is not considered in the literature. The past is conceived from an evolutionary, unilinear and materialistic perspective which shows the non-updated nature of the ideas found in those illustrations. The shift from hunter-gatherer to farmer is presented as a revolution and not as a process. The illustrations suggest not only the domestication of plants and animals, but of people themselves, transforming wild landscapes into domesticated landscapes.

Conclusions

The images that illustrate these books create a fringe and stereotypical universe, whose iconic elements harmonize with the children's representations concerning archaeology. The 'cave man image', for example, is so well-known that it arouses no questions. Moser and Gamble (1997, 205) affirm that 'There is something so familiar about the caveman stereotype that it seems to have been in existence long before prehistoric archaeology appeared on the scene'.

In the same way, the reproduction of scenes similar to those experienced by children makes the past delightful. That is the case with illustrations which show a typical photo taken from a family album: the tall and broad-shouldered father, the shorter mother by his side and holding a baby in her arms, with another child standing in front (Girardet and Salas 2000; Masson 2007). Or it could be a 'kitchen' scene, where the mother oversees the cooking of food inside a leather receptacle on the fire, while a child observes the scene licking his/her lips (Masson 2007). According to Moscovici (1978), the strange is made familiar in the process of constructing the representation, so that the new information can fit into the previously established repertoire of images.

The coincidence verified between those illustrations and the research carried out with children in Brazil (Bezerra 2003, 2005; Cury 2006; Funari 2006; Thomaz 2001) raises two considerations on the one hand, that the iconography in those books influences the image of archaeology that they construct; on the other hand, that the illustrations reveal themselves as an echo of childhood representations and are thus immediately accepted and incorporated into the children's literary repertoire regarding the discipline (Figure 7.1).

It is also a disturbing reality that Brazilian children learn about archaeology and prehistory through these stereotypes. Besides this, the books written by Brazilian authors depict images that do not represent Brazilian pre-colonial landscapes. The images are inspired by Anglo-Saxon patterns (Sousa 2003), be they in the stereotypical representation of Brazilian Indians or in the way that prehistoric populations are described. Furthermore, the majority of those stories do not even include the knowledge produced by archaeology, in Brazil or overseas, regarding the Brazilian context. The underrepresentation and/or misrepresentation of Brazilian prehistory in children's literature, in particularly in favor of European prehistory, means that Brazilian children learn about the past through a biased lens coloured by a colonialist perspective.

Furthermore, social representations of archaeology are linked to the processes of configuring conduct towards social life (Moscovici 1978, 77). I suggest, based on previous research (Bezerra 2003, 2005), that they are designed according to ideas and concepts that individuals learn from popular culture, from interpersonal discussions and so on. Those concepts are the starting point for elaborating theories about the discipline and the past that end up constituting attitudes which concern the object of the representation itself, in this case archaeology. Mapping and understanding those representations contributes towards interpreting perceptions and attitudes of the child audience regarding archaeology. This has direct implications for preserving the archaeological heritage.

The distortions and the damage caused to archaeology by those representations are increased by the influence of another group of representations that found many of the icons presented here. When representations of science, gender, the elderly, family, the Indian, the East, caves and humanity merge with the images of the discipline, archaeology '(...)ceases to exist as such and is converted into an equivalent (...)' (Moscovici 1978, 59, my translation), into an alternative archaeology, an Archaeology as Allegory.

Finally, the debates about narratives of the past, multivocality and the Poetics of Archaeology, have suggested that all those reconstructions, simulations, interpretations and visual representations are also part of the research process (Moser 2001, 281). Understanding the context in which they were conceived opens up the possibility of assessing the impact of scientific knowledge in their composition (Holtorf 2006; 2007a; 2007b; Moser 2001). It also points to the iconic discourse of Archaeology as a visual artefact that constructs, and is constructed by, both the present and the past.

Acknowledgements

I want to thank the anonymous reviewers for their useful suggestions and comments.

Bibliography

Bachelard, G. 2008. *A Poética do Espaço.* Martins Fontes, São Paulo.

Bhabha, H. 2007. O Local da Cultura. Belo Horizonte, Ed UFMG.

Benjamim, W. 2002. *Reflexões Sobre a Criança, o Brinquedo e a Educação.* São Paulo, Livraria Duas Cidades, Ed. 34.

Bezerra, M. 2003. O Australopiteco Corcunda ou As Representações Sociais da Arqueologia para as Crianças: um estudo de caso no Brasil. *Anais XII Congresso da Sociedade de Arqueologia Brasileira,* 1-6. RJ, SAB.

Bezerra, M. 2005. Make Believe Rituals: Reflections on the Relationship between Archaeology and Education through the Perspective of a Group of Children in RJ, Brazil. *Archaeologies* 1(2), 60-70.

Bird, S.E. and Von Trapp, C. 1999. Beyond Bones and Stones. *Anthropology News* Oct, 9-10.

Cury, M. X. 2006. Para saber o que o público pensa sobre arqueologia. *Revista Arqueologia Pública* 1, 31-48.

De Boer, W. 1999. Metaphors We Dig By. *Anthropology News* Oct, 7-8.

Eco, U. 2009. *Seis Passeios pelo Bosque da Ficção.* São Paulo, Companhia das Letras.

Emmott, K. 1994. A child´s perspective on the past: influences of home, media and school. In R. Layton (ed), *Who needs the past? Indigenous values and archaeology,* 21-44. London, New York, Routledge.

Figueiredo, L.A.V., Travassos, L.E.P., Silva, A.S. da 2009. A Caverna no Cinema: análise preliminar de paisagens naturais e simbólicas. *Anais do XXX Congresso Brasileiro de Espeleologia.* Montes Claros, Minas Gerais, Sociedade Brasileira de Espeleologia. www.sbe.com.br/anais30sbe, accessed on 10/01/2009.

Fundação Instituto de Pesquisas Econômicas 2007. *Pesquisa e Produção e Vendas do Setor Editorial Brasileiro – Relatório 2006.* São Paulo, FIPE.

Funari, R. dos S. 2006. *Imagens do Egito Antigo: um estudo de representações históricas.* São Paulo, Annablume, Unicamp.

Gero, J. and Root, D. 1996. Public Representations and Private Concerns: Archaeology in the Pages of National Geographic, in R. Preucel and I. Hodder (eds.), *Contemporary Archaeology: a reader,* 531-548. Oxford, Blackwell Publisher.

Gosden, C. 2004. *Archaeology and Colonialism: cultural contact from 5000 BC to the Present.* Cambridge, Cambridge University Press.

Grupioni, L.D. 1996. Imagens Contraditórias e Fragmentadas: sobre o lugar dos índios nos livros didáticos. *Revista Brasileira de Estudos Pedagógicos* 186, 409-437.

Hernández, F. 2000. *Cultura Visual, Mudança Educativa e Projeto de Trabalho.* Porto Alegre, Artmed.

Hodder, I. (ed.) 2001. *Archaeological Theory Today.* Cambridge, Polity Press.

Holtorf, C. 2006. Experiencing Archaeology in the Dream Society. In I. Russell (ed.), *Images, Representations and Heritage,* 161-176. New York, Springer.

Holtorf, C. 2007a. *Archaeology is a Brand: the meaning of archaeology in contemporary popular culture.* Ill. Q. Drew, Walnut Creek, Left Coast Press.

Holtorf, C. 2007b. An Archaeological Fashion Show: how archaeologists dress and how they are portrayed in the media, in Childrens´s literature, in T. Clack, and M. Brittain (eds.), *Archaeology and the Media,* 69-88. Walnut Creek, Left Coast Press.

Ingold, T. (ed.) 1994. *What is an Animal*. London, New York, Routledge.

James, S. 1997. Drawing Inferences: visual reconstruction in theory and practice. In B.L. Molyneaux (ed.), *The Cultural Life of Images: visual representations in Archaeology*, 22-48. London, New York, Routledge.

Livraria Cultura
www.livrariacultura.com.br, accessed on 29 February 2012.

Livraria Saraiva
www.livrariasaraiva.com.br, accessed on 29 February 2012.

Lopes, E. S. de L. and Park, M. B. 2007. As Representações Sociais de Crianças Acerca dos Velhos e a Influência do Contato Intergeracional durante o Projeto de Resignificação da Memória Cultural 'Jarina tem Memória'. *Estudos de Psicologia* 12 (2), 141-148.

Molyneaux, B.L. (ed.) 1997. *The Cultural Life of Images: visual representations in Archaeology*. London, New York, Routledge.

Moraes, A. G. de, Vianna, D. M.,Freitas, J. D. de, Reis, J. C. de O., Pinto, K. N. and Braga, M. A. B. 1990. Representações sobre Ciência s suas Implicações para o Ensino da Física. *Caderno Catarinense de Ensino da Física* 7(2), 120-127.

Moscovici, S. 1978. *A representação social da psicanálise*. RJ, Zahar.

Moser, S. 2001. Archaeological Representations: the visual conventions for constructing knowledge about the past. In I. Hodder (ed.), *Archaeological Theory Today*, 262-283. Cambridge, Polity Press.

Moser, S. and Gamble, C. 1997. Revolutionary Images: the iconic vocabulary for representing human antiquity. In B.L. Molyneaux (ed.), *The Cultural Life of Images: visual representations in Archaeology*, 184-212. London, New York, Routledge.

Ministério do Trabalho e Emprego 2010.
http://www.mte.gov.br/, accessed on 15 January 2010.

Ramos, J.F. and Olschowsky, J. 2009. *As Representações Sociais de Cientistas em Filmes de Animação Infantil. XXXII Congresso Brasileiro de Ciências Sociais da Comunicação*. Curitiba, Sociedade Brasileira de Estudos Interdisciplinares da Comunicação.

Ricon, L.E. 2005. Cientista ou Criança? As representações sociais do cientista nos desenhos animados infantis. *III Seminário Internacional: as redes de conhecimento e a tecnologia*. RJ, UERJ. http://www.lab-eduimagem.pro.br/frames, accessed on 20 August 2009.

Russell, I. (ed.) 2006. *Images, Representations and Heritage*. New York, Springer.

Russell, L. 1997. Focusing on the past: visual and textual images of Aboriginal Australian in museums. In B.L. Molyneaux (ed.), *The Cultural Life of Images: visual representations in Archaeology*, 230-248. London, New York, Routledge.

Said, E. 2001. *Orientalismo: O Oriente como Invenção do Ocidente*. São Paulo, Cia das Letras.

Schaan, D.P. 2009. A Arqueologia Brasileira nos Trinta Anos da SAB, in D.P. Schaan and M. Bezerra (eds.), *Construindo a Arqueologia no Brasil: A Trajetória da Sociedade de Arqueologia Brasileira*, 281-300. Belém, GKNoronha.

Shobat, E. and Stam, R. 2006. *Crítica da Imagem Eurocêntrica*. São Paulo, Cosac and Naif.

Souza, G. P. C. B. de 2006. *A Literatura Infanto-Juvenil Brasileira Vai Muito Bem, Obrigada!* SP, Difusão Cultural do Livro.

Spielberg, S. (dir.) 1981. *Raiders of the Lost Ark*. 115 minutes, Universal Pictures.

Spielberg, S. (dir.) 1984. *Indiana Jones and the Temple of Doom*. 118 minutes, Universal Pictures.

Spielberg, S. (dir.) 1989. *Indiana Jones and The Last Crusade*. 127 minutes, Universal Pictures.

Spielberg, S. (dir.) 1993. *Jurassic Park*. 101 minutes, Universal Pictures.

Spielberg, S. (dir.) 2008. *Indiana Jones and the Kingdom of the Crystal Skull*. 122 minutes, Universal Pictures.

Thomaz, L.V. 2001. Entre Lápis e Papéis: a arqueologia no imaginário infantil. *Anais do XI Congresso da Sociedade de Arqueologia Brasileira*, 1-8. RJ, SAB.

Tilley, C. 1998. Archaeology as socio-political action in the present, in D.S. Whitley (ed.), *Reader in Archaeological Theory: Post-processual and Cognitive Approaches*, 315-330. London, New York, Routledge.

Tuan, Y. 1980. *Topofilia: um estudo da percepção, atitudes e valores do meio ambiente*. São Paulo, DIFEL.

Zeder, M. A. 1997. *The American Archaeologist: a profile*. Walnut Creek, London, New Delhi, Altamira Press.

Zilberman, R. 2003. *A Literatura Infantil na Escola*. SP, Global.

Examined Sample

Disney, W. 1996. *Os Arqueólogos*. Edição Especial, 155, São Paulo, Abril.

Fairbairn, E. 2000. *A Tumba do Faraó: uma aventura arqueológica*. Rio de Janeiro, Garamond. Ill. M. A. Fairbairn and A. A. Fairbairn.

Funari, P.P. de A. 2001. *Os Antigos Habitantes do Brasil*. São Paulo, UNESP. Ill. I. V. Stever.

Girardet, S. and Salas, N. (ill.) 2000. *A Gruta de Lascaux*. SP, Cia das Letrinhas.

Gusmão, J. 2006. *Aventura no Vale do Catimbau*. Recife, Bagaço.

Hoffman, G. and Lebrun, F. 1999. *No Tempo das Cavernas*. 4ed, SP, Scipione.

Larry, H.I. 2008. *Zac Power: a tumba amaldiçoada*. São Paulo, Fundamento Educacional. Ill. A. Hook and A. Oswald.

Leite, M. 2006. *O Clube da Capivara*. São Paulo, Escala Educacional. Ill. A. Abu e A. Camanho.

Loibl, E. 1994. *O Mistério do Índio Voador*. São Paulo, Cia Melhoramentos. Ill. J. de O. S. Filho-Máqui.

Loibl, E. 2002. *Perigo na Grécia*. 3ed, São Paulo, Melhoramentos.Ill. R. Mello.

Loibl, E. 2006. *Aventura no Egito*. São Paulo, Melhoramentos. Ill. J. de O. S. Filho.

Loibl, E. 2008. *O Segredo do Ídolo de Barro*. São Paulo, Melhoramentos.

Masson, P. 2007. *Mini-Larousse da Pré-História*. São Paulo, Larousse do Brasil. Ill. D. Balicevic.

Olivieri, A. C. 2000. *Pré-História*. 10ed., São Paulo, Ática. Ill. M. de Sant´Anna.

Olivieri, A. C. 2008. *Pré-História*. 14ed., São Paulo, Ática. Ill. Líbero.

Pavanello, R. 2009. *Bad Pat: a avó do Tutancâmon*. São Paulo, Fundamento Educacional. Ill. B. Pisapia.

Pirozzi, R. 2007. *A Menina e o Tigre-Dente-de-Sabre: uma viagem pelo mundo da arqueologia*. São Paulo, Cia Ed. Nacional. Ill. A. Turoulin.

Prominska, E. 2004. *As Aventuras de Paulina no Nilo*. São Paulo, Cortez. Ill. H. Grudzien and D. Grudzien.

Rius, M. and Vergés, G. e O. 1997. *Viajando Através de: Da Pré-História ao E*gito. São Paulo, Scipione.

Rodrigues, R. M. 2003. *O Homen na Pré-História*. São Paulo, Moderna. Ill.G. Delphim.

Sousa, M. de 2003. *Manual da Pré-História do Horácio*. São Paulo, Globo. Ill.M.Sousa.

Stine, R.L. 2007. *Goosebumps: a maldição da tumba da múmia*. São Paulo, Fundamento Educacional.

A LOOK IN THE MIRROR AND THE PERSPECTIVE OF OTHERS: ON THE PORTRAYAL OF ARCHAEOLOGY IN THE MASS MEDIA

Diane Scherzler

Abstract

This chapter focuses on the question of what typifies the quality of a journalistic representation of archaeology. To this end it compares the respective views of archaeologists and journalists. Can the quality criteria of archaeology be transferred to journalism at all? It explores how journalists understand their role and their task with respect to the relationship between archaeology and the public at large. Why does the journalistic description of archaeology differ from the way the profession portrays itself? Where is the friction between science and journalism? Furthermore, this text suggests that when analysing how it is presented in the media, archaeology should also turn its attention to phenomena which have hardly been considered so far, such as medialisation and monopolistic influences on public opinion.

Keywords: Archaeology, accuracy, communication, mass media, journalism, television, radio, press, medialisation

Introduction

If an archaeologist asks me what I do, and my reply includes the words 'science communication' and 'mass media', their reaction is usually quite predictable: 'It's great that somebody is finally explaining to the media how archaeology works, because the things journalists write about our profession and about the past are often completely wrong!' They are very surprised when I reply that while journalists should know more about archaeology, archaeologists could also do much to improve the quality of media reporting. Since 2002, I have been gaining experience at the interface between archaeology and the mass media as editor and author at one of Germany's largest public service media organisations. As a prehistorian I am involved with archaeological topics time and again: I regularly interview archaeologists and report on their research. I am very anxious to improve the collaboration between science (particularly archaeology) and journalism, which is why I teach science communication, provide media training courses for archaeologists who want to improve their interaction with journalists, and advise scientific organisations on their media relations. Between 2003 and 2010, I have thus been able to work and discuss with some 350 archaeologists from different countries and specialist fields. Their views on the media world will be incorporated into this chapter in addition to my experiences as a science journalist.

Many archaeologists do not appreciate how their field and how the past is presented in the media. They often regard archaeological reports on television, on the radio or in the press as odd or annoying (cf. Holtorf 2007a, 105). Some archaeologists who participated in one of my media training courses had previously counted the errors which journalists (actually or supposedly) make or smiled at the simplifications their colleagues use in interviews. They still like to peer suspiciously at the media popularity of a colleague (see Hale 2006, 236).

In this chapter, I would like to focus on a subject which archaeologists like very much to discuss: which representation of the past and of archaeology in the mass media is acceptable, and what is to be rejected? What are the characteristic features of journalistic quality? I will discuss this by comparing the respective views of archaeologists and journalists. The actual journalistic system, with which most archaeologists are not familiar, deserves a closer look. I will therefore also allow a number of experienced science journalists to have their say. It is they who make it possible to produce a professional, practical view of things from the journalistic system. This can put the subject in a completely different light than if archaeologists discuss journalism only with other archaeologists, as is often the case. Cinema films, incidentally, are not included in the journalistic formats; they shall nevertheless be dealt with in passing owing to their impact on the public image of archaeology. I would initially like to briefly deal with the relevance of the issue for archaeology.

Does archaeology really need to rely on the media?

The mass media are the most important factor for the relationship between archaeology and the public: what people see on television and in the cinema, what they read in the newspaper and hear on the radio greatly influence their perception of what archaeology is. A survey carried out for the Society for American Archaeology shows that 56% of adult US Americans learn about archaeology from television, 33% from magazines, 33% from books and 24% from newspapers (Ramos and Duganne 2000, 16). In contrast, archaeologists' own efforts by means of cultural events or in local archaeological or historical societies, for example, meet with little public interest, however, with 1% each (Ramos and Duganne 2000, 18). Surveys in Sweden, Canada and Great Britain provide very similar results: television is the dominant source of information on archaeology (Holtorf 2007a, 52-54). For many people, the mass media are even the only source of information about the sciences (Luhmann 1996, 9; Schäfer 2007, 14). The mass media are, moreover, the place where, in society, 'the legitimation of science is most strongly negotiated' (Schäfer 2007, 18; cf. also Raupp 2008, 389). If scientific organisations or individual researchers are named in the media and are sought after as interview partners, politicians tend to judge this as an indicator for social relevance (Peters *et al.* 2008, 88). Scientific disciplines, institutions and players, therefore, put emphasis on not only appearing in the media, but also exerting a positive influence on the assessments of themselves, where possible. Success here also increases the probability of financial support (Schäfer 2007, 20-21). The same also applies to archaeology and to the long-term survival of quality archaeological research (Brittain and Clack 2007, 26; Ascherson 2004, 156). For these – and, of course, for several other reasons as well – it is absolutely imperative for archaeology to come to terms with the mass media.

What constitutes a quality representation of archaeology?

Which media representation of the past can an archaeologist approve of? A film dealing with all the angles which are important to an archaeologist? A radio report which the archaeologist checked when it was finished? How important is the use of specialist terminology? Is the expression 'Iron Age' acceptable in place of 'La Tène A'? Is the phrase 'several thousand years ago' too imprecise and thus to be rejected? What about tabloid newspapers: is it acceptable to have an article on archaeology next to a pin-up girl? What is the minimum length a radio report must have in order to still reasonably present the facts? What should one think about the use of stereotypes: gold, Atlantis, hidden treasure? While there are examples for the presentation of the past in the media which all or no archaeologist finds acceptable, the attitudes of my seminar participants often differ: something which one archaeologist still finds acceptable is already not acceptable to another. Neither is there an all-encompassing and generally valid definition of journalistic quality (Lehmkuhl 2006a, 14), but rather a large number of criteria for this – we will come back to some of them below. One also has to extend the field of vision: after all, it is not only the archaeologist who defines what an appropriate presentation of archaeology in the media is. I therefore now want to compare the quality criteria of archaeologists and journalists.

The perspective of archaeology

Archaeologists regularly discover omissions, mistakes, exaggerations, distortions, stereotypes and sensationalism in the media (see Ascherson 2004, 145 ff., 154; Brittain and Clack 2007, 17, 23). They analyse the mass media from the perspective of the discipline (Benz and Liedmeier 2007, 153) and apply scientific criteria to journalistic reports in order to determine the quality of a film, an article or a radio broadcast: factual correctness, completeness of all scientifically important aspects and the communication of the limitations of data are but some of these criteria. 'After all, it is my own

research the journalist is writing about! And everything should be correct.' is what an archaeologist would perhaps say. Many of the archaeologists I work with are therefore of the opinion that how the past is presented should depend on them in the end. They perceive reputable journalists as being those who produce long television broadcasts or newspaper articles for a well-educated audience or readership and who can prepare themselves for a topic with corresponding thoroughness (I am reminded of those journalists who perceive an archaeologist to be more 'real' the larger the dig, the more valuable the finds and the more impressive the technology used). Neal Ascherson (2004, 155) considers it advantageous for good reporting if the journalist has a degree or some experience in archaeology. William E. Boyd (1995, 52) perceives successful newspaper reports and radio interviews to be those which follow his press release very closely, sometimes even word for word, and take up the issues which he himself considered to be the most important. Archaeologists are more inclined to accept media reporting which presents archaeology in a way which corresponds to their own expectations and perceptions (Holtorf 2007a, 31). Jon C. Lohse (2007, 3) also commented on Mel Gibson's film *Apocalypto* (Gibson 2006) from the perspective of scientific correctness: 'Anyone who cares about the past should be alarmed; if most moviegoers who see the film use it to formulate their understanding of what pre-Columbian life was like, Apocalypto will have set back, by several decades at least, archaeologists' efforts to foster a more informed view of earlier cultures.' Kenneth L. Feder (1995, 14) also considers the mass media's 'nonsense about our discipline' as a permanent adversary of his efforts to create an archaeologically informed public.

The power of the media to create a media reality which is so perfect that its effects can make it seem more real than reality, on the one hand, and on the other the power to influence the masses by virtue of their prevalence, is also possibly perceived by some archaeologists as a threat to their authority to interpret the past.

The perspective of journalism

Journalists apply journalistic criteria to journalistic reports to determine the quality of an article. One of my priorities as a journalist is to be understood by my reader, listener or viewer. If this is not the case and the reader thus stops reading, or indifference leads the listeners or viewers to switch to a different station, the report has failed. If an archaeologist who is interviewed by a journalist is therefore not prepared to leave behind the linguistic style of the scientist and explain their work in a way that is interesting and comprehensible to the respective audience, then the journalist has difficulty in using those statements. The television author Christian Frey has for many years been making documentaries on the history of the 20th century which are shown in prime time slots on the public service television channels in Germany. He says: 'The ideal interview partner for me is a scientist who, on the one hand is, of course, preferably brilliant in their field but who is also prepared to accept the laws of journalism. They should be comprehensible in the interview, maybe even funny and entertaining.' (pers. comm. 28 Aug 2009). The television writer and producer Friedrich Steinhardt, who is responsible for series of history and science documentaries on German public service television, holds a very similar view. He particularly values interview partners whose 'enthusiasm and love of the topic' is evident (pers. comm. 3 March 2010).

Both film makers therefore consider additional factors, which play only a marginal role in science at most, to be important apart from expertise. The requirements which they place on a media-friendly interview partner have, in my opinion, nothing to do with the frequent complaint of sensationalism of the media: a scientist who talks about their research in a monotonous voice and in technical jargon and thus does not make the crucial point is hardly understood by the audience, who therefore do not want to listen to him/her (which archaeologist would like that?). Moreover, as a science journalist I have repeatedly found that unstructured, long-winded statements are very difficult or impossible to cut to the ever short air time or length of text. It is then down to the journalists to filter out the important parts of the whole statement. This is very time-consuming and also increases the likelihood of mistakes, which editors like to avoid. These archaeologists are therefore only asked for an interview if there is no other option. Comprehensibility is thus a very important (but by no means the only) factor which decides which scientists journalists like to collaborate with and which are therefore publicly visible (cf. Peters 2008, 115).

Moreover, the media also apply criteria to archaeological topics which are fundamentally different from those of the discipline. Judith Rauch, editor of the successful German monthly illustrated print magazine 'bild der wissenschaft' says, for example: 'In a magazine it is important that the issues can be illustrated well. […]. Our magazine unfortunately has to drop even interesting subjects if there are no ideas at all about illustration' (pers. comm. 16 Sep 2009). Television, too, places its own particular demands on a topic: 'The more tangible a story, i.e. the more it is a story with a protagonist and a conflict, with a beginning, a progression and an end, the better it can be represented on television,' says Christian Frey (pers. comm. 28 Aug 2009). 'Evidence is sacrificed to story' is the complaint of Christopher Hale (2006, 238) about television and thus describes a weakness of the medium which manifests itself in the choice of topics: 'Television is not suited to communicating abstract connections,' explains Frey (pers. comm. 28 Aug 2009). It follows that these topics or these aspects of a topic have only a slim chance on television. Archaeologists have already noticed that certain activities such as the digging are frequently shown in the press and on television, other tasks – literature research for example – are very rarely shown (Benz and Liedmeier 2007, 170; Holtorf 2007b, 86).

Christian Frey explains why this is so in his medium: 'Everything that can be shown in pictures, which contains action, can be transported well on television. This is much more interesting for the viewer […] than a scientist studying literature, for example. Just imagine a film about studying the sources of the New Testament. If you were only to show someone who is bent over the Qumran scrolls all the time, then quite simply nobody would watch it' (pers. comm. 28 Aug 2009). The television author Tamara Spitzing is herself an archaeologist. She confirms Frey's assessment: 'How can one visualise literature studies? […] I also want to make a visually nice film, which pleases the eye. I must therefore show something which is visually attractive.' (pers. comm. 4 Aug 2009). I think that if television shows archaeologists in stereotype on a dig, it may have something to do with the lack of imagination of some journalists. When assessing the quality of television reports, however, the nature of the medium, as described above, should also be taken into consideration.

Incidentally, the quality criteria which archaeologists and journalists respectively apply to a journalistic report can also directly contradict each other. I would like to illustrate this by using two examples. Firstly, although the complaint of archaeologists regarding the many errors in the media cannot be repudiated, on closer inspection some turn out to be simplifications and omissions. Both are obligatory in journalism and do not automatically cause factual errors. If a journalist has to explain the importance of Hannibal in no more that 500 words, for example, but their readership has at best only heard the name of the general and has not received any formal higher education, then the journalistic challenge is precisely to build information bridges across an enormous number of omissions, which give those who had not previously been interested in the subject a rough idea of it and arouse their curiosity for more. Completeness of information cannot therefore be a criterion for good journalism. Judith Rauch, too, says: 'We will never be able to be complete. After all, journalism consists in selecting what is important for the reader. Never completeness!' (pers. comm. 16 Sep 2009). Secondly, if a journalist sticks word for word to a press release of an archaeologist, and additionally relies on a single source - Boyd (1995) describes such a case and considers this to be journalistic quality - then from the perspective of the media this is not a careful way of doing things, but rather evidence of a lack of journalistic quality; if the issue was a political one, journalists would call this 'announcement journalism' or 'obsequious reporting'.

I would now like to consider in detail three areas where not only the differences between science and journalism again become apparent, but which also actually cause friction between the two disciplines.

Fields of conflict between journalism and archaeology

Journalistic independence

In my view, what lies behind the above-mentioned expectation of many archaeologists that good science journalism passes on their results to the public in as 'unadulterated' a form as possible, is the perception that journalistic communication works in basically the same way as the inter-specialist one, and the prime concern is to educate an ignorant public. It is also based on the assumption that archaeology is without hidden interests and a neutral provider of scientific truth. Finally, this also demonstrates the view that the journalist is the intermediary, the translator, science's transmission belt into society (see Samida 2006, 157; Brittain and Clack 2007, 30; cf. Kohring 2004, 166-167), an instrument of archaeology, even, to accomplish its objectives (see Ascherson 2004, 156). On closer inspection, however, none of these three points applies: extra-disciplinary communication simply obeys different laws to the ones within the discipline (Peters and Jung 2006, 33-34), and education of the public is by no means the only objective of science journalists. Archaeology does have interests, one only has to think of the desire to point out the lack of research funds in the media, to entice visitors to an exhibition or to show one's own work in a favourable light. And, finally, the journalist is not primarily the intermediary and never the translator who has to (this is implied by the term) accurately stick to the archaeologist's text (Scherzler 2007, 190-191). The public at large quite rightly expects a journalist to provide a sound insight from a point of view which is as neutral as possible, and frequently also an assessment of the facts in order to be able to form its own opinion from this. And therefore the majority of journalists do not see themselves as intermediaries who transport archaeology and its findings into society, not as those who have to ensure the research is accepted by the public at large (Randow 2003), but as representatives, as scouts of the audience in the world of science. The communication scientist Matthias Kohring (2004, 177) writes: 'The trustworthiness of journalism, and this is not a new realisation, depends directly on the distance it keeps from the object of its reporting (this distinguishes it fundamentally from PR).' The desire to keep a distance is also the reason why journalists resolutely reject copy approval of a finished report by the archaeologist in most cases. The editorial statutes of the British newspaper 'The Guardian' state that no-one is accorded the right of copy approval, an interview partner is allowed to look at the text or quotes used only under certain circumstances (Guardian 2007, 2; re. copy approval see also Rögener 2008, 260). Archaeologists often regret this, because they see copy approval as a way of avoiding errors (see Levy 2007, 173). It is also possible to interpret archaeologists' desire to authorise as an attempt to transfer intra-scientific procedures – the proofreading of scientific publications – to extra-scientific communication, where the archaeologist see themselves as the author of the newspaper article, film or radio broadcast to some extent (Peters 2008, 112-113; Peters et al. 2008, 79). Journalists, however, do not consider the source of their information, in this case the archaeologists, as the author of their report at all, but as its subject (Peters and Jung 2006, 33). Journalism research views the close proximity of journalists to science, the presentation of science as a supposed source of superior knowledge and the strong emphasis on scientific success, as deficits of journalism (Lehmkuhl 2006a, 22-23; Schneider and Raue 2003, 13). The observation of science from the viewpoint of other social areas, i.e. according to extra-scientific viewpoints, is the basis of journalistic quality, however. After all, an important function of journalism is to observe the mutual dependencies of a differentiated society, in this case the relationship between archaeology and society (Kohring 2004, 177). This produces a picture of archaeology in the public mind which is slightly independent of its self-portrayal and thus deviates from it. The social scientists Hans Peter Peters and Arlena Jung write on this issue (2006, 28): 'This journalistic procedure must not be misunderstood as a deficit or a quality problem. It is the only strategy which gives a large lay audience access to science.' This is the only way to have a real dialogue between archaeologists and society from which I feel the discipline could also gain valuable views and suggestions. The science researcher Ulrike Felt (2007) even views science communication as a 'space to get involved in collective thought experiments with society.'

The selection criteria of journalism

Which archaeological topics attract the attention of journalists and which do not? As has been mentioned above, journalists put an archaeological topic into a broader, non-scientific context which is of relevance and interest to the respective audience. Information which is disseminated by the media must therefore satisfy certain criteria, so called news factors that can be weighted differently depending on the medium and its addressees. Journalists take care that an issue concerns a large number of people, for example, that it is new and that it is set in the spatial or social vicinity of the addressee. There are a few further such factors, which can include the fact that a scientific issue has consequences, that it represents a conflict, that it generates emotions and opinions or that it is entertaining (Ruhrmann and Göbbel 2007). The higher the number of news factors a story has, the higher the probability that it is taken up in the media. It thus becomes evident that scientific relevance is only one such news factor, usually not even the most important one (see also Lehmkuhl 2006b, 102). This also explains why journalists often select different topics and stress other aspects of an issue than an archaeologist would. Incidentally, the news factor 'conflict' can, in my opinion, be quite problematic for an appropriate representation of archaeology: academic disputes often receive more attention in the media than consensus. Moreover, the media repeatedly focus their reporting on outsiders, the literary scholar Raoul Schrott on the subject of Troy, for example (see the film *Der Fall Troja (The case Troy)*, ZDF 2010).

The media transform archaeology

Good science journalism must not be equated to the imparting of science, because it does not submit to the vested interests of archaeology (cf. Kohring 2004, 172). The media do not present archaeology on a one-to-one basis, i.e. in the way the discipline sees itself - they do not consider this to be their job in the slightest. Rather one can say that a transformation is achieved via the media (cf. Lehmkuhl 2007, 9). Scientific and journalistic reality can deviate from each other. Journalism also uses other means to represent its 'reality', as already outlined by Weingart (2001, 238; cf. Stollorz 2008, 573).

What leads to friction in these three areas has hopefully become apparent: the mass media do not fulfil the aforementioned expectations which many archaeologists have of them. Moreover, the presentation of archaeology and the past is in the hands of journalists, which is usually difficult for scientists to accept (cf. Peters 2008, 112-114). The reasons for this are correct in my view, however, given journalism's observer function. In practice, scientists do have influence on what and how the mass media report on their discipline. One example is the information for journalists provided in advance by the great journals such as 'Nature' and 'Science' which is tailor-made to the needs of the media and which provides them with a way of influencing the reporting to a significant degree (cf. Stollorz 2008, 575).

Journalism has its own perspective and its own criteria

Quality criteria for journalism can therefore not be derived from how true to detail and how comprehensively it reports on science, nor to what extent the journalistic presentation is 'correct' in the eyes of the researcher. To produce high-quality journalistic work means, for example, to inform truthfully, neutrally and to the best of one's knowledge and belief. Accuracy (but not in the sense of completeness, rather in the sense of correctness), balance and independence are among the fundamental values of good journalism (see Thomson Reuters Corporation 2008, 3). The topicality and relevance of the topic are essential for quality, as is careful research and checking of sources. Journalistic quality is also measured by how well journalism fulfils its social function: can society gain an impression of archaeology from the journalistic report, regardless of how archaeology presents itself (c.f. Kohring 2004, 178)?

From a methodological point of view, I therefore feel it makes no sense at all for archaeologists to judge journalistic reports according to the criteria they apply to academic articles. Many of these criteria have no validity at all in journalism! Archaeologists who lament the many 'inaccuracies' and the 'inappropriate' angles on the topic

taken by journalists have often fundamentally misunderstood the role of the media themselves (Weingart 2001, 238; Holtorf 2007c, 152). The way the media presents the discipline and its protagonists is not a look in the mirror, it is not an accurate self-reflection. Instead of being confronted with their reflection, the media presentation of their research confronts the archaeologist with the view the others have of them. That is possibly not always pleasant.

Journalism is anything but perfect

So far we have mainly considered quality journalism. Unfortunately, it is necessary to mention that journalistic ideals are not always realized under the daily pressure to meet deadlines which exists in some editorial offices. As in many other professions there are, of course, also journalists who are always willing to sacrifice the scientific facts and the most probable interpretations of a finding for a sensationalist headline, and editors for whom the same approach to a topic over and over again suffices. This even happens in media concerns which champion journalistic quality, explains Tamara Spitzing: 'I know of television editors who want to have the scientist being portrayed or giving an interview presented as a character, and preferably a character like Indiana Jones. This primarily concerns broadcasts for prime time television. If the archaeologist is nothing like Indiana Jones, but maybe more of a very shy researcher, the author is supposed to 'carve out' an adventurer. As the author, one therefore has to sometimes really protect the protagonists involved in one's broadcast' (pers. comm. 04 Aug 2009). It is a fact that some editors who assign journalists to a topic have stereotypes in their mind – and journalism is also a commodity: magazines need their circulation, broadcasting its ratings. A dig enhanced with adventure, gold and photogenic archaeologists fits perfectly. Factual errors also frequently occur in journalism (Silverman 2007, 11), and it is the task of the editorial offices to work very hard in order to keep the number of errors as low as possible and thus maintain the trust of the public in the mass media. Sometimes journalists simply know too little of science and this can lead to serious errors of judgement. There once was a discussion in my editorial office about one of my articles on a dig in Herxheim in the Rhineland-Palatinate, Germany, for example. A colleague asked why I had reported on this excavation when the archaeologists could not present a concluding interpretation of their findings. Would it not have been better to wait until the complete results were available? The journalist (a young reporter who did not specialise in science) had no appreciation whatsoever that research is a process and that scientific discussion is not a sign of perplexity, but serves to provide insight. Individual journalists, e.g. from the 'news' department, are also unfamiliar with the significance of scientific publications as a quality criterion. They believe that something which is still unpublished is the latest research and therefore particularly interesting. The reader is requested not to rashly transfer these examples to the complete media world! They are intended to show that stereotypes and a lack of knowledge on the part of journalists can really cause science to be poorly presented in individual cases – poorly not only from the viewpoint of archaeology, but also from the perspective of good journalism and also from society's perspective, which then does not really learn anything about archaeology. These cases must be distinguished from those which can simply be attributed to the intrinsic styles and tasks of journalism, however.

Medialisation, overload scenarios and monopolistic influences on public opinion

Let us return to the beginning: if a journalist writes 'Iron Age' instead of 'La Tène A', or if they make an individual researcher the protagonist of a broadcast (instead of acknowledging all 35 team members), or if an attractive, naked blonde is shown next to the article, this is, in my opinion, something archaeology should and simply must come to terms with. It seems to me very important, however, to point out some aspects of the interaction between science and journalism on which archaeologists have so far focused very little or not at all. Under the permanent scrutiny of the media, archaeology may possibly change by reacting to the supposed expectations of the mass media and the public, and by strongly orienting itself towards the logic used by the media to impart information – so-called medialisation (cf. Weingart 2005, 151 ff). An investigation needs to be carried out into the extent to which it already applies to the discipline. One indication of a medialisation of archaeology is provided by a press release (University of Tübingen, 14 May 2009) by Tübingen archaeologists which relates to an article in 'Nature' and whose title is guided quite strongly by the supposed expectations of journalists: 'A Venus figurine from the Swabian Jura rewrites prehistory'. On nature.com (2009) the Venus from the Hohle Fels Cave is even called a 'Prehistoric Pin-Up', whereas the actual academic article is linguistically conservative: 'A female figurine from the basal Aurignacian of Hohle Fels Cave in southwestern Germany' (Conard 2009, 248). One of the dangers of such medialisation is that the selection logic of the media over-shapes the rationality of archaeology at some stage, that the discipline makes itself the 'extra' of media productions (Raupp 2008, 388). If scientists go still one step further and use the media instead of specialist journals to increase their standing, if the press conference becomes more important to them than the specialist publication, if they receive research funds on account of their (media) prominence and not primarily on account of their academic reputation, archaeology must tackle such overdrives. Marcus Brittain and Timothy Clack (2007, 36-37) cite a deception by the Japanese archaeologist Fujimura Shinichi which archaeologists explain by Shinichi's desire for recognition in the media, and for which the media had possibly to be held accountable to some extent. Apportioning blame in this way seems to be too simple in my view, nevertheless the desire for media attention may have triggered the deception. Another example of

overdrive comes from palaeontology: in May 2009, the Norwegian palaeontologist Jørn Hurum caused a worldwide stir with the 47-million year old fossil called 'Ida'. The attention was not only focused on the primeval primate from the Messel pit in Germany, but also on the manner in which Hurum approached the public: in collaboration with the History Channel he organised a very professionally orchestrated media event. This comprised a very lavish film documentation with the slogan 'This changes everything', the book 'The Link: Uncovering Our Earliest Ancestor', the 'Revealing the Link' website and an exclusive deal with ABC News. The British BBC and the German ZDF were also subsequently involved with the marketing of the fossil (Arango 2009). The participating scientists compared the significance of the find to the moon landing and Kennedy's assassination (Arango 2009). The German palaeontologist Jens Franzen, who participated in the investigation of the fossil, called it 'the Eighth Wonder of the World' in the film and equated the significance of the specialist publication to the impact of an asteroid on Earth (sic!). In the specialist publication at PLoS ONE the tone is significantly more moderate, however; it states, for example: 'Note that Darwinius masillae [i.e. 'Ida'] [...] could represent a stem group from which later anthropoid primates evolved, but we are not advocating this here [...]' (Franzen et al. 2009). The main thing that makes one wonder is the fact that Hurum had already sold the rights to the media reporting for a lot of money before the find had undergone any sort of peer review process at all (Arango 2009). Tim Arango, a reporter for the New York Times, queried this critically (incidentally a nice example of the observer function of the media). Hurum replied: 'Any pop band is doing the same thing. Any athlete is doing the same thing. We have to start thinking the same way in science' (Arango 2009). Hurum proudly told the science journalism researcher Markus Lehmkuhl (2009, 11): 'We have made "Ida" an icon of evolution with less than two weeks of press work.' He freely admitted that the deliberately chosen slogan 'The Link' was suitable for generating the association with the 'missing link' in the public mind, something which the fossil by no means is (Lehmkuhl 2009, 13). So we can see how the strong orientation towards the mass media can lead to very questionable self-presentations of science. The case of 'Ida' is still an exception. Much more frequent is the following phenomenon, which possibly also applies to archaeology: since many journalists prefer to interview scientists who they already know can express themselves well and go into the questions posed, it is always the same experts who appear in the press and on radio and television. It is often the case that not more than a handful of scientists dominate one topic in the media. Such monopolistic influences on public opinion endanger a balanced presentation of scientific topics and also their quality, i.e. there could also be inexperienced or very controversial scientists among the media stars, because there is hardly any connection between media prominence and scientific reputation (Salzmann 2005, 6). The problem of the monopolistic influence on public opinion is caused, on the one hand, by the journalist, since it is so much easier to interview scientists who are known to be media compatible than to put a lot of effort into looking for different interview partners. On the other hand, it is also the fault of archaeology, where, as I see things, too few researchers want to deal with journalists at all or are prepared to abide by the rules of the media. One reason why incorrect statements of individual archaeologists, faulty presentations by journalists and especially films such as the *Indiana Jones* series (Spielberg 1981, 1984, 1989, 2008), *Apocalypto* (Gibson 2006) or *Lara Croft: Tomb Raider* (West 2001) make such a large impact is because they are scarcely accompanied or countered by archaeology. A few angry articles in archaeological journals do not reach the public at any rate. Tamara Spitzing would also like to see archaeologists more on the offensive: 'On the one hand, German archaeologists say about the media: 'Oh, they always get everything wrong. They don't understand me, either.' On the other, something can be mega-wrong in the media, but no scientist says anything about it in public. And this is why scientists also make a significant contribution to the fact that a few things are left wrong' (pers. comm. 4 Aug 2009; cf. also Schadla-Hall 2004, 263).

Conclusion

In this chapter, I have attempted to explain three things: firstly, the method of assessing journalistic reports in accordance with the intra-disciplinary criteria of archaeology can scarcely lead to sound results; journalistic criteria are needed instead. Secondly, it is right and proper from the viewpoint of the theory of journalism that the presentation of archaeology in mass media differs from its self-portrayal. Thirdly, when turning its attention to the media, archaeology should also look at so far neglected phenomena such as medialisation, overdrive scenarios and monopolistic influences on public opinion. Most important for me, however, is to encourage archaeologists to get involved with journalists. A qualitatively demanding presentation of archaeology and the past in the mass media is a goal which means a lot to good journalists as well as to archaeologists. This is why I think it is important that archaeologists do get involved when journalists are looking for an interview partner or have a question. And finally, archaeology itself can also profit enormously from contact with the sections of the public to whom the mass media have ready access.

Acknowledgements

I would like to cordially thank my discussion partners who devoted time to me and provided me with valuable insights into their journalist work: Christian Frey, Judith Rauch, Tamara Spitzing and Friedrich Steinhardt. I am also obliged to the three anonymous referees for their comments and suggestions on a previous version of this paper.

Bibliography

Arango, T. 2009. Seeking a Missing Link, and a Mass Audience. It is science for the Mediacene age. *The New York Times*, 18 May 2009. http://www.nytimes.com/2009/05/19/business/media/19fossil.html?_r=1&scp=1&sq=hurum&st=cse accessed on 29 February 2012.

Ascherson, N. 2004. Archaeology and the British Media. In N. Merriman (ed.), *Public Archaeology*, 145–158. London, Routledge.

Benz, M. and Liedmeier, A. K. 2007. Archaeology and the German Press, in T. Clack and M. Brittain (eds.), *Archaeology and the Media*, 153–173. Walnut Creek, Left Coast Press.

Boyd, W. E. 1995. Media coverage of an archaeological issue: Lessons from the press release of initial radiocarbon dating results of a possible pre-Cook European ship at Suffolk Park, northern New South Wales. *Australian Archaeology* 40, 50-55.

Brittain, M. and Clack, T. 2007. Introduction: Archaeology and the Media, in T. Clack and M. Brittain (eds.), *Archaeology and the Media*, 11–65. Walnut Creek, Left Coast Press.

Conard, N. 2009. A female figurine from the basal Aurignacian of Hohle Fels Cave in southwestern Germany. *Nature* 459, 248-252.

Feder, K. L. 1995. Ten years after. Surveying misconceptions about the human past. *Cultural Resource Management* 18 (3) (Archaeology and the Public), 10–14.

Felt, U. 2007. Wissenschaftskommunikation neu denken. Zur Repositionierung der Universität in einer Wissensgesellschaft. Talk at the Symposium 'Wissenschaftskommunikation im öffentlichen Raum. Welche Rolle spielen die Universitäten?' 12 Apr 2007. Berlin.

Franzen, J. L., Gingerich, P. D., Habersetzer, J., Hurum, J. H., Koenigswald, W. von and Smith, B. H. 2009. Complete Primate Skeleton from the Middle Eocene of Messel in Germany: Morphology and Paleobiology. *Public Library of Science (PLoS ONE)*. http://dx.plos.org/10.1371/journal.pone.0005723 , first published: 19 May 2009 (accessed on 10 June 2009).

Gibson, M. (dir.) 2006. *Apocalypto*. 139 minutes. Touchstone Pictures.

Guardian, The 2007. Guidelines. The Guardian's Editorial Code. Updated April 2007. http://image.guardian.co.uk/sys-files/Guardian/documents/2007/06/14/EditorialCode2007.pdf (accessed on 4 May 2010).

Hale, C. 2006. The Atlantean Box. In G. G. Fagan (ed.), *Archaeological Fantasies. How pseudoarchaeology misrepresents the past and misleads the public,* 235–258. Abingdon, New York, Routledge.

Holtorf, C. 2007a. *Archaeology is a brand! The meaning of Archaeology in contemporary popular culture.* Oxford, BAR Publishing.

Holtorf, C. 2007b. An Archaeological Fashion Show. How Archaeologists Dress and How they are Portrayed in the Media, in T. Clack and M. Brittain (eds.), *Archaeology and the Media,* 69–88. Walnut Creek, Left Coast Press.

Holtorf, C. 2007c. Can you hear me at the back? Archaeology, communication and society. *European Journal of Archaeology* 10(2-3), 149–165.

Kohring, M. 2004. Die Wissenschaft des Wissenschaftsjournalismus. Eine Forschungskritik und ein Alternativvorschlag. In C. Müller (ed.), *SciencePop. Wissenschaftsjournalismus zwischen PR und Forschungskritik,* 161–183. Graz, Nausner & Nausner.

Lehmkuhl, M. 2006a. Defizite im Wissenschaftsjournalismus. In W. Göpfert (ed.): *Wissenschafts-Journalismus. Ein Handbuch für Ausbildung und Praxis,* 14–25. Berlin, Econ.

Lehmkuhl, M. 2006b. Auswahlkriterien für Wissenschaftsnachrichten. In W. Göpfert (ed.): *Wissenschafts-Journalismus. Ein Handbuch für Ausbildung und Praxis,* 98–104. Berlin, Econ.

Lehmkuhl, M. 2007. Es gibt ein Risiko. *wpk Quarterly*1, 8–11.

Lehmkuhl, M. 2009. 'Wir haben den ganzen Job selbst gemacht!'. Interview with the Norwegian scientist Jørn Hurum. *wpk Quarterly* 2, 11–13.

Levy, J. E. 2007. Archaeology, Communication, and Multiple Stakeholders: From the Other Side of the Big Pond. *European Journal of Archaeology* 10 (2-3), 167–184.

Lohse, J. C. 2007. Apocalypto. Letter to the editor. *The SAA Archaeological Record* 7(2), 3.

Luhmann, N. 1996. *Die Realität der Massenmedien.* Opladen, Westdeutscher Verlag.

Nature.com (2009): Prehistoric pin-up. Trailer and full film.
http://www.nature.com/nature/videoarchive/prehistoricpinup/ accessed on 29 February 2012.

Peters, H. P. 2008. Erfolgreich trotz Konfliktpotenzial - Wissenschaftler als Informationsquelle des Journalismus, in H. Hettwer, M. Lehmkuhl, H. Wormer and F. Zotta (eds.), *WissensWelten. Wissenschaftsjournalismus in Theorie und Praxis,* 108–130. Gütersloh, Bertelsmann-Stiftung.

Peters, H. P., Heinrichs, H., Jung, A., Kallfass, M. and Petersen, I. 2008. Medialization of Science as a Prerequisite of Its Legitimization and Political Relevance, in D. Cheng, M. Claessens, T. Gascoigne, J. Metcalfe, B. Schiele and S. Shi (eds.), *Communicating Science in Social Contexts. New models, new practices,* 71–92. Dordrecht, Springer.

Peters, H. P. and Jung, A. 2006. Wissenschaftler und Journalisten. Ein Beispiel unwahrscheinlicher Co-Orientierung. In W. Göpfert (ed.), *Wissenschafts-Journalismus. Ein Handbuch für Ausbildung und Praxis,* 25–36. Berlin, Econ.

Ramos, M. and Duganne, D. 2000. Exploring Public Perceptions and Attitudes about Archaeology. Report by Harris Interactive on behalf of the Society for American Archaeology.
http://www.saa.org/Portals/0/SAA/pubedu/nrptdraft4.pdf accessed on 29 February 2012.

Randow, G. von 2003. Scientific Journalism - a Risky Business. Acceptance speech for the European Science Writers Award on 13 Jun 2003. http://www.euroscience.net/article2.html accessed on 29 February 2012.

Raupp, J. 2008. Der Einfluss von Wissenschafts-PR auf den Wissenschaftsjournalismus, in H. Hettwer, M. Lehmkuhl, H. Wormer and F. Zotta (eds.), *WissensWelten. Wissenschaftsjournalismus in Theorie und Praxis,* 379–392. Gütersloh, Bertelsmann-Stiftung.

Rögener, W. 2008. Das Ende der Langsamkeit! Veränderungen im Arbeitsalltag freier Wissenschaftsjournalisten, in H. Hettwer, M. Lehmkuhl, H. Wormer and F. Zotta (eds.), *WissensWelten. Wissenschaftsjournalismus in Theorie und Praxis,* 257–260. Gütersloh: Bertelsmann-Stiftung.

Ruhrmann, G. and Göbbel, R. 2007. Veränderung der Nachrichtenfaktoren und Auswirkungen auf die journalistische Praxis in Deutschland. Concluding report for netzwerk recherche e. V. http://www.netzwerkrecherche.de/docs/ruhrmann-goebbel-veraenderung-der-nachrichtenfaktoren.pdf accessed on 29 February 2012.

Salzmann, C. 2005. Was Einstein und Frankenstein gemein haben. Warum Wissenschaftler zu Medienstars werden - und was die Soziologie darüber weiß. *wpk Quarterly* 2, 5–6.

Samida, S. 2006. *Wissenschaftskommunikation im Internet. Neue Medien in der Archäologie.* Munich, Reinhard Fischer.

Schadla-Hall, T. 2004. The comforts of unreason. The importance and relevance of alternative archaeology. In N. Merriman (ed.), *Public Archaeology*, 255–271. London, Routledge.

Schäfer, M. S. 2007. *Wissenschaft in den Medien. Die Medialisierung naturwissenschaftlicher Themen.* Wiesbaden, VS Verlag für Sozialwissenschaften.

Scherzler, D. 2007. Journalists and Archaeologists. Notes on dealing constructively with the mass media. *European Journal of Archaeology* 10 (2-3), 185–206.

Schneider, W. and Raue, P. 2003. *Das neue Handbuch des Journalismus.* Reinbek, Rowohlt.

Silverman, C. 2007. *Regret the Error. How media mistakes pollute the press and imperil free speech.* New York, Union Square Press.

Spielberg, S. (dir.) 1981. *Raiders of the Lost Ark.* 115 minutes, Universal Pictures.

Spielberg, S. (dir.) 1984. *Indiana Jones and the Temple of Doom.* 118 minutes, Universal Pictures.

Spielberg, S. (dir.) 1989. *Indiana Jones and The Last Crusade.* 127 minutes, Universal Pictures.

Spielberg, S. (dir.) 2008. *Indiana Jones and the Kingdom of the Crystal Skull.* 122 minutes, Universal Pictures.

Stollorz, V. 2008. Ist der Platz zwischen allen Stühlen der richtige Ort? Essay über die Frage, was Wissenschaftsjournalismus heute soll, in H. Hettwer, M. Lehmkuhl, H. Wormer and F. Zotta (eds.), *WissensWelten. Wissenschaftsjournalismus in Theorie und Praxis*, 566–582. Gütersloh, Bertelsmann-Stiftung.

Thomson Reuters Corporation 2008. Handbook of Reuters Journalism. A Guide to Standards, Style and Operations. Second, fully revised online edition. http://handbook.reuters.com/index.php, accessed on 18 April 2012.

University of Tübingen (ed.) 2009. Eine Venusfigur von der Schwäbischen Alb schreibt die Urgeschichte neu. Archäologe der Universität Tübingen berichtet in der Zeitschrift Nature über sensationelle Funde. Press release, 14 May. http://www.uni-tuebingen.de/uni/qvo/highlights/h72-venus.html, accessed on 18 April 2012.

Weingart, P. 2001. *Die Stunde der Wahrheit? Das Verhältnis der Wissenschaft zu Politik, Wirtschaft und Medien in der Wissensgesellschaft.* Weilerswist, Velbrück.

Weingart, P. 2005. *Die Wissenschaft der Öffentlichkeit. Essays zum Verhältnis von Wissenschaft, Medien und Öffentlichkeit.* Weilerswist, Velbrück.

West, S. (dir.) 2001. *Lara Croft: Tomb Raider.* 100 minutes. Paramount Pictures.

ZDF 2010. *Der Fall Troja (The case Troy).* 'Terra X' television series. 31 January 2010.

'LOOTING' UNVEILED, ARCHAEOLOGY REVEALED:
CASE STUDIES FROM WESTERN GREECE

Ioanna Antoniadou

Abstract

This paper explores non-professional physical interactions with the material past, as articulated by the digging and collecting of antiquities by two locals of Kozani. It stems from a larger ethnographic research project conducted in the municipality of Kozani in northern Greece and it considers the instigation, form and implications of non-professional engagement with antiquities. The necessity for such a concern lies in the advancement of our knowledge regarding the factors that influence public perception and treatment towards the material past.

Keywords

non-professional digging, collecting, looting, symbolic capital

Introduction

In a discussion about physical encounters with the material past, one might ask: what makes people engage with antiquities in particular? Belk (1995: 139) argued in his study of collecting, '[j]ust as it was natural to paint madonnas and seek relics of saints in a time and place when Christianity was the centre of sacred power, and to assemble cabinets of automata, wonders from the New World, and natural curiosities in a time and place in which science was emerging as the sacred centre, so too it is natural to collect and revere mass-produced objects and artistic depictions of such things in a consumer society in which consumer goods have become the central focus of our dreams and desires.'

This account reflects a fundamental notion upon which this paper is premised, namely, the idea that 'centres of sacred power' produce foci of 'dreams' and 'desires' and as such, determine the object to be collected. Accordingly, if we are concerned with a time and place where national 'imagination' (see Anderson 1991; Gourgouris 1996) renders the material past sacred for the nation, then antiquities become the object of physical engagement and a popular category for collecting.

This paper concerns such time and place where, the pursuit of non-professional physical engagement with the past is instigated by the desire for antiquities, which, official archaeology considers 'sacred' (see Hamilakis and Yalouri 1999). In the examples examined here, this desire involves not so much the connection with the 'sacredness' that the archaeological past officially embodies, but the capacity to wield its symbolic significance, and adapt it to idiosyncratic taste. As such, in the two examples considered here, the desire for and subsequently the physical engagement with the past is about manoeuvring an established 'sacredness' and attaching alternative symbolic meaning to objects. Physical access to antiquities, however, is officially controlled by state archaeology (i.e. Archaeological Ephorates) in Greece. As such, any non-professional attempt to assert physical control over antiquity challenges legal and ethically accepted standards of behaviour.

With regards to the two non-professionals considered here, the 30th Archaeological Ephorate in Kozani asserted that their undocumented digging and unauthorised collecting prevent the safety of the material past, pursue self-serving interests and ultimately oppose official archaeological authority and ethics (Karamitrou-Mentesidi, pers. comm., August 2007). Yet, the need to dig deeper than this perception of opposition to official discourse is crucial. In what follows, I argue that these actions confront a profound facet of official state archaeology, namely, its exclusive physical control over the material past and its power to determine the meaning of antiquity. Concurrently, however, a profound correspondence with official discourse lies behind this resistance, because both official and non-professional agents endorse and defend a shared objective: the control over antiquity and antiquity's symbolic power.

This study is drawn from a larger research project on non-professional engagements with the material past within local communities in Kozani. It follows the trajectory of 'bottom-up' ethnographies, which provide alternative outlooks towards the 'looting' phenomenon. In particular, they re-consider the moral basis behind monolithic treatments of non-professional engagements with the past and also carefully explore the socio-cultural and political reasons that trigger their development (see Matsuda 1998; Maury 1996; Hollowell 2006a; 2006b). Overall, what they essentially illustrate is that economic profit is not the sole motive behind looting. In some places this phenomenon coincides with the support of corrupt governments (see Stark and Griffin 2004) or with economic disintegration and struggle for survival (see Matsuda 1998; Maury 1996; Politis 2002; Hollowell 2006b). In others, surface collecting is linked with the production of a sense of locality and identity (see Labelle 2003; Colwell-Chanthaphonh 2004). Evidently, the conditions and meanings surrounding the so-called 'looting' acts are far from uniform. For that reason, this paper attempts to defend what this great diversity calls for: a contextual approach towards unofficial and illegal engagements with the past, as opposed to the tradition of blanket conceptualisation (cf. Renfrew 2000).

National imagination and the sacredness of antiquity

During a process of national 'imagination' in Greece, antiquity became not only an essential reference point for defining Hellenism, but also the material basis for legitimising the Greek nation (Hamilakis 2007). The past was rendered 'sacred' for the national significance that it came to embody (see Hamilakis and Yalouri 1999). Through practices of demarcating and purifying archaeological sites (see Hamilakis 2007: 85-99; Herzfeld 1991; 2006) ancient remains were gradually transformed into symbolically important monuments, which not only represented the nation but *were* the nation (see Yalouri 2001; 2010). The symbolic power incorporated into ancient remains called for, as well as profoundly defended, the official conceptualisation and execution of the past's protection and stewardship. Moreover, this symbolic value that objects came to embody was often exchanged for ideological or economic profits for the purposes of nation-building (see Hamilakis and Yalouri 1996).

In such a context, for a site or an object to become symbolic capital, that is, to incorporate sacred, national symbolic value, it was not only required to occupy a physical space within the national topography, but, more importantly, to articulate a symbolic place within national imagination. One of the implications of this selective process is the symbolic marginalisation of some sites: while certain sites represent or even are the nation – such as the Acropolis (see Yalouri 2001) or the tomb of Phillip II (see Hamilakis 2008) – others are overlooked by the national narrative and, by extension, excluded from the national symbolic capital (see Demetriou 2010; Hamilakis 2006).

The discourse schematically described here is to a very large extent prevalent to this day (see Hamilakis 2008; Kokkinidou 2005). The concept that the past is the property of the Greek nation still lies at the core of modern Greek archaeology (see current Archaeological Law of Greece, Hellenic Republic 2002). This idea not only preserves the particular 'sacredness' of antiquity (one that maintains the centrality of antiquity in relation to the nation), but also the ethical reasoning and defence of a particular kind of protection and stewardship. The archaeological ethic to protect and steward antiquity underpins the project of modern archaeology and legitimises the politics of its exclusive physical control over antiquity and over its symbolic power.

Such articulation of symbolic capital manifests a power inequality which limits the physical access to archaeological sites and the production of narratives within an official domain (for exceptions see Stroulia and Sutton 2010). Evidently, archaeological practice entails an inherent dominance and exclusiveness which can potentially lead to various forms of resistance. If non-professional engagement with the past is viewed, therefore, in relation to this power imbalance, then the idea of social conflict emerges as a profound condition that needs to be considered if we are to understand what underlies a seeming opposition to official archaeological authority and ethics.

The place

Kozani's peripheral unit and its namesake capital city are located in northern Greece, north of the Aliakmonas river valley. Kozani is the seat of the periphery of western Greek Macedonia, which is also comprised of the peripheral units of Florina, Kastoria and Grevena. Its antiquity drew the attention of many scholars and travellers from as early as the 19th century. The first systematic archaeological excavations in Kozani commenced in 1983, revealing the ancient city of Aiani, which is 23km south of the city of Kozani. Soon after the first excavations were conducted, Aiani was established as one of the most archaeologically significant places in Greek Macedonia.

Particular emphasis was placed upon the site of *Megali Rachi* and its Archaic and Classical phases (6th and 5th centuries BC) for its numerous built tombs and pit-graves, as well as its architectural remains and public buildings. The excavations led to the identification of the site as the ancient city of Aiani, which was further identified as the ancient capital of the Hellenistic kingdom of *Elimeia* (see Karamitrou-Mentesidi 1996; 2005). Today the site of *Megali Rachi*, together with all archaeological heritage of Kozani and Grevena, is managed by the 30th Archaeological Ephorate of Prehistoric and Classical Antiquities, which is located in the town of Aiani. Its jurisdiction covers all matters regarding the excavation, protection, conservation, study and representation of the two prefectures' archaeological heritage.

George

George is a 70 year old retired architect, who currently lives in Velos, a village south of the city of Kozani. His engagement with the material past took the form of digging, collecting and publicly displaying antiquities from around his village from 1983 until the mid 1990s. In our conversations he has often expressed his love for archaeology, while at the same time stressing that his involvement was very different from that of professional archaeologists. As he said, 'had I been an archaeologist, I would probably have ended up being like most archaeologists. This way, however, I am a "different" archaeologist, because it is a hobby for me. It is not a science with [technocratic] duties and stuff like that... stuff which reduces it to a common practice. Like me and architecture, when I worked on legal procedures checking the legality of residences. And it ended up being a common practice [...] Nobody ever said "what a

mark George has made as an architect!". The same would have happened had I become an archaeologist'. [1]
He asserted that when he started collecting, he had full support from his fellow villagers, who would report and hand over to him any ancient finds they would come across in their lands. He once said to me: 'I don't understand... I must have been lucky. In just a few years I managed to collect so many objects. From people's homes, basements... someone had it inside their closet. It had been found in the field.' He eventually assembled various categories of remains and stored them in the local Cultural Centre.

There he also kept a logbook for the finds, where he included a photo, a general description, possible interpretation, the context of the find's discovery (which usually involved the names of land-owners), and the name of the person who handed it over to him. He said to me that people frequently asked to see the items they had given him, and he always willingly did so, because he wanted to reassure them that the finds are in good hands. George consistently argued in our conversations that whatever he did, he did for the benefit of his village in pursuit of its 'self-definition' through the knowledge of the local history. He once held that 'our grandfathers drank from those cups', whilst pointing at his manuscript of records, asserting his sense of duty towards the heritage of his village.

He has written and published a book on his interpretations of the ancient history of Velos. He mentioned to me that through this book he proves – contra to official claims – that the location of the capital of the ancient kingdom of 'Elimeia' is not Aiani, but his village. Today his aspiration is to convince the Ministry of Culture, based on this argument, to allow him to legitimately entitle the archaeological collection as that of the capital of 'Elimeia' (contra to Aiani's official declaration as the capital of Elimeia). He stressed to me that this would render his archaeological collection as unique. In his words: 'If the inscription for our collection simply says 'Archaeological Collection' then it is like a child of an unknown father. But if it states the place where these antiquities came from, then it makes a huge difference'.

On the other hand, according to the official archaeological perspective, George is an example of disobedience to official authority and of impingement on archaeological ethics. Soon after the establishment of the Archaeological Ephorate in the prefecture of Kozani in 1983, his conflict with official archaeology began. The Archaeological Ephorate had argued that George had failed to register to the nearest archaeological authority the antiquities he had found and held, and therefore was considered to have conducted illegal excavations, for which he should be penalized. Eventually, George was taken to court (George, pers. comm., 2007). It is important to note that no relevant court records exist, since all court records from 1988 to 1994 were lost in a fire. George, however, asserted that he was found innocent, which was also confirmed by the Director of the Archaeological Ephorate in Kozani (Karamitrou-Mentesidi, pers. comm., 2007).

Eventually, the archaeological collection George had created remained in Velos. On 22 June 1993, the Directory of Prehistoric and Classical Antiquities (Department of Museums) awarded the Cultural Association of Velos the licence to hold the antiquities George had collected on its behalf. According to the official record of this award, the antiquities would remain under the supervision of the 17th Archaeological Ephorate, which, together with the local council, would stipulate the terms for the antiquities' preservation, safety and manner of display. When I asked him if he continues his engagements with antiquities he replied: 'I don't. I am tired. I am tired of all the conflicts and the fuss. It was not an easy thing to deal, you know, with all the conflicts and the fuss. And the local chiefs did not approve of me going against the Archaeological Service. It is hard to go against these kinds of Services. How can I say this now...let's say it is a secluded discipline. Nobody enters and nobody leaves from there [...] Archaeology is like the Vatican. Nobody knows what is going on in there'.

The creation of a local symbolic capital

Since the beginning of the archaeological excavations in Kozani, the region's material past has been increasingly establishing itself within the 'national narrative'. This is evident from popular but also archaeologically based statements, such as 'this is the birthplace of the kingdom of Macedonia' (see Karamitrou-Mentesidi 1996). A turning point was when Aiani concreted a symbolic and a physical space in the Greek national narrative. Archaeological narratives about Aiani established a seminal reference point for the region's past and (its) Greek Macedonian identity.[2] Its status as a significant archaeological site and tourist attraction became well established on a national and international level. Evidently, the endowment of the material past with national symbolic power and the consequent operation of antiquity as symbolic capital are conditions prevalent in Kozani. One may ponder, though: does that leave any room for other localities to contribute to the national narrative, or to participate in the national symbolic capital? (cf. Appadurai 1995; Hamilakis 2006; Herzfeld 2003).

The beginning of archaeological excavations failed George's loyalty towards officially-driven narratives, as he witnessed the construction of symbolic capital being

[1] All translations are my own and the names of individuals and places have been changed.

[2] In 2001 I conducted ethnographic research in the village of Aiani, where I explored the way archaeology affected everyday life. The results showed that officially constructed archaeological narratives participated in the construction of the contemporary local 'Macedonian' identity.

restricted to official control and emphasising one place alone. In the attempt to elevate Kozani for its cultural and historical significance, he foresaw the exclusion of his locality from becoming a potential symbolic resource. In realising that the official symbolic capital centred around the capital of Elimeia, the ultimate glory of the ancient past of Kozani would be immediately concentrated exclusively in the place of Aiani. Effectively, George feared that Velos, just like any other physical space around Aiani, would be rendered less significant in symbolic value, and would thus play a marginal role in the national narrative. He therefore became determined to include his place and his voice into the national discourse.

He created local pride in the past of his local community, founded on the premise that Velos was 'Elimeia' instead. That way, he felt that he challenged the neighbouring symbolic capital, which, he thought, had unjustly attracted the dominant symbolic authority with regards to Kozani's past. The message, though, as I understand it, is not that George's actual objective was to threaten the official symbolic capital. Instead, he wanted to be included in it. He found himself on the other side of the wall which separates the visible from the invisible part of the symbolic space and the national narrative. He therefore made a move that would prevent such outcome. He pursued unofficial collecting as a vehicle for controlling the past of a local community and therefore indulging in the compensation that only officially-empowered places indulge in.

Nikos

Nikos is a 74 year old retired architect from Lake, a small village west of the city of Kozani. He started engaging with antiquities in the late 1970s and perceives himself as an avid devotee of archaeology. The routine of his current engagement involves going to spots where he knows that objects lie 'hidden'. After stocking himself with plastic bags for potential items, he sets off by foot, with his wooden walking stick for the long trek ahead. Then he collects surface items, items he considers in need of rescue, and brings them home. He keeps them for a variable while, until he decides it is time to give them up to archaeologists.

The local Archaeological Ephorate knows about Nikos' surface collecting activities, as it often receives from him relics that he finds. The Director of the Ephorate has mentioned his contribution by name in the official Archaeological Newsletter every time Nikos has indicated archaeological sites and delivered archaeological finds. On the other hand, archaeologists regard such activities considerably harmful, as they believe that he causes irreparable damage to the archaeological context of objects (Karamitrou-Mentesidi, pers.comm., August 2007). He has often been warned to cease removing artefacts from their provenance and was advised to simply indicate the sites that he discovers, if he wants to appropriately assist official practice. These

instructions, however, fail to prevent Nikos. Instead, he considers himself as someone who protects archaeology and actively assists the work of archaeologists. One explanation for turning a blind eye to official orders could be that he feels that he compensates for the alleged 'damage' he poses by delivering his collections to the archaeologists. In fact, Nikos asserts that he removes objects only to give them to archaeologists.

Nikos had known for many years about the existence of archaeological sites around his village. He started collecting in the late 1970s, when no archaeological activities were being conducted yet in the prefecture of Kozani. His first collecting incident occurred in 1978, after he discovered a number of relics – Neolithic potsherds and clay figurines – when he conducted an occupational assessment for the provision of a building licence of one area near his village. A few years after the first systematic archaeological excavations began in 1983 in the prefecture of Kozani in Aiani, Nikos presented these objects to the archaeologists. He hoped that they would provide a motive for professional research to focus on his village, so that, as he hoped, 'signposts would be placed in the archaeological sites to indicate that we have something really important here'. However neither the time, nor the financial resources were available to allow further excavations besides those in Aiani. He therefore kept the objects. In his own words, 'I kept them. I said when the right time comes I will present them [to the archaeologists] so they take care of them. I showed them in '84-'85 [to archaeologists] but they were really busy at the time. And so I kept them… until another opportunity arose with the sanctuary's excavation due to the Egnatia construction.' Nikos waited until 1993, when once again, he indicated to the archaeologists the same sites and handed the objects over, along with two hundred copper coins (Hellenistic/Roman) which he, at some point, had also collected from there. It took another five years for systematic excavations to commence, with financial resources coming from the construction company of a central motorway.

Such a development was fundamentally important to Nikos, because he thought it would produce certain compensations. One type of compensation concerned the recognition of his contribution, which would defend and legitimise his treatment of the past. He hoped that his amateur involvement with the material past would finally be recognised and applauded by official archaeologists. Another compensation that he greatly anticipated concerned the elevation of local archaeology. In particular, he hoped that, with the arrival of professional archaeologists, ancient ruins – whose existence was gradually 'threatened' and whose function remained incomprehensible – would be preserved and studied. Illustrative of this was when Nikos stressed that 'it is a great joy to bring out [things] from the darkness, from the ground or from caves… objects from a culture are brought to light… things that humans created once and since then have for years and years remained obscure and unknown. I believe that the joy and the devotion that the archaeologist feels are great'. Another time, he argued that archaeology 'brings out and pushes forward what remains hidden; how those who have passed away had lived and created their culture. These have to be unearthed; they cannot be left to rot'.

Nikos endorsed to a great extent the ideological foundation of official archaeology, in that he condoned the premise that the past incorporates an immense significance due to which it needs to be protected. He defended it as such, by delivering the objects to the Archaeological Ephorate. Nevertheless, the point that triggers speculation is when he – despite official guidelines – removes objects from their provenance, and then keeps them for a temporary, yet never specific period of time before he hands them in. Is there a deeper meaning in this inconsistency of his behaviour? Could it be hiding an ambivalent resistance to the official practice he strives to participate in?

The creation of personal symbolic place

Nikos often acknowledges the fact that he cannot preserve the objects in a professional manner. He once mentioned that '[i]t would be wrong to keep them in my shed, as I possess neither the scientific knowledge for their preservation nor the technical tools and environment.' Yet, for the time that he keeps them, he manages to indulge in a physical engagement with the material past, which, in turn, links to important connotations. He may not offer professional treatment to the objects he brings home, he nevertheless singularises, combines, classifies them; he austerely, yet intimately, cleans them and then he stores or displays them inside his shed. Such processes articulate a control over objects, which further enables him to create new products – the collections – (Belk 1995), or, as Stewart (1984) beautifully once put it, a 'little world'.

Earlier, I discussed how and why Nikos participates in the project of official archaeology through delivering these collections. But what about before that? How do his 'little worlds' compensate whilst he keeps hold of them? A closer look at the stage preceding the act of delivering the objects uncovers a kind of subliminal resistance to the official agenda, as he indulges in a private and emotional consumption that official archaeological practice in fact forbids. The objects that Niko delivers to archaeologists become the matter of scientific research, the embodiment of a national narrative, since they concern the culture 'that once humans created'. This symbolic meaning, however, juxtaposes the less grand, yet more intimate, meaning that he vests the objects with before he takes leave of them. This time, objects relate to him and his culture, as opposed to human culture in general.

He often emphasizes the emotional aspect of his engagement with remains by vesting the objects with nostalgic memories and narratives. Nikos' following

account, as told after he returned from one of his collecting expeditions, is illuminating. He held a plastic bag full of Neolithic animal bones and whilst showing them to me, he said: 'These are toys. We used to play with these as children. And as you can see, so did the ancients'. Equally, when he showed to me Neolithic grinding stones and loomweights which he kept collecting regularly from one site, his response was the same: 'We used these the same way the ancients did'.

The personal symbolic meaning with which he vests the objects at times contradicts official narratives. Interesting in this respect is his interpretation of the coins that he discovered, for it entails an idiosyncratic observation based upon a local practice: 'On one coin was written 'Epirus', another said 'Amphipolis', another said 'Thessaly'. They were brought from distant places…from I don't know where! And another four and a half thousand coins like mine were found! And there was one found from Sinope of Pontus [the Black Sea], which was left by a passer-by, who lit a candle, made a libation and placed his offering. [...] But archaeologists argue that this place was Apollo's Treasury because it housed treasure [that had been offered to Apollo]. But how could this be when no golden or even silver coins were ever found? I believe that people, for thousands of years, left coins there as offerings. I found the pots with which they made libations and 'reached' God. They [the ancients] would leave their offering, in the same way people do now, when they light a candle and leave a small coin.'

These accounts reflect a profound attachment to the material past premised on connecting the latter to what is emotionally meaningful: nostalgic memories and local practices. I believe that through such a process Nikos manages to capture and control those symbolic meanings. Here I agree with McCracken's (1988: 104-117) suggestions regarding the displacement of cultural meaning upon 'locations on the continua of time and place'. McCracken (1988) gives the example of a 'golden age', which he describes as a largely fictional moment when social life is imagined to have conformed perfectly to cultural ideals. This way, he argues, 'locally unobtainable ideals' are given 'empirical demonstration' and thus are made to resemble 'practical realities', which only exist, however, in a distant location (McCracken 1988: 104-117).

Equally, Nikos keeps the objects under his ephemeral control because that way they facilitate the displacement and preservation of what is symbolically valuable to him: nostalgic moments. The relics that Nikos collects capture the meaningful past in the present, and preserve it in a material form that is within immediate reach. His active engagement with remains of the past not only allows for an escape into a nostalgic world, but also sustains the hope that past experiences are still practicable because they were once practised. The ephemeral control over the past represents one unique form of unofficial, physical engagement, because it involves an ambivalent position towards official archaeology, and a complex perception of the past.

Conclusion

What has been attempted so far was to illustrate two forms of non-professional engagement with the material past, which involve two forms of reaction to the official control of the material past. According to the official archaeological perspective, both George and Nikos represented an 'obvious' opposition to official authority and an impingement on archaeological ethics, given the destruction of the archaeological context and the mistreatment of objects that – to their understanding – both locals had participated in. However, this approach does not adequately represent the dynamics that underlie George's and Nikos' assertion of control over objects and the development of their idiosyncratic perceptions.

Dominant notions and practices that lay at the foundation of official archaeological practice – such as the idea that the past incorporates symbolic power and that its control leads to further ideological or other profits – permeated the locals treatments of the objects to such a degree, that one should perhaps query *whether these engagements were indeed cases of obvious conflict with official discourse.* In the context of this paper, the aspiration to wield antiquity's symbolic power permeated both official discourse, as well as George's and Nikos' attitudes towards the material past. Therefore, it is not that George and Nikos opposed official discourse as a whole, since to a significant degree *they rather complied with its most fundamental premises.* Furthermore, the so-claimed 'obvious' misbehaviours did not aspire to prevent the stewardship or the protection of the past. Instead, what was confronted was state archaeology's exclusivity in executing antiquity's stewardship and protection and in defining antiquity's sacredness. In light of this, it is fair to conclude that a contextual approach towards non-professional engagements with the past is fundamental, because it moves beneath the surface of acts that are religiously condemned as unethical. It reveals a far more complex interconnection of dynamics. More importantly, it mirrors a significant degree of the accountability of official discourses, which cannot afford to be overlooked.

The fact that George and Nikos pursued resistance to official discourse signals the failure of the official agenda to integrate non-professional engagements with the past and indicates the crisis of the formation of symbolic capital, with its inherently marginalising tendency. Within the officially established symbolic capital, the term 'sacred' is opposed to ordinary and suggests that a significant part of objects and meanings is not good enough to deserve a space. This is why George's and Nikos' resistance also implies a rejection of the very framework through which recognition takes place. It is a call for an alternative framework for constructing 'sacredness', where less 'grand' antiquities

and less authorized voices are allowed a space within the perceptions and embodiments of symbolic power.

Bibliography

Anderson, B. 1991. *Imagined Communities*. London, Verso.

Appadurai, A. 1995. The production of locality. In R. Fardon (ed.), *Counterworks: Managing the Diversity of Knowledge*, 204-255. London, Routledge.

Belk, R. W. 1995. *Collecting in a Consumer Society*. London, Routledge.

Colwell-Chanthaphonh, C. 2004. Those objects of desire. Collecting cultures and the archaeological landscape in the San Pedro Valley of Arizona. *Journal of Contemporary Ethnography* 33(5), 571-601.

Demetriou, O. 2010. The Cyclops, the Sultan, and the empty post: sites and histories in Turkish(re)appropriations of the Thracian past, in A. Stroulia and S. B. Sutton (eds), *Archaeology in Situ: Sites, Archaeology, and Communities in Greece*, 221-240. Lanham, MD, Lexington Books.

Gourgouris, S. 1996. *Dream Nation. Enlightenment, Colonization and the Institution of Modern Greece*. Stanford, Stanford University Press.

Hamilakis, Y. 2006. The colonial, the national and the local: legacies of the 'Minoan' past, in Y. Hamilakis and N. Momigliano (eds), *Archaeology and European Modernity: Producing and Consuming the 'Minoans'*, 145-62. Padova: Botega D'Erasmo, Creta Antica 7.

Hamilakis, Y. 2007. *The Nation and Its Ruins. Antiquity, Archaeology and National Imagination in Greece*. Oxford, Oxford University Press.

Hamilakis, Y. 2008. Decolonising Greek archaeology: indigenous archaeologies, modernist archaeology and the post-colonial critique, in D. Damaskos, and D. Plantzos (eds), *A Singular Antiquity. Archaeology and Hellenic Identity in twentieth-century Greece,* 273-284. Athens, Benaki Museum.

Hamilakis, Y. and Yalouri, E. 1996. Antiquities as symbolic capital in modern Greek society. *Antiquity* 70 (267), 117-129.

Hamilakis, Y. and Yalouri, E. 1999. Sacralising the past. Cults of archaeology in modern Greece. *Archaeological Dialogues* 6(2), 115-135.

Hellenic Republic, 2002. *On the Protection of Antiquities and Cultural Heritage in General (Law No. 3028/2002).*

http://www.unesco.org/culture/natlaws/media/pdf/greece/gre_law_3028_engtof.pdf , accessed on 29 Febrtuary 2012.

Herzfeld, M. 1991. *A Place in History. Social and Monumental Time in a Cretan Town.* Princeton, Princeton University Press.

Herzfeld, M. 2003. Localism and the logic of nationalist folklore: Cretan reflections. *Comparative Studies in Society and History* 45(2), 281-310.

Herzfeld, M. 2006. Spatial cleansing: monumental vacuity and the idea of the West. *Journal of Material Culture* 11(1/2), 127-149.

Hollowell, J. 2006a. St. Lawrence Island's legal market in archaeological goods, in N. Brodie, M. Kersel, C. Luke and K. Walker-Tubb (eds), *Archaeology, Cultural Heritage and the Antiquities Trade*, 98-132. Gainesville, FL, University Press of Florida.

Hollowell, J. 2006b. Moral arguments of subsistence digging, in C. Scarre and G. Scarre (eds), *The Ethics of Archaeology: Philosophical Perspectives on Archaeological Practice*, 69-96. Cambridge, Cambridge University Press.

Karamitrou-Mentesidi, G. 1996. *Aiani.* Athens, Ministry of Culture.

Karamitrou-Mentesidi, G. 2005. *Aiani. The Exhibition and the Archaeological Museum.* Kozani, Publishers of the Archaeological Museum of Aiani.

Kokkinidou, D. 2005. *The Past and Power: Dimensions of Archaeology in the Greek Society and Education.* Thessaloniki, Vanias.

Labelle, J. 2003. Coffee cans and folsom points: why we cannot continue to ignore the artefact collectors, in L. J. Zimmerman, K. D. Vitelli and J. Hollowell-Zimmer (eds), *Ethical Issues in Archaeology*, 115-127. Walnut Creek, CA, AltaMira Press.

Matsuda, D. 1998. The ethics of archaeology, subsistence digging, and artefact looting in Latin America: point, muted counterpoint. *International Journal of Cultural Property* 7, 87-97.

Maury, S. P. 1996. *Surviving the rainforest: the realities of looting in the rural villages of El Peten, Guatemala.* http://www.famsi.org/cgi-bin/print_friendly.pl?file=95096, accessed on 29 February 2012.

McCracken, G. 1988. *Culture and Consumption.* Bloomington, Indiana University Press.

Politis, K. 2002. Dealing with the dealers and tomb-robbers: the realities of the archaeology of the Ghor es-Safi in Jordan, in N. Brodie and K. Walker-Tubb (eds), *Illicit Antiquities*, 257-267. London, Routledge.

Renfrew, C. 2000. *Loot, Legitimacy and Ownership: the Ethical Crisis in Archaeology.* London, Duckworth.

Stark, M. and Griffin P. B. 2004. Archaeological research and cultural heritage management in Cambodia's Mekong Delta: the search for the "Cradle of Khmer Civilisation", in Y. Rowan and U. Baram (eds), *Marketing Heritage: Archaeology and the Consumption of the Past*, 117-142. Walnut Creek, CA, AltaMira Press.

Stewart, S. 1984. *On Longing. Narratives of the Miniature, the Gigantic, the Souvenir, the Collection.* London, Duke University Press.

Stroulia A. and Sutton S. B. 2010 (eds.). *Archaeology in Situ: Sites, Archaeology, and Communities in Greece.* Lanham, MD, Lexington Books.

Yalouri, E. 2001. *The Acropolis: Global Fame, Local Claim.* Oxford, Berg.

Yalouri, E. 2010. Between the local and the global: the Athenian Acropolis as both national and world monument, in S. Buck Sutton and A. Stroulia (eds), *Archaeology in Situ: Sites, Archaeology and Communities in Greece*, 131-158. Lanham, MD, Lexington Books.

VISUAL COLLISION?
PREHISTORIC ROCK ART AND GRAFFITI IN AN ARMENIAN LANDSCAPE

Fay Stevens

Abstract

The aim of this paper is to present an 'alternative' or 'other' view to the possible reasons and motivations behind the production of images at archaeological sites. Fusing together a palimpsest of rock art imagery from a volcanic site in Armenia and the production of contemporary urban graffiti, notions such as the possible rationale behind the creation of these images and how they reflect the textures of social relationships will be explored. I consider, through the making and varying presentations of these images, how the material production of imagery is a visual deposition, depicting a visual stratigraphy and interplay between the possible flux or stability (depending on ones perspective) of the world people live/d in.

Keywords

rock art, graffiti, identity, social relations, Armenia

Introduction

In 2006, I was invited to visit the site of Ukhtasar (Armenia) on a small scale trip that aimed to look at an archaeological site rich in prehistoric rock art and to consider ways of studying the prehistoric rock art further.[1] Armenia, sometimes referred to as part of the Eastern Europe/Newly Independent States (NIS Republics), is a culturally rich and politically complex country. Bordering Turkey, Azerbaijan, Iran and Georgia, its archaeological record reflects its diverse cultural and social contacts with European, Middle Eastern, and Asian influences, while also acting as an independent and unique region itself (Panossian 2006). Its archaeology includes concentrations of rock art that are known on the Aragat and Gueghama mountain ranges, while sites including the Bronze Age cemetery and Iron Age hillfort of Lchashen and the site of Artik identify Armenia as a region with broad trade and exchange networks (cf. Xnkikyan 2002; Martinossian 1969, 1981). The site of Ukhtasar is located within the prominent mountain range of Syunik in south-eastern Armenia (Figure 10.1). Situated at c.3,300 meters above sea level within an extinct volcano, Ukhtasar is inaccessible for much of the year, with accessibility only possible in the summer months. However, while the site

is known of, and to some extent recorded, it is little understood.

The site was first discovered by archaeologists in the 1960s and documented by Karakhanian and Safian in their 'Rock Carvings of Syunik' (1970). They noted '*graphic and voluminous*' (Karakhanian and Safian 1970 45) rock carvings located horizontally or vertically on the flat surfaces of rocks which they recorded with schematic monochrome drawings of the depictions. They dated the rocks depicting imagery to be broadly from the 5th millennium BC to the 2nd millennium BC, based on stylistic traits (images of animals, human figures, carts and abstract imagery) with Syunik and other regions of Armenia and Asia Minor (Karakhanian and Safian 1970 46). The concentration of rock art is located within the inner landscape of the crater and is found on a number, but not all, of the boulder streams that shape the site. Rock art is depicted on surfaces that are flat, have a black and shiny patina and striations that are the outcome of glacial action. As such, the surface of the rock, on which the rock art appears, looks polished, is reflective and highly visible.

When we began to engage with and think about how we might record the prehistoric rock art, I became more aware of the contemporary rock carvings that also appear on the site. This was considered by the other participants to be 'graffiti', mostly relating to recent conflict with Azerbaijan. In fact, as I understand it (the situation is constantly in flux), the site of Ukhtasar is situated at a contested border that marks a position between Armenia and unnamed territory (this perspective varies according to ethnicity and political leaning). These contemporary carvings comprise text that is often accompanied by animal and abstract imagery. The contemporary carvings are located alongside the earlier prehistoric images, as well as on rock surfaces without prehistoric imagery. On first viewing, these prehistoric and contemporary images appear to collide and a majority of the participants in the group commented on how the contemporary 'graffiti' 'interfered' with the prehistoric art and was not worthy of study. As I became more aware of the 'graffiti', I started to see how it interacted with the prehistoric rock art, rather than colliding or clashing with it. To me there seemed to be an interplay of image-making taking place between the contemporary and prehistoric images. As such, I conducted my own independent research into the contemporary image making, referred to as 'graffiti'. I started to consider the potential of breaking away from art historical methods of enquiry that have been applied to the interpretation of rock art and the shamanistic reasons and motivations behind the construction of the images (not to dispute these as invalid perspectives, rather to offer an alternative). I developed an interest in

---

[1] The invitation was on behalf of a former continuing education student who had submitted coursework on the prehistoric rock art on the site and was interested in studying the prehistoric rock art further. Other participants included her husband (who works in Armenia and is a keen amateur archaeologist) and a small group of Armenians (some of whom worked in tourism), who were interested in the archaeology of the prehistoric rock art at the site.

Figure 10.1: Map of Armenia, highlighting the Syunik region in which the site of Ukhtasar is located.
Source: http://www.embassyconsulates.com/armenia/maps-of-armenia.html
accessed on 29 February 2012.

the construction and location of the graffiti and its interaction with the earlier prehistoric imagery. I started to wonder if there was a history of image-making in this location that reflects the varying textures of social relationships played out there.

Independently, I started to observe and record the contemporary graffiti, to see if there were any shared qualities between these multi-temporal images and, if so, how might these qualities inform our understanding of the reasons and motivations behind the production of imagery at Ukhtasar.

Contextualising graffiti

Graffiti is an inscriptive act whose definition changes, depending upon the context in which it is used. Broadly speaking, the term graffiti has generally been reserved for the trangressive adornment or defacement (depending one's point of view) that marks, scars and defaces public spaces, associated with subservice social acts of resistance by marginal groups, often defined as 'urban activists' who seek to challenge the political order of the 'establishment'. It tends to be featured as one of the activities targeted by legislation outlawing 'anti-social behaviour' (along with littering, fly posting, spitting, public drunkenness and other behaviours). Research into graffiti has, however, revealed a wider, more nuanced range of reasons and motivations behind its production. These range from an interesting social analysis of graffiti

in public washrooms/toilets (Stocker *et al.* 1972), to a consideration of class, sexuality and ethnic composition of the community (Sechrest and Flores 1969). Such studies have considered that graffiti may reveal changes in customs (cf. Stocker *et al.* 1972), be an outcome of 'crisis in command' and represent an attempt at governance and regulation (Hermer and Hunt 1996). There is also 'official graffiti' that serves as a mediator of social reality, such as warning signs, road signs, prohibitions, directions and advisories (Hermer and Hunt 1996) and graffiti as 'street art' (e.g. Bowen 1999), where it functions as both aesthetic practice and criminal activity.

There are a number of contemporary graffiti artists who have gained notoriety as both criminals and artists in their interplay of the aesthetic and criminal aspects of image-making. These include: Blek le Rat (France), Pixnit (USA) and Banksy (UK). Banksy, although now considered as famous, is an 'unknown' graffiti artist known for his work from around the 1980s onwards. This work mainly takes the form of challenging and controversial stencil images that 'miraculously' appear overnight in highly visual public places. More recently, his work has raised his profile across the globe and he now exists as a famous icon of the global graffiti community. His images offer ironic commentaries on politics, poverty and on the quality of living in urban environments, while his politicized imagery at the dividing wall in the occupied west bank of Ramallah is representative of broader social and political pictorial challenges to the structure of society (Figure 10.2). Banksy has used his status as a 'graffiti artist' to visually highlight the implications and outcomes of conflict within society. As such, he has recently become referred to as an 'arts hero' and his identity has transformed from a so-called anti-establishment 'vandal' to that of 'artist'. As an outcome of its changing identity, graffiti appears to be going through a process of re-invention, crossing the boundaries of street culture, youth culture, and the art community. However, while this may be attractive to many artists it also places them in contradictory relationships.

In spite of this, archaeologists have tended to approach the study of rock art as aesthetic vs. graffiti as troublesome, rock art as regulated vs. graffiti as random. If we draw upon graffiti's newly re-shaped cultural identity, however, we can adopt another archaeological viewpoint. For example, it has been suggested that archaeologists should view graffiti in the same way that we understand the ground we excavate (Parno 2010, 650), prompting us to reconsider the methodologies and questions we apply to an archaeological analysis of visual media. From another perspective, Schofield (2010, 71-81) prompts us to assess what precisely distinguishes prehistoric cave paintings and similar forms of ancient 'art' from contemporary 'graffiti', questioning why archaeological investigations of such activity may be any less legitimate than the study of prehistoric 'art' forms? Conceivably, these ideas stress that we should re-engage with graffiti as a powerful material force and consider the materiality of graffiti and the rhythms and scales of temporality in which graffiti works (e.g. Buchli 2010, 101). Indeed, as archaeologists, we should consider graffiti as an act that connects the maker to a place through the very act of image-making/writing and the demands it makes on artists/writers' bodies e.g. through place, location, skills in production, time and environmental factors (Halsey and Young 2006, 278). Moreover, this image-making is a performative act in terms of its creation but also in how it is 'read' and engaged with (cf. Shanks and Tilley 1992, 18). In a contemporary context, we understand graffiti as a form that acts deliberately to recreate the meanings of places and an attempt to instigate social change. Why not consider this within an archaeological context? Why not study both the prehistoric and contemporary image-making at Ukhtasar simultaneously, with an interest in considering the social relationships that bring about the production of image-making? This is not to say the reasons and motivations behind image production are the same. Rather, that they may somehow be relational. From this, we can, perhaps, move aside from the separateness of the archaeology of rock art and the contemporary practice of graffiti, to archaeologies of social practice associated with image-making.

Method

For this paper, I draw specifically on the work of Macdonald, whose ethnographic research of graffiti in London and New York introduced her to 'a sub-cultural world with its own rules, rewards and social hierarchy' (2006, 293). Macdonald considered what she refers to as a 'creative interplay' between graffiti-writing and the creation of identity (specifically drawing upon the graffiti of young men). She argued that there is a much deeper level of creativity at play in graffiti and that graffiti is a recourse in which people can build their identities (Macdonald 2006, 293). In her paper 'The spray-can is mightier than the sword' (2006), Macdonald noted how the production of contemporary graffiti follows a series of certain rules. It is favoured by the people who make it, it is found in urban environments, it should be executed in public surfaces and be highly visible – it is then considered to be successful. Interestingly, this highly visible requirement for the 'success of the image' is recognized but rarely understood; its meaning is private. Macdonald identifies three key processes at play in the production of contemporary urban graffiti: positioning, piecing and symbolic exchange.

In order to work towards and understanding of the production of 'graffiti' at Ukhtasar, I will draw upon the analogy put forward by Macdonald by outlining the processes of positioning, piecing and symbolic exchange of graffiti at the site. To contextualize my approach, I will consider Macdonald's contemporary processes with 'prehistoric' images, as a route into exploring the production of both prehistoric and contemporary image-making at Ukhtasar.

Positioning

At a basic level, graffiti claims fame, respect and recognition – it is about making a name. This is achieved by the production of a simple prolific inscription of word and/or image in the form of a signature and uses coverage, quality and visibility as tools of success. In contemporary terms, this is called tagging. The graffiti writer[2] uses words or a word symbol (tag), as a visibly recognisable signature and image to mark his or her passage through various locales in the community.

Figure 10.3 depicts and compares examples of a London graffiti tag and images at Ukhtasar. While the London graffiti (Figure 10.3, images A, D, G) illustrate recognizable tags in the form of text and figurative image, at Ukhtasar I started to observe images that follow this pattern: a simple prolific inscription, highly visible and repetitive. By far the most prolific prehistoric image is that of what are thought to be Bezoar goats. In fact, Karakhanian and Safian (1970) state that rock carvings in Armenia are commonly known as 'Itsagir',

---

[2] Graffiti artists both historically and today, refer to each other and themselves as 'writers' (Bowen 1999, 24).

Figure 10.2: Ramallah checkpoint 2005, Banksy (2006, 141). '**Segregation Wall, Palestine**. Palestine is now the world's largest open-air prison and the ultimate activity destination for graffiti artists' (Banksy 2006, 136). Image courtesy of the artist.

i.e. goat-letters (Karakhanian and Safian 1970, 45). The goat at Ukhtasar is distinguished by its shape, size and shape of horn and varying gestures that depict movement.

It seems that the Bezoar goat evidently played a significant role in the lives of the people who carved the images of the animal at Ukhtasar. Indeed, the site is considered to be an important place in transhumance activities of the past inhabitants of the landscape; for around nine months in the year, the rocks are covered with thick snow and the site is only accessible during the summer months. If we take lead from the reasons and motivations behind the production of contemporary tags, we might wonder if the goat letter might also act as a visibly recognisable signature and image that marks passage through and within various locales, representative of the people who associated themselves with the goat and with this particular place[3] (Figure 10.3, image B). Moreover, it might be possible that the goat somehow marks the success of the people who actively depicted this animal at this location. Likewise, the contemporary 'graffiti' at Ukhtasar also includes stylised animal imagery (Figure 10.3, image F)[4]. This suggests that animal imagery plays a significant role in people's relationship with the site, within a broad temporal trajectory. Overall, images (both prehistoric and contemporary) are located in highly visible places, thus providing a vantage point and specific locale from which social relations might be articulated and depicted.

Piecing

Pieced images comprise a surface that can be covered with a range of tags and images that relationally piece together over the designated surface. They are larger and more elaborate, with recognisable stylistic imagery that represents variations of the maker's (i.e. the piecer's) name, in which the piecers use style as recognition of their success. Both tagging and piecing are about competing for reputation and respect, working to outdo each other (Macdonald 2006). Piecers use style as recognition of their success.

Figure 10.3 (images D, E, F) illustrates and compares examples of piecing in London graffiti and possible piecing at Ukhtasar. There is a number of what are referred to archaeologically as 'complex' images in the prehistoric rock art at Ukhtasar. Here, rock surfaces with multiple images, often juxtaposing and seemingly random, depict a wide range of various images (animal, human, abstract) on the majority of surfaces (Figure 10.3, image E). This practice continues into the production of contemporary 'graffiti' at the site (Figure 10.3, image F), although less frequently. Here, the contemporary concept of piecing in graffiti art is a useful visual and social tool. Perhaps, rather than a collection of random motifs, the rock surface portrays a visual dialogue, in which images relate to each other and contemporary image-making interacts with prehistoric images at the site. While this is not so prolific with the contemporary graffiti at the site, there are a number of surfaces at Ukhtasar on which contemporary 'graffiti' interacts with prehistoric 'art' or where there is a sequence of pieced 'graffiti' on a rock surface.

Symbolic Exchange

Symbolic exchange refers to larger more elaborate stylised imagery. The exchange of imagery enables writers to mark their identity and to animate an image. Graffiti makers know that this symbolic exchange/ language is private to their sub-group and its inaccessibility to outsiders adds to its success (Macdonald 2006). Moreover, the position of different tags is important, it presents a hierarchy, e.g. above/below – contact/no-contact etc.

Figure 10.3 (images G, H, I) illustrates and compares examples of a symbolic exchange in London graffiti and possible symbolic exchange at Ukhtasar. Here, a sequence of repetitive and layered image-making is evident. Whilst the example of London graffiti (Figure 10.3, image G) illustrates some form of linearity, the prehistoric rock art (Figure 10.3, image H) illustrates human, animal and abstract images juxtaposed at various angles and positions, with evidence for overlaying in cases. The example of contemporary graffiti at Ukhtasar (Figure 10.3, image I) is particularly interesting, in that it depicts the scrubbing out and erasing of a previous image/text[5]. This destruction of images can be said to be an indication of their power and affective achievement, i.e. that they provoke a response and are therefore successful by evidence of their destruction (Buchli 2010, 103; cf. Peteet 1996). Here, we can see some form of visual exchange taking place, where recognition and repetition (across time) of material forms (images such as the goat, human body) can actively create relationships, mediating between and across identities/contested groups, ideas and places.

Discussion

By interfacing the production of contemporary graffiti in urban landscapes with prehistoric rock art and graffiti located in a volcanic crater in Armenia, I aimed to explore whether there might be any discernable cross-temporal pattern or structure and, if so, if it is possible to gain an understanding of the social and cultural construction of the landscape at Ukhtasar. I also wanted to explore the lexical identifiers we use when it comes to describing and categorizing art and graffiti. Ukhtasar is a place of varied and diverse social practices; its art is socially formed, not just a collection of dispassionate visual depictions. So, what is an authentic perspective in the interpretation of these multi-vocal, multi-temporal images? If they do interact, what are the reasons and motivations behind their social and cultural production? Gell prompts my discussion, for he states that we need to understand art objects as part of social relations, enmeshed in the texture of social relationships, rather than as merely reflective or representative of them (Gell 1999[1992], 161; 1998).

---

[3] I am not insinuating that the 'goat-letter' is a TAG *per se*, but rather that the production of repetitive images of goats at Ukhtasar might act as an identifier, of some sort, for prehistoric people visiting the site.

[4] It is also interesting to note that image C appears to have fused stylistic traits of both goat and missile.

---

[5] Image C also depicts partial scratching out of the image.

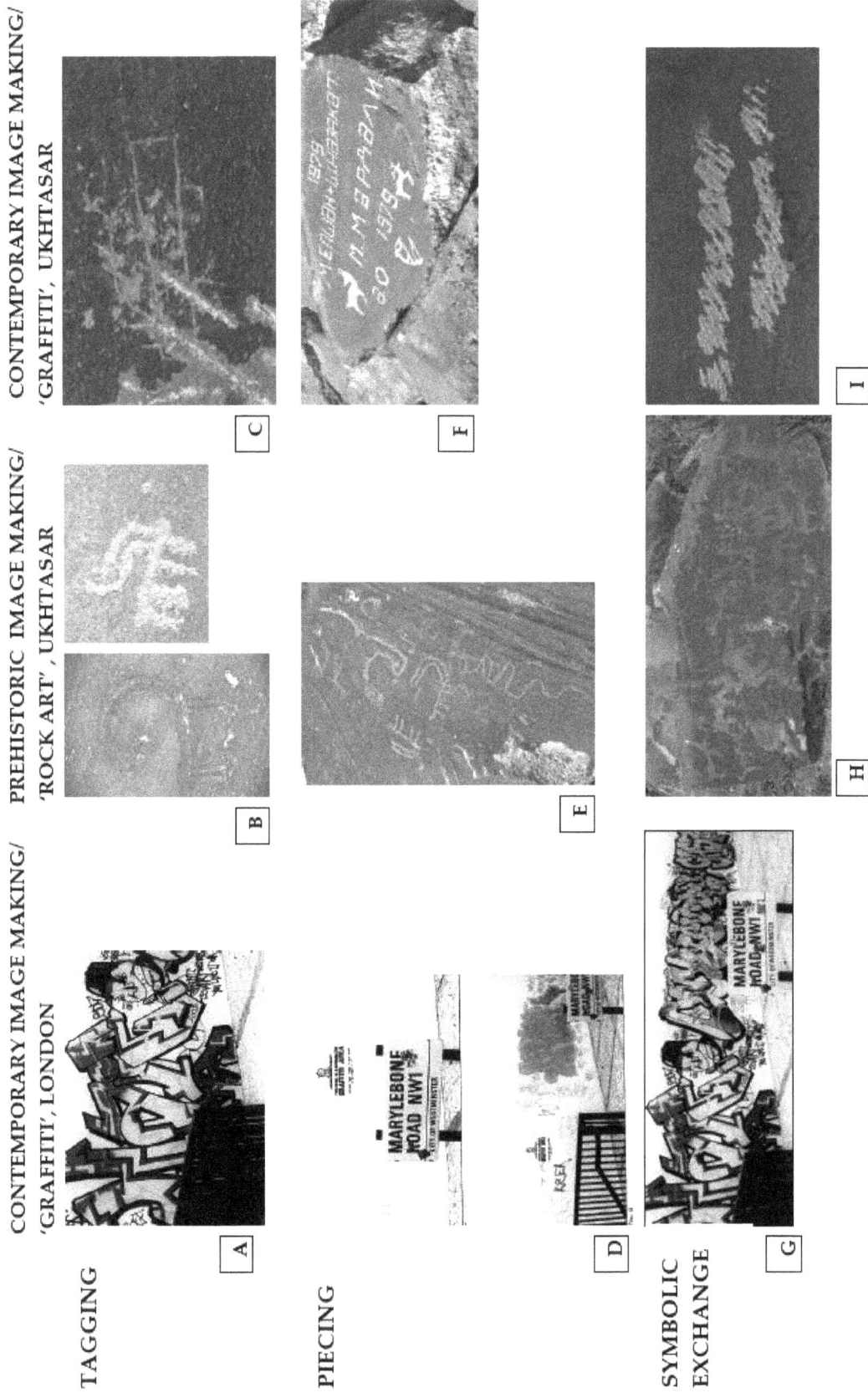

Figure 10.3: Comparing the process of tagging, piecing and symbolic exchange in contemporary graffiti (Banksy 2006) with prehistoric and contemporary image making at Ukhtasar. Photographs by the author.

Graffiti, as has been illustrated, presents an interest in resisting – or bringing about – changes to landscapes. If we remind ourselves that tagging, piecing and symbolic exchange are about competing for reputation, a visual recognition of an image-maker's success and respect and a process of graffiti artists/writers working to outdo each other, we can perhaps see this being played out across a broad temporal perspective at Ukhtasar. In fact, should we even talk of graffiti as a singular phenomenon, or could we say that different forms of graphic marking interact with their contexts in ways that are shaped by their linguistic, iconic and territorial significations and, in turn, inflect their specific context with different meanings (cf. Chmielewska 2007, 147)? A consideration of graffiti, within this context, can awaken us to otherwise hidden arguments. It can insinuate different ways of approaching the world of Ukhtasar and re-affirm places of social discussion (cf. Schacter 2008, 60). For itself, graffiti does more than signify or reflect: it is contextualized in sets of power relations and structures (Peteet 1996) and can be employed as a means of implicit and explicit claims over a contested materiality, since it can be transformed to adapt to social meanings (e.g. Orengo and Robinson 2008). As such, I am not stating that the graffiti at Ukhtasar reflects the social and cultural production of prehistoric image-making; rather, that it is drawing upon the prehistoric images to articulate social and cultural transformation within its contemporary context.

The image-making at Ukhtasar in many respects portrays a process of visual deposition, in which the act of leaving a mark on a place, in turn, leaves a cultural and metaphorical mark on the person (cf. Halsey and Young 2006). Perhaps, the practice of contemporary mark making at Ukhtasar served to highlight and actively fix the identities of those whose relationship with the landscape was in a process of conflict and flux. Here, the concept of identity was/is complicated and paradoxical, culturally situated in time, place and society and at once imposed on others and self-imposed (cf. White and Beaudry 2009, 210), where the act of inscription functioned as an unsanctioned devotional offering, token, votive offering or souvenir (cf. Owen 2010). Here, graffiti can be considered to provide a sounding board for thinking about different attitudes in society (cf. Cowdell 2010) and operate as a signifier of memory and identity (cf. Oliver and Neal 2010, 2). By referencing prehistoric rock art, the graffiti at Ukhtasar can therefore be considered as conveying a form of attachment to place, perhaps where the identity of the image-maker is re-imagined in the reality of conflict and contestation that we know has taken place in the more recent history of the site.

Conclusion

'Every image of the past that is not recognized by the present as one of its own concerns threatens to disappear irretrievably'

(Benjamin 1968, 255)

The objective of this paper, is not to dispute or challenge some of the more established models put forward for the production of prehistoric image-making. Rather, it offers a perspective that draws upon 'fringe' or 'other' images from a more contemporary perspective, as a route into considering the possible reasons and motivations for the multi-temporal production of images at Ukhtasar. What is interesting about Ukhtasar is that we see both 'types' of images (prehistoric rock art/ contemporary graffiti) in place. Urban graffiti is often seen as being 'in process' i.e. that society is in process and that there are many voices simultaneously working through and communicating the texture of society[6] (cf. Stevens 2007, 84-87). Indeed, image-making cannot be created and apprehended 'transparently' (Moser and Smiles 2005, 2). Rather, image-making and viewing are always contextualized within social, cultural, geographical and temporal milieu. Perhaps we are seeing similar social processes at play across a broader temporal perspective at Ukhtasar.

Traditionally, rock art is presented as a 'mainstream' cultural marker in archaeology, in the sense that we have a wealth of material to work with. Graffiti at archaeological sites, on the other hand, has been viewed as too 'alternative' to be taken into account. Yet the majority of archaeological sites associated with rock art also include image-making that is referred to as 'graffiti'. My intention in drawing upon the image-making at Ukhtasar was to start to consider the role of archaeology and archaeologists in the creation of meaning, not just about the prehistoric past, but about the wider temporality of an archaeological site. The visuality of recent conflict is easily evident at Ukhtasar, in the form of graffiti and military shrapnel, and the impact of this evidence affected how I started to engage with the site in a variety of ways. Images do not collide at Ukhtasar – they are far more nuanced and relational and the site richer and more meaningful as an outcome of considering the 'other past' of visual production.

Acknowledgement

This paper was presented at the European Association of Archaeologists Conference, held in Zadar, Croatia in 2007. I would like to thank Anna and Eleni for running a stimulating, thought-provoking session and for their efforts in putting together this collection of papers.

[6] Ukhtasar is a remote site, although it is visited by a wide-range of archaeologists and tourists. Generally, contemporary graffiti has been overlooked at archaeological sites, although, as the bibliography in this paper highlights, there is a renewed interest in considering graffiti (of whatever date) as a significant attribute of a site. It is not the intention of this paper to make any political comment on the nature of the conflict between Armenia and Azerbaijan, or indeed on any conflict that has been referred to in this paper.

Bibliography

Benjamin, W. 1968. (Trans. Zohn) *Illuminations*. New York, Schocken Books.

Bowen, T.E. 1999. Graffiti Art: A Contemporary Study of Toronto Artists. *Studies in Art Education A Journal of Issues and Research 1999* 41/1, 22-39.

Banksy 2006. *Wall and Piece.* London, Random House Group Ltd.

Buchli, V. 2010. Afterword, in J. Oliver and T. Neal (eds.), *Wild Signs: Graffiti in Archaeology and History*, 101-103. British Archaeological Reports International Series 2074, Studies in Contemporary and Historical Archaeology.

Chmielewska, E. 2007. Framing [Con]text. Graffiti and Place. *Space and Culture* 10(2), 145-169.

Cowdell, P. 2010. In London you're never more than 10 feet from a rat (stencil): The rat and urban folklore, in J. Oliver and T. Neal (eds.), *Wild Signs: Graffiti in Archaeology and History,* 93-101. British Archaeological Reports International Series 2074, Studies in Contemporary and Historical Archaeology.

Gell, A. 1998. *Art and Agency.* Oxford, University Press.

Gell, A. 1999 [1992]. The Technology of Enchantment and the Enchantment of 'Technology'. In Gell, A. *The Art of Anthropology: Essays and Diagrams,* 159-186. London, Athlone Press.

Halsey, M. and Young, A. 2006. 'Our desires are ungovernable': Writing graffiti in urban space. *Theoretical Criminology* 10, 275-306.

Hermer, J. and Hunt, A. 1996. Official Graffiti of the Everyday. *Law and Society Review* 30(3), 455-480

Karakhanian, G. H. and Safian, P. G. 1970. *Rock Carvings of Syunik.* Yerevan, The Archaeological Monuments and Specimens of Armenia.

Macdonald, N. 2006. The spray-can is mightier than the sword: graffiti writing and the construction of masculine identity, in J. Maybin and J. Swann (eds.), *The Art of English: Everyday Creativity,* 293-302. Basingstoke, Palgrave Macmillan.

Martinossian, A.A. 1969. *Monuments and Specimens of the Bronze Age. Settlements and Sepulcres of the Late Bronze Age.* Yerevan, The Archaeological Monuments and Specimens of Armenia, Volume 2.

Martinossian, A.A. 1981. *The Rock-Carvings of the Gegham Mountain Range.* Yerevan, The Archaeological Monuments and Specimens of Armenia, Volume II.

Moser, S. and Smiles, S. 2005. Introduction, in S. Moser and S. Smiles (eds.), *Envisioning the Past. Archaeology and the Image*, 1-13. Oxford, Blackwell.

Oliver, J. and Neal, T. 2010. Introduction, in J. Oliver and T. Neal (eds.), *Wild Signs: Graffiti in Archaeology and History*, 1-4. British Archaeological Reports International Series 2074, Studies in Contemporary and Historical Archaeology.

Orengo, H. A. and Robinson, D. W. 2008. Contemporary engagements within corridors of the past. Temporal elasticity, graffiti and the materiality of St Rock Street, Barcelona. *Journal of Material Culture* 13(3), 267-286.

Owen, K. 2010. Traces of Presence and Pleading: Approaches to the Study of Graffiti in Tewkesbury Abbey, in J. Oliver and T. Neal (eds.), *Wild Signs: Graffiti in Archaeology and History,* 35-47. British Archaeological Reports International Series 2074, Studies in Contemporary and Historical Archaeology.

Panossian, R. 2006. *The Armenians. From Kings and Priests to Merchants and Commissars*. London, C. Hurst & Co.

Parno, T.G. 2010. 'What the Frak is F**K?' A Thematic Reading of the Graffiti of Bristol, in J. Oliver and T. Neal (eds.), *Wild Signs: Graffiti in Archaeology and History,* 61-71. British Archaeological Reports International Series 2074, Studies in Contemporary and Historical Archaeology.

Peteet, J. 1996. The Writing on the Walls: The Graffiti of the Intifada. *Cultural Anthropology* 11(2), 139-159.

Sechrest, L. and Flores, L. 1969. Homosexuality in the Philippines and the United States: The Hand-writing on the Wall. *The Journal of Social Psychology* 79, 3- 2.

Schacter, R. 2008. An Ethnography of Iconoclash. *Journal of Material Culture* 13(2), 35-61.

Schofield, J. 2010. 'Theo loves Doris': Wild-signs in Landscape and Heritage Context, in J. Oliver and T. Neal (eds.), *Wild Signs: Graffiti in Archaeology and History,* 71-81. British Archaeological Reports International Series 2074, Studies in Contemporary and Historical Archaeology.

Shanks, M. and Tilley, C. 1992. *Re-constructing Archaeology: Theory and Practice.* Second Edition. London, Routledge.

Stevens, F. 2007. Identifying the Body: Representing Self. Art, Ornamentation and the Body in Later Prehistoric Europe. In J. Sofaer (ed.), *Material Identities*, 82-99. Oxford, Blackwell.

Stocker, T.L., Dutcher, L.W., Hargrove, S.M. and Cook, E.A. 1972. Social Analysis of Graffiti. *American Folklore Society* 85 (338), 356-366.

White, C, L. and Beaudry, M. C. 2009. Artifacts and Personal Identity, in T. Majewski and D. Gainster (eds.), *International Handbook of Historical Archaeology*, 209-228. New York, Springer.

Xnkikyan, O. S. 2002. (Translated by Vatche Ghazarian) *Syunik During the Bronze and Iron Ages*. Barrington USA, Mayreni Publishing.

THE COLOURS OF THE PAST

Cornelius Holtorf

The editors of the present volume set themselves the task of exploring the variety of archaeologies (in the plural) that co-exist in the present. These archaeologies may be considered as 'mainstream' or as 'alternative'; they may or may not be academically sound; they may be able to command public attention or they may gain currency only about specialists, and they may serve a variety of different agendas.

The ten contributions assembled here explore the creations, characteristics, contexts and consequences of some very diverse archaeologies that differ in their perspectives, approaches and appeal from academic and professional archaeologies. As one might expect, these archaeologies create other pasts than those academic and professional archaeologists are familiar with and often also other pasts than they are prepared for.

What all pasts have in common – mainstream or not and whatever their agenda – is, however, that they rely on particular meanings and express themselves in particular narratives about the past. Indeed, archaeology is commonly seen as the stuff of exciting stories rather than as a tool for getting answers to specific questions about the past. Archaeological stories have the potential to move people and interest them in a particular aspect of (studying) the past, whether they are laypeople or highly educated specialists. These stories can be complex and their messages may not always be popular or delightful. I have argued elsewhere (Holtorf 2010b) that telling stories and meta-stories about archaeology or the past is one way of making a real and widely appreciated contribution to very many peoples' lives. As popular culture aptly demonstrates, such stories do not only entertain large audiences but also connect with some of their most common fantasies, needs and desires. In an insightful essay, the culture historian Nina Witoszek (2012) recently argued that whatever professional archaeologists may make of the historical explanations advocated by the legendary alternative archaeologist Thor Heyerdahl, he posed three important challenges to his academic colleagues. These challenges do not concern the specific stories about seafaring and other achievements of ancient civilizations but instead they concern the archaeological meta-stories he told for a global audience and which are well worth remembering even now. The first one has to do with passion, longing and romance created by Heyerdahl's enchanted adventures in a disenchanted world. The second challenge is about the environmental, pacifist and social agenda that can be found in Heyerdahl's projects, whatever else they may have been investigating at the same time. Finally, Heyerdahl has been questioning the myth of ethnic purity which is so prominent in many founding stories linked to archaeological sites and finds around the globe. As Witoszek suggests, professional archaeologists in the mainstream would do well to ask themselves whether they can learn from this broad agenda that Heyerdahl embraced and communicated to his global audience. Archaeological story-telling is an opportunity for archaeology to fulfil itself in contemporary society by directly improving the quality of peoples' lives, providing meaning, stimulation and guidance in various ways. The present volume, too, gives ample evidence of this potential of archaeology.

In their introduction, Anna Simandiraki-Grimshaw and Eleni Stefanou are taking up a number of questions that run through the contributions that follow. Important is their commitment in this volume not to want to debunk alternative archaeologies but rather trying to understand better how they work and what roles they play in society. The book in its entirety poses the intriguing question whether it is possible in all cases to keep mainstream and alternative archaeologies strictly apart and, perhaps more importantly, on what grounds the border may be policed, and by whom (see also Holtorf 2005).

In the remainder of my commentary here I am going to concentrate on exploring one question which Anna Simandiraki-Grimshaw and Eleni Stefanou posed in the session on which this book is based: *What is the impact of present diverse archaeological readings on the past itself?* In other words, can 'other' pasts, deriving from a variety of archaeologies in the present, have any impact on the past itself? What is that proposition supposed to mean? What could it mean?

At face value it seems absurd to assume that any meaning or narrative about the past could have an impact on the past itself. After all, within our conventional concept of linear history, the past happened before the meanings and narratives it attracts today, and it can thus not be affected by them. Indeed, one could point out that the past at large has *caused* the contemporary world in which other pasts emerged, and the cause by necessity precedes the effect. Most certainly, the former cannot in turn be an effect of the latter. In this thinking, the past is understood as another physical reality that is different from our own physical reality primarily due to its distance in linear (measurable, physical) time.

However, as Anna Simandiraki-Grimshaw and Eleni Stefanou indicate in that question they were raising, there are other ways of perceiving the relation between archaeologies in the contemporary world and the pasts itself.

If reality is defined as the sum of contemporary human experiences and social practices, even the reality of the past is contemporary insofar as it emerges from contemporary human experiences and social practices.

The past can therefore be evoked and presenced through experiences that are perceived as non-mediated and immediate, as for example in games and virtual reality, role play and TV docu-soaps. As a consequence, contemporary practices have an impact on the past itself; indeed they create the past in the present. According to this view, the past is not a physical reality distinct from our own, but a particular kind of flavour that is contained in the mix of specific human experiences and social practices in the present (Holtorf forthcoming). Seen from this perspective, even time travelling can become possible in the present, not as a product of the imagination but very much as a part of reality. Intriguingly, such time travel experiences and associated social practices have become ubiquitous and popular, in some cases replacing other ways of packaging the past for popular consumption (Holtorf 2010a).

Much like ice cream scoops, the flavour of the past in the present can have a number of different colours. In preposterous histories in which events and processes of subsequent periods inform our understanding of earlier ones these colours can colour the past as such. As the historian of art and literature Mieke Bal (1999: 100) put it, every reuse of pre-existing material changes it. Really, this is not preposterous at all but a result of the way in which we understand the past.

According to the German philosopher Hans-Georg Gadamer (1900-2002), understanding is always interpretation, and it means to use one's own preconceptions so that the meaning of the object can be made to speak to us (Gadamer 1975: 358). Understanding is thus not a merely reproductive but a very productive process, and interpretations will always keep changing during the reception history of what is being understood.

> *Time is no longer primarily a gulf to be bridged, because it separates, but it is actually the supportive ground of process in which the present is rooted. Hence temporal distance is not something that must be overcome. This was, rather, the naive assumption of historicism, namely that we must set ourselves within the spirit of the age, and think with its ideas and its thoughts, not with our own, and thus advance towards historical objectivity. In fact the important thing is to recognise the distance in time as a positive and productive possibility of understanding. It is not a yawning abyss, but is filled with the continuity of custom and tradition, in the light of which all that is handed down presents itself to us.*
>
> (Gadamer 1975: 264-5)

Gadamer argues that the 'true' historical object is not 'an object' at all, but a relationship which comprises both the reality of history and the reality of historical understanding. This he calls the 'principle of effective-history' (1975: 267). Not only does the power of effective history determine in advance what seems to us to be worth enquiring about, but we also find that, by following the criterion of intelligibility, the other presents itself 'so much in terms of our own selves that there is no longer a question of self and other' (Gadamer 1975: 268).

Hence an interpretation can be made richer not only by continuous study of the object, but also by better understanding the themes and issues of its effective-history. And this is indeed one important rationale for investigating the reception history, for example, of archaeological monuments (Holtorf 2000-2008: 3.10).

The colours of the past have to do with the 'identity of the past' (Shanks 1992: 114; cited after Cremo) and thus with particular ontologies brought to bear on the past. Michael A. Cremo, for example, is very explicit in his chapter about adopting an ontology that incorporates nonmaterial substance, intelligence and agency. As a direct outcome of that ontology Cremo can consider his archaeology to be an integral part of his yoga, his meditation and his spiritual discipline. Suggesting that we humans do not evolve up from matter but down from pure consciousness, Cremo hopes that consciousness will be restored to its original pure state and that this restoration should be the main purpose of human existence.

Tera C. Pruitt discusses in her chapter a past with a rather different identity. The Bosnian pyramids, supposedly discovered since 2005 by the Bosnian business man Semir Osmanagić, are firmly linked to stories about himself as an adventurer-hero fighting for truth against a corrupt establishment and about the sites in question as a sensational Bosnian heritage. To Pruitt, the pyramids constitute a hyperreal history drawing on a simulacrum of the sites at which he has been working. In her view, Osmanagić may not only literally be carving pyramids out of roughly pyramid-shaped hills, he is also creating, or indeed inventing, the pyramids by repeatedly asserting in public that there are pyramids. Pruitt brings the nature of this invention to the point by citing a local business owner who stated: 'If they don't find the pyramid, we're going to make it during the night. But we're not even thinking about that. There *are* pyramids and there *will be* pyramids.' Ironically, Pruitt to the same extent dis-invents the pyramids when she categorically asserts: 'The hills are simple geological formations; no matter how hard Osmanagić may search, he will not produce verifiable evidence of a supercivilization.'

The past which Liv Nilsson Stutz discusses is not commonly considered to be invented in the same way as the Bosnian pyramids. But it certainly is at least as non-scientific and non-academic. Her topic are indigenous pasts among contemporary Native Americans. Her case-study is Kennewick Man/The Ancient One and the conflicting claims to it by white scientists and Native Americans. To Nilsson Stutz it is very clear that the conflict is in parts about 'fundamentally different understandings of the past' which arguably amount to different pasts. Whereas the scientists were interested in learning more about the history of the peopling of the North American continent, the native American tribes claimed that based on traditional knowledge they already knew that they had lived in their regions since the beginning of time.

Similarly divergent understandings of the past are discussed by Paul Hubbard and Robert S. Burrett in relation to Zimbabwean archaeologies. Here, a variety of diverse pasts exist besides each other, from academic to racist to alien-related and other fringe pasts. These pasts co-exist in parallel universes in which mainstream professional archaeologists and fringe authors have no direct communication.

As Anna Zalewska's discussion demonstrates, such conflicting pasts can even be identified in an analysis of the content of educational textbooks over the past century. Interestingly, Zalewska accounts for different interpretations of the site of Biskupin by pointing to the archaeologists' own processes of socialization and education as effectively resulting in different pasts. Here, the past becomes very clearly a social construction of the present and it mirrors in various ways the conditions from which it originates.

Similarly, Marcia Bezerra has been looking at children's worldviews of archaeologists and the past as they are reflected in a number of stereotypical elements in children's literature. Going beyond an acknowledgment and appreciation of the past as a contemporary construct and a reflection of the children's worldviews, Bezerra discusses alternative representations of archaeology and the past in terms of social representations. Social representations use familiar objects in order to represent unfamiliar concepts. Bezerra sees a risk that such representations, as allegories of archaeology and the past, distort and damage the very core of the discipline of archaeology so that it ultimately risks ceasing to exist. The problem is however that a social and historical perspective, as it is advocated in several of the other contributions to the volume, reveals how difficult it can be to divide accurate from distorted representations of the past and archaeology. Does the discipline of archaeology really offer anything else than its own social representations, using familiar images and stories to represent unfamiliar concepts and ideas?

Moving from children's literature to mass media, Diane Scherzler discusses the significance of medialisation, whereby the past is being presented to journalists in terms that are assumed to result in more media attention. Such mediatised parts do not reflect the archaeologists' own process of socialization and education, and the colour of their own particular pasts, but rather how they picture the colour of the journalists' pasts.

Ioanna Antoniadou and Fay Stevens studied non-professional engagements with the material and sacred past that are disobedient to the rules established by official authority. Whereas Antoniadou's example are illicit collections through which two looters have been laying claim to a sacred past, Stevens focusses on contemporary graffiti artists apparently interfering with prehistoric art but arguably representing an 'other past' which recreates the meaning of a place by articulating social and cultural transformation. Both papers are powerful reminders of the existence of other practices in relation to archaeological heritage than those sanctioned by the relevant state authorities.

The volume as a whole illustrates aptly that, whatever their colour, archaeologies in present-day society have a profound impact on the past and its remains. In telling stories about the past, they give expression to particular meanings and values. In recent decades it has become common to accept indigenous communities' versions of the past and archaeological sites as legitimate alternatives to standard scientific accounts and approaches that all too often have become hegemonic. The epistemologies and intellectual traditions between those pasts may differ, but they share a commitment to give the past and archaeology meaning and significance in our present. The same courtesy should now be extended to other alternative archaeologies, deriving from yet other epistemologies and intellectual traditions and giving the past and archaeology meaning and significance in our present in yet another way.

Next time you encounter an alternative archaeology, you may be sufficiently curious about the kind of past it creates that you want to get close enough to make out its colour.

Bibliography

Bal, M. 1999. *Quoting Caravaggio: contemporary art, preposterous history*. Chicago, University of Chicago Press.

Gadamer, H.-G. 1975. *Truth and Method.* London, Sheed and Ward.

Holtorf, C. 2000-2008. *Monumental Past: The Life-histories of Megalithic Monuments in Mecklenburg-Vorpommern (Germany).* Electronic monograph. University of Toronto, Centre for Instructional Technology Development. http://hdl.handle.net/1807/245, accessed on 19 May 2012.

Holtorf, C. 2005. Beyond crusades: how (not) to engage with alternative archaeologies. *World Archaeology* 37, 544-551.

Holtorf, C. 2010a. On the Possibility of Time Travel. *Lund Archaeological Review* 15-16, 2009-2010, 31-41.

Holtorf, C. 2010b. Meta-stories of archaeology. *World Archaeology* 42 (3), 381-393.

Holtorf, C. forthcoming. On Pastness: A Reconsideration of Materiality in Archaeological Object Authenticity. *Anthropological Quarterly*.

Witoszek, N. 2012. The World after Thor Heyerdahl: Challenges to Archaeology in the Twenty-First Century. *European Journal of Archaeology* 15 (1), 146-151.